the angry years

Also by Colin Wilson:

Non-Fiction

The Outsider Cycle:
The Outsider
Religion and the Rebel
The Age of Defeat
The Strength to Dream
Beyond the Outsider

Rasputin and the Fall of the Romanovs
The Brandy of the Damned (Essays on Music)
Eagle and Earwig (Essays on Books and Writers)
Introduction to the New Existentialism
Poetry Mysticism
Shaw – A Study of his Work
The Occult
Mysteries
Beyond the Occult
New Pathways in Psychology
Order of Assassins
Autobiography: *Dreaming to some Purpose*
The Quest for Wilhelm Reich A Criminal History of Mankind
The Misfit: A Study of Sexual Outsiders
Rogue Messiahs

Fiction

Ritual in the Dark
Adrift in Soho
The Schoolgirl Murder Case
The Philosopher's Stone
The Mind Parasites
The Killer
The God of the Labyrinth
The Glass Cage
The World of Violence
Necessary Doubt
Man Without a Shadow
The Black Room
The Space Vampires
The Janus Murder Case
Spider World: The Tower
Spider World: The Delta
Spider World: The Magician
Spider World: Shadowland

the angry

COLIN WILSON

years

The Rise and Fall of the
Angry Young Men

ROBSON
BOOKS

First published in the United Kingdom in 2007 by
Robson Books
151 Freston Road
London
W10 6TH

An imprint of Anova Books Company Ltd

ISBN 10: 1 86105 972 8
ISBN 13: 9781861059727

A CIP catalogue record for this book is available from the British Library.

10 9 8 7 6 5 4 3 2 1

Typeset by SX Compsong DTP, Rayleigh, Essex
Reproduction by Spectrum Colour Ltd., Ipswich
Printed and bound by Creative Print & Design, Ebbw Vale, Wales

This book can be ordered direct from the publisher.
Contact the marketing department, but try your bookshop first.

www.anovabooks.com

Contents

Acknowledgements

Many friends have read this book, either in whole or in part, and made valuable comments. First in the list I should mention Bill Hopkins, who suggested the book, even though I felt I had covered much of it in my autobiography *Dreaming to Some Purpose*. I am glad he persisted.

My publisher Jeremy Robson offered enthusiasm and kindly concern at a critical stage.

John Sutton made warm comments that also spurred me on.

Other friends who have read it while it was in progress are Howard Dossor, Ted Brown and Chris Nelson – the latter also sent me a useful article about John Braine's last days.

My friend Brad Spurgeon, of the *New York Herald Tribune*, was kind enough to supply me with the information about Sartre's daily intake of alcohol, tobacco and drugs from *Le Ventre des philosophes: Critique de la raison diététique* by Michel Onfray.

My old friend and editor, Paul Newman, not only read the book chapter by chapter but typed the Analytical Table of Contents and Bibliography.

Other friends who have been helpful have been Christopher Logue, Laura Del Rivo, David Mason, Maurice Bassett and Geoff Ward. Arnold Wesker made some helpful comments about John Osborne, and about the section on himself. Doris Lessing likewise offered useful insights and some excellent advice. So did Ronald Duncan's daughter Briony Lawson. Antoni Diller read the section on Stuart Holroyd and was also able to communicate some useful facts.

Another old friend, Professor Dale Salwak, was able to help me locate some essential material, while Professor Richard Bradford, author of the two best critical studies of Philip Larkin and Kingsley Amis, was able to point me in the right direction.

Finally, I wish to thank the *Observer* newspaper and Longman's publishers for allowing me to quote Kenneth Tynan's original review of *Look Back in Anger*, and Bloomsbury publishers for permission to quote from *The Diaries of Kenneth Tynan*, edited by John Lahr. Messrs Faber & Faber gave permission to quote from Philip Larkin's prose and poetry.

Colin Wilson
November 2006

Analytical Table of Contents

Preface
The Angry Young Men and the satire movement of the 1950s. Why the Angry Young Men aroused hostility in the critics. 'Class barriers'. Why my second book was panned. Rousseau's 'Man is born free'. Why Rousseau is central to this book. *The New Héloïse* and *The Social Contract*. For Rousseau, sexual revolution came before social revolution. 'Sexual underprivilege'. Why the British were unworried about the French Revolution. Lord Russell throws a Frenchman's shoes out of the window. Ireland and India. Osborne's Jimmy Porter on his in-laws. My girlfriend's parents and the 'horsewhipping incident'. *Look Back in Anger* and *The Outsider* arrive in the same month in 1956. Osborne is chased down the Charing Cross Road.

1 Getting Launched
London in 1951. Where was the postwar literary generation? The British Museum Reading Room. London landladies. Angus Wilson's *Hemlock and After*. Marriage breakdown. Laura Del Rivo and Bill Hopkins. 'You are a man of genius – welcome to our ranks.' Paris. George Plimpton and the Café Tournon. *Merlin* and Samuel Beckett. *Watt*. Christopher Logue and Alex Trocchi. Bill Hopkins in Paris. Paris and existentialism. Dostoevsky and the firing squad. Girodias and dirty books. A Christmas job in Leicester. Joy Stewart. Flax Halliday. The Christmas show. Joy agrees to come to London. I decide to sleep outdoors to save rent. Writing in the British Museum. Meeting Angus Wilson. Wain, Amis and Larkin. Alfred Reynolds and Bridge. Stuart Holroyd. Working in the Coffee House. Writing *The Outsider*. Suicide and the romantics. Victor Gollancz expresses interest. My mother's illness. Notting Hill. My first literary party. Iris Murdoch. Meeting John Wain. First publicity interview. *The Outsider* becomes a bestseller. Non-stop publicity. The Angry Young Man label. Kenneth Tynan launches *Look Back in Anger*.

2 He That Plays the King
Tynan at Oxford. 'Have a care for that box, my man – it is freighted with golden shirts.' His taste for masturbation and female posteriors. He begins to write theatre reviews. His pornography collection. 'Just a thong at twilight.' He marries Elaine Dundy. She objects to being flogged. His career

as a director stalls. *He That Plays the King* makes his reputation. His London debut in *Hamlet*. A bad review lands him a job. He pans Vivien Leigh. The Broadway scene. Sacked from the *Evening Standard*. The *Observer* under Astor. Tynan as a 'Right Man'. Campaigns against Loamshire and the Lord Chamberlain. The Royal Court opens. Angus Wilson's *The Mulberry Bush*. *Look Back in Anger* opens to poor reviews. Tynan saves the day. I take Joy to see it and hate it. A press officer invents the Angry Young Men. Tynan attacks *The Outsider*.

3   The First Wave

'Kingsley Amis tries to push me off a roof'. Amis's schooling. He meets Larkin at Oxford. Their devotion to masturbation. Larkin's scathing intellectual judgements. They collaborate on soft porn. Amis is called up. His seductions. Larkin's *Jill*. Monica Jones: Amis 'didn't know who he was'. Larkin becomes a librarian. He seduces Ruth Bowman. Amis fails his doctorate. *A Girl in Winter*. Amis seduces Hilly Bardwell and makes her pregnant. Larkin in Belfast. Patsy Strang reads his masturbation diaries. Amis writes *Lucky Jim*. John Wain broadcasts an extract on the BBC. Success. Wain's *Hurry on Down*. Amis's infidelity to Hilly. The cultural saboteur. Amis's review of *The Outsider*. My letter to Amis causes lifelong paranoia. Meeting Amis. *That Uncertain Feeling*. Hilly writes 'I FUCK ANYTHING' on Amis's back. Wain's second novel a failure. Wain's persistent touch of bitterness. Larkin applies for librarianship at University of Hull.

4   Court Intrigues

Devine asks me to write a play. Nigel Dennis. Failure of *Cards of Identity*. My plunge from 'intellectual stardom'. The horsewhipping scandal. Pursued by the press to Ireland. Gollancz advises me to get out of London. We move to Cornwall. Samuel Beckett's *Endgame*. *The Entertainer*. *The Death of God*. Devine's rejection note. Ronald Duncan describes my play as 'a child's TV serial'. In spite of which, he and I become friends. 'A natural bigamist'. Success of *This Way to the Tomb*. Fame and sexual temptation. Duncan's affairs with Petra and Antonia. Smashing crystal vases with high-heeled shoes. Ronnie persuades Rose Marie she is lesbian. 'But I don't like it.' Devine engineers the failure of Duncan's *Don Juan*. Influence of Tynan on Devine's politics. Tynan and Christopher Logue form an alliance.

5   The Paris Input

Tynan invites Logue to see *Look Back in Anger*. I meet Logue at an *Encounter* party. Alexander Trocchi in London. He tells Logue he is going to New York to take heroin. Trocchi's childhood and youth. Paris on a travelling scholarship. Jane Lougee. His wife moves to Madrid. He launches *Merlin*. Logue's suicide attempt. Pornographic books for Maurice Girodias. Publication of *The Story of O*. Trocchi decides to research domination and submission. He joins *Situation Internationale*. The Society of the Spectacle. Debord orders him to break all contact with former friends. He abandons *Merlin*. London. He impregnates a schoolteacher. An abortion party. He leaves for America. The Beat Generation in Paris. Ginsberg reads *Howl*. Seized by US customs. Ginsberg persuades Girodias to publish *The Naked Lunch*. William Burroughs shoots his wife. Maurice Girodias and *The Ginger Man*. Donleavy takes Girodias to court. John de St Jorre's *Venus Bound: The Erotic Voyages of Olympia Press*. Robert Pitman and Donleavy. Nabokov and *Lolita*. Graham Greene launches Nabokov to fame. *Lolita* and sexual underprivilege. How sexual advertisements reached twentieth-century London. 'It is not a woman I want – it is *all* women.' The Paris Vice Squad raids Girodias. The French minister of justice lifts the ban on *Lolita* and *The Story of O*.

6 'As for Living . . .'

Terry Southern's *Candy*. Southern's New York agent breaks with Girodias. *Candy* is sold to Putnam's. Lancet's pirated edition. Girodias goes bankrupt. Donleavy buys Olympia Press. The Hollywood lifestyle destroys Southern's talent. Trocchi in New York. Heroin addiction. *Cain's Book*. 'As for living, our servants can do that for us.' Romanticism and lassitude. Girodias publishes the Beckett trilogy. Beckett's laziness. Bellacqua 'the most indolent man who ever lived'. Beckett in Dublin and futility syndrome. The war years. Revelation on Dunlaoghaire Pier. 'It was like resolving to go naked.' Decides to write a play. *Waiting for Godot* rejected five times before Roger Blin accepts it. It makes Beckett famous. 'The play where nothing happens, twice.' Writes *The Unnameable* to establish his credentials as nihilist. The nadir of romanticism. Beckett versus Proust. Girodias publishes *The Naked Lunch* and makes Burroughs famous. 'Nothing is true, everything is permitted.' Henry Miller's *Tropic of Cancer*. My *Sex Diary of Gerard Sorme* judged obscene in Boston. My return to London. *The Outsider*. Cornwall and hostile reception of *Religion and the Rebel*.

7 Joe for King

Room at the Top. 'Remember the name, John Braine . . .' Joe's interest in sex. The defeat premise in modern literature. Joy and I meet Braine. How *Room at the Top* came to be written. The colonel's daughter. Failure of bid to become a writer. Braine and I share a pied-à-terre. The ménage at 25 Chepstow Road. Tom Greenwell and Stuart Holroyd. *Emergence from Chaos* is panned. The brawl outside the Court. *The Vodi*. Film version of

Room at the Top. Braine and John O'Hara. John Osborne and Tony Richardson and the film of *Look Back in Anger*. *The World of Paul Slickey* flops. Osborne flees with Jocelyn Rickards. Robert Pitman introduces me to *Saturday Night and Sunday Morning*. *Loneliness of the Long Distance Runner*: 'Very trying Communist propaganda'. *The Death of William Posters. A Tree on Fire. The Flame of Life*. Arnold Wesker. *The Kitchen. Chicken Soup with Barley*. Devine commissions *Roots*. Wesker's disillusionment with Communism. *I'm Talking about Jerusalem. Chips with Everything*. The concept of 'Promotion'. Wesker is appointed director of Centre 42. An attempt backed by the TUC to bring art direct to the people. *Their Very Own and Golden City*.

8   Declaration

Braine's depression; he begins to drink too much. The Ibsen syndrome. Amis's self-image problem. *I Like It Here*. Updating *Clarissa*. 'The only reason that I like girls is I want to fuck them.' *The Egyptologists*. Elizabeth Jane Howard. Hilly Leaves Amis. Bill Hopkins suggests *Declaration*. Bill's *The Divine and the Decay*. Its unprecedentedly hostile reception. Bill and I in Hamburg. La Mettrie: The human race will never be happy until we accept that we are machines pure and simple. Maine de Biran. The launching party for *Declaration*. Bill Hopkin's 'Ways Without a Precedent'. Belief in the heroic. Stuart Holroyd's 'A Sense of Crisis'. My 'Beyond the Outsider'. H G Wells compares man to the earliest amphibians. Amis declines to contribute to *Declaration*. Wain's 'Along the Tightrope'. The writer's task is to 'humanise the environment'. Osborne's 'They Call it Cricket': I want to make people feel not think. Tynan's 'Theatre and Living'. 'A society where people care more for what you have learned than from where you learned it.' Lindsay Anderson: 'Get Out and Push'. His part in the British film revival. Doris Lessing: from Rhodesia to London. *The Grass is Singing. The Children of Violence* series. 'A small personal voice'. *The Golden Notebook. The Four-Gated City*. Surviving nuclear catastrophe.

9   Downhill

Osborne and Jocelyn Rickards flee to Capri. 'He had talent for fucking up other people's lives, and his own.' Robert Shaw in New York. Osborne's affair with Penelope Gilliatt. Osborne, Tony Richardson and Jocelyn Rickards take a villa in the South of France. George Devine's nervous breakdown. Osborne's 'I hate you England' letter. Osborne goes to Venice to meet Gilliatt. 'I'm going to behave badly again, my darling'. Osborne and Gilliatt flee to Hellingly Mill, pursued by the press. Osborne, Richardson and Devine work together on the film of *Tom Jones*. *Plays for England*. The success of *Luther. Tom Jones. The Blood of the Bambergs*.

Under Plain Cover. A Patriot for Me. Inadmissible Evidence. Devine collapses on stage. Osborne leaves Penelope Gilliatt for Jill Bennett. *A Bond Honoured* commissioned by Tynan. Its failure. Tynan's decline. Success of *The Dud Avocado.* Tynan flees on pornography charges. Elaine starts a divorce case. Tynan as 'Right Man'. 'If you ever write another book, I'll divorce you.' Tynan's become theatre critic of *New Yorker.* 'Social game-hunting'. Tynan in Cuba. Tenessee Williams and Hemingway. Elaine instructed to call Hemingway 'Papa'. Tynan upsets Hemingway. 'I've been apologised to by a Nobel Prizewinner.' Elaine goes off with a Scottish laird. Tynan breaks her nose. Tynan and Mary McCarthy. His mother dies insane. Tynan has a mental breakdown. The National Theatre: Olivier: 'How shall we slaughter the little bastard?' Literary manager. *Hamlet* with Peter O'Toole. Clashes with the board. His marriage to Kathleen Gates. He says 'fuck' on television. *Oh Calcutta!* Rolf Hochhuth's *Soldiers.* The board rejects it. A libel suit. Resigns from the National Theatre. Emphysema. A new affair: Nicole.

9   Iris Murdoch and the Gospel of Promiscuity

Origins of existence-philosophy: Kirkegaard, Sartre and Camus. Iris on *The Outsider. Under the Net. Pierrot Mon Ami.* Canetti forbids Iris to sleep with John Bayley. Canetti's egoism. *Flight from the Enchanter.* Rudolf Nassauer and *The Hooligan. Auto da Fé. Crowds and Power.* My trip to St Anne's. Pub crawl in the Edgware Road. Magical realism in *The Sandcastle.* Success of *The Bell* worries Iris. *A Severed Head.* She and Priestley turn it into a play. Iris's obsession with promiscuity. Parallel with D H Lawrence. Frieda Lawrence's affair with Otto Gross. Lawrence accepts 'the gospel of promiscuity'. *Mr Noon.* The religious approach to sex. *The Plumed Serpent.* Lawrence and William Blake. *Why Mrs Blake Cried.* The Moravian Chapel in Fetter Lane. 'Religious ecstasy through sexual means'. Blake's advocacy of promiscuity. An all-night orgy. Beyond existentialism.

11   'Now That My Ladder's Gone . . .'

A trip to Leningrad with John Braine. John's alcoholism. He arrives back home unexpectedly. John Wain on the boat to England. *Life at the Top.* John quarrels with Bill Hopkins. Launching *Penthouse. The Jealous God.* John moves to Woking. *The Crying Game. Stay With Me Till Morning.* Braine's death. His last books. Amis's marriage to Jane begins to sour. *The Green Man.* Amis's alcoholism. *Girl 20. The Alteration.* Amis becomes impotent. *Jake's Thing.* Amis becomes aware that he never liked women. Jane walks out. Getting his own back. *Stanley and the Women.* Amis's final novels. *The Biographer's Moustache.* The Garrick Club. Amis's death. Why Amis and Wain quarrelled. Wain is elected professor of poetry at

Oxford. *A Winter in the Hills*. The final trilogy. 'I was a pretty selfish sod.' Philip Larkin's last years. His affair with Maeve Brennan. He sleeps with his secretary. Increasing fame. *The Whitsun Weddings*. The Monitor programme. Alvarez attacks him. 'Books are a load of crap.' 'Now that my ladder's gone.' Larkin's fear of death. Cancer of the oesophagus. Amis attends his funeral.

12 Watch It Come Down

One of the most spectacular declines in the history of British theatre. Osborne's bitterness about Jill Bennett. Her weekend in Cornwall. The break up of the marriage. He drives on to a traffic island. *The Hotel in Amsterdam. Time Present. The Charge of the Light Brigade. West of Suez.* 'They've shot the fox.' *A Sense of Detachment.* 'This must surely be an end to his career in the theatre.' 'You've really fucked up your life, haven't you?' *The End of Me Old Cigar. Watch It Come Down.* 'Money back!' Osborne leaves Jill Bennett. The curious affair of *The Entertainer* revival. A £100,000 overdraft. The move to Clun. Jill Bennett commits suicide. Osborne adds a vindictive chapter to *Almost a Gentleman*. Writing a sequel to *Look Back in Anger*. *Déjàvu* is rejected. He is found to be diabetic. 'John Osborne, ex-playwright'. The Writers' Guild award for Lifetime Achievement. Osborne is booed. He dies of pernicious anaemia on Christmas Eve 1994. Tynan in California. He spanks a black girl. Forced to jump from a balcony. 'Bankruptcy, emphysema, paralysis of the will – and now this!' The trip to Spain with Nicole. The count and countess spank a dishonest maid. 'It is fairly comic and slightly nasty but it is shaking me like an infection . . .' 'A diabolical dream'. The disastrous summer. Burst blood vessel in penis. Wallet stolen twice. 'Life itself is my enemy'. His death at 53. Alex Trocchi's attitude to Tynan. He becomes a celebrity in Greenwich Village. 'Miss Hicks of Hicksville'. Gives himself a fix on television. Lyn is arrested. Trocchi flees back to England. Lyn joins him in London. A twelve grains-a-day habit. Guy Debord excommunicates him. The International Writers' Conference in Edinburgh. Trocchi tries to kick heroin in Herne Bay. Lyn dies in Guy's Hospital. His son Mark contracts cancer of the throat. Trocchi opens a market book stall. The final trip with Jane Lougee. A successful operation for lung cancer. He dies of lobal pneumonia. His ashes are stolen from *his* mantelpiece.

Epilogue

Romanticism and optimism. Rousseau and nature. Wordsworth: 'Bliss was it in that dawn to be alive'. The new pessimism. The tragic generation. The case of Iris Murdoch. *The Time of the Angels*. Seduction and incest. The decline of fall of existentialism. The non-existence of God. Philosophy as a search for meaning. Bertrand Russell: 'The vastness and fearful passionless

Preface

The last book written about the 'Angry' movement of the 1950s was Humphrey Carpenter's *The Angry Young Men*, subtitled 'A Literary Comedy of the 1950s', which was published in 2002.

The justification for the present work is that Carpenter's short book, an unashamed potboiler, was totally out of sympathy with the writers he was discussing. In his view, the really significant movement of the mid-century was the satire trend that began with *Beyond the Fringe* and the television series *That Was the Week that Was*. By comparison, he felt that their predecessors, the 'Angry Young Men', were beneath serious consideration.

Now I certainly had no objection to the satire movement. I bought the record of *Beyond the Fringe* as soon as it appeared, and watched *That Was the Week that Was* every Saturday night – I even appeared in one of its later incarnations. But I regarded it as lightweight anti-authoritarian entertainment, like Groucho Marx's song 'Whatever it is, I'm against it'.

I have, as will appear, my own reservations about the Angry Young Men. But what made them interesting as a group was that John Osborne, John Braine, Alan Sillitoe, Stan Barstow, Arnold Wesker and myself were all from working-class backgrounds. Although I was frankly indifferent to the class issue, being more interested in science and philosophy, the others, driven by a detestation of the class system that had been around since William the Conqueror, were the first *group* of working-class writers that had ever existed. Before that, the majority of writers had come from middle- or upper-class backgrounds, and been to university. As Peter Lewis remarked in *The Fifties* (1978), speaking of the heroes of Osborne, Braine and Sillitoe: 'All of them are up against class barriers symbolised by some character who is the concentrated essence of all that the hero and, one assumes, the author hates most in Fifties England.'

Lewis goes on to point out that the 'establishment' hated them. They didn't mind being satirised by one of themselves, like Aldous Huxley or George Orwell, but they wouldn't take criticism from a working-class writer, as D H Lawrence had discovered to his cost. Lewis sees the violent attacks on my second book *Religion and the Rebel* as a class reaction. 'There could scarcely be a better illustration of how the Establishment operates. Having taken a naïve and over-confident young writer at his own valuation, with one accord the literary mandarins made him a sacrificial scapegoat and reasserted their natural prejudice against anyone who had come up from the ranks. It is a unanimity which is sinister and unreal.'

It is worth remarking that Humphrey Carpenter, who dismissed the Angry Young Man movement as a 'comedy' of the fifties, was the son of a former bishop of Oxford.

So why, in spite of failing to share their sensitivity about the class system, do I regard the Angry Young Men as worth writing about? Because, unlike the satirists who followed, the movement was based on a real political protest that hoped to get something done, to change things as Rousseau and Cobbett and Godwin had wanted to change things. That is why they deserve to be taken more seriously than satirists who fire their arrows and then duck.

Now although I had always had my reservations about political idealism, this was on grounds of realism, not of conservatism. As Bernard Shaw pointed out, Jean-Jacques Rousseau's assertion that men are born free is wishful thinking. 'We are all born in a slavery to nature that compels us to work x hours a day, as cows are compelled to graze, on pain of death by hunger, thirst and exposure.' We are also slaves to our biological instincts and emotions. So although I loved Shelley's poetry, I was dubious about his belief that man could become free by over-throwing tyrants.

This did not make me a cynic about rebellion. When I read Byron's lines in *Don Juan:*

> The mountains look on Marathon –
> And Marathon looks on the sea;
> And musing there an hour alone
> I dream'd that Greece might still be free,

my scalp tingled in a way that convinced me that freedom was, in some real sense, a human possibility. Rousseau and Shelley were simply approaching it too simplistically.

So although I felt Peter Cook, Jonathan Miller and the team of *That Was the Week that Was* were marvellously stimulating, they were not concerned with the kind of freedom that interested me, or even that interested Osborne, Braine, Sillitoe and Wesker. Braine said about the hero of *Room at the Top*: 'Joe doesn't want to do away with the class system. But he would say that from now on it's achievement that counts. It shouldn't matter who your father was.' And in saying that, he was expressing the spirit of rebellion that had kicked and struggled since Rousseau, and had finally brought about the French Revolution.

Which is why Rousseau's name is evoked so many times in this book: because he was virtually the patron saint of the Angry movement.

Since few people nowadays know anything about him, I may be as well to begin by summarising his life and achievement.

Born in 1712 in Switzerland, one of the least class-ridden countries in Europe, he was the son of a watchmaker, and therefore in no sense one of the poor and oppressed. But when his father abandoned him at the age of twelve, he experienced the sense of social insecurity that haunted him for the rest of his life and fuelled his protest against the system. He became a wanderer, worked as a lackey in aristocratic households, tried becoming a trainee priest, then became the lover of a woman who – for reasons we can only surmise – had been given a pension by the king of Sardinia.

He was almost 40 when he became famous for an essay on whether art and science had improved the lot of mankind. His answer was a surprising no. Art and science, he said, have only made man more corrupt and vicious. Civilisation is the culprit, and with civilisation came private property, tyranny and injustice. Man will not be happy until he has returned to Nature and regained lost innocence.

Rousseau's yearning caught the spirit of the age, and he became the most celebrated thinker in France. His novel *The New Héloïse* (1761) went on to spread his fame across Europe.

It describes how a penniless tutor becomes the lover of his aristocratic pupil Julie, and it argues that if a couple are in love, they have a right to consummate it in defiance of society. The scandal was immense, since in France a girl's virginity was her chief commercial asset.

It was two years later that Rousseau published the work that established his reputation as a political rebel, *The Social Contract*, with its famous opening sentence 'Man is born free and is everywhere in chains'. It was in this that Rousseau developed his argument that civilisation has caused man to be enslaved by authority, and that government should rest upon the consent of the governed. The ideal society would be that which gives the individual the most freedom to intervene in state affairs.

But it is important to emphasise that the sexual revolution of *La Nouvelle Héloïse* came before the political revolution of *Le Contrat Social*. The sense of sexual underprivilege preceded the sense of social underprivilege; sexual rebellion inspired social rebellion, not vice versa. And sexual rebellion would become one of the most important strands in the revolution inaugurated by Rousseau. Here we have touched on one of the central themes of this book.

Similar ideas on religion, expressed in his novel of education, *Émile*, led to condemnation by the Church, and he was forced to flee to Geneva, then (when his house was stoned) to England, at the invitation of the philosopher David Hume. But the phlegmatic British temperament was alien to Rousseau, who soon hurried back to Paris. There his paranoia increased until he became virtually insane, and he would eventually die of apoplexy at the age of 66.

This paranoia is again something we shall note repeatedly in the saga of the Angry Young Men.

Still, for all his self-pity and persecution mania, Rousseau changed the world. In the year after his death came the storming of the Bastille, and the downfall of the aristocracy. The angry philosopher had done more than anyone to light the powder train.

France was ready for it. Since the reign of Louis XIV the nobles had been ruining the country with their extravagance and their insolence. In Louis's reign, an aristocrat could ride along in his carriage and take potshots at peasants standing in their doorways as if they were game. When his minister Colbert tried to bring prosperity by encouraging trade and industry, the king undid his efforts by exempting the nobles from taxes. After Louis's death in 1715, the population soared and the towns were filled with unemployed farm labourers; yet with the poor starving, the nobles still expected to be exempt from taxes. No wonder the people cut their heads off.

Now in England, the ascendancy of the governing classes had always been so complete that no one had ever thought of questioning it. True, if the mob was outraged by some aristocratic scandal, they were likely to throw stones and rotten eggs at the gilded carriages of their betters; but on the whole they were good-humoured about it. No one had thought seriously about revolution since the days of Watt Tyler. The British ruling class was so confident that they allowed foreign revolutionaries to come and live in England; it didn't bother them if a bearded German named Marx was writing a book on economics in the British Museum Reading Room, or if anarchists were advocating throwing bombs at Speakers' Corner.

This self-assurance could be infuriating to foreigners, as in this example from Martin Page's *The Lost Pleasures of the Great Trains*:

> Another Englishman travelling on the continent, Lord Russell, was acclaimed for putting a native with whom he was sharing a compartment in his place. As the train drew out of the station the foreigner proceeded to open his carpet-bag, take out a pair of slippers, and untie the laces of his shoes.
>
> 'If you do that, sir,' proclaimed the great Victorian jurist, 'I shall throw your shoes out of the window.'
>
> The foreigner remarked that he had a right to do as he wished in his own country, so long as he did not inconvenience others. Lord Russell demurred. The man took off his shoes, and Lord Russell threw them out of the window.

In Ireland the British conquerors behaved like this with depressing frequency, drawing upon their heads the kind of hatred that finally brought about their downfall after the executions of 1916. In India in 1919, a massacre of nationalist protesters would lead to the same result.

It was this kind of Englishman who aroused John Osborne's sarcasm in *Look Back in Anger*. This is Jimmy Porter on the in-laws who had gatecrashed his wedding:

'Mummy was slumped over her pew in a heap – the noble, female rhino, pole-axed at last! And Daddy sat beside her, upright and unafraid, dreaming of his days among the Indian Princes, and unable to believe he'd left his horsewhip at home.'

For me, that last phrase would prove prophetic when, not long after the *succès fou* of my first book *The Outsider*, which launched me into a vertiginous notoriety two weeks after Osborne's play, my girlfriend's middle-class family burst into my London flat, her father waving a horsewhip and shouting 'Wilson, the game is up', and tried to remove her by force. It seems that her sister had got hold of a diary of mine when I was visiting Joy in hospital, and garnered some rather peculiar ideas, such as that I was a homosexual with half a dozen mistresses, and probably meant to sell Joy into white slavery.

The resulting scandal hit the front pages of the newspapers, and the publicity destroyed any chance I had of being taken seriously as a writer thereafter. My publisher Victor Gollancz, who regarded me as his *protégé*, advised me that if I did not leave London, I would never write another book. Which is how we came to move to Cornwall – where, nearly half a century later, with Joy in the next room, I am writing these words.

This was typical of the publicity that had swirled around the Angry Young Men ever since that day in May 1956 when *The Outsider* and *Look Back in Anger* had been reviewed almost simultaneously, and would continue when John Osborne found himself besieged by journalists in a country cottage after he had eloped with somebody's wife.

This kind of thing had nothing whatever to do with literature, and made the serious critics (who suspected us of courting publicity) cynical and hostile. My second book, *Religion and the Rebel*, received an unprecedented roasting at the hands of the critics who had praised *The Outsider*. Osborne's second play *The Entertainer* escaped the same fate largely because the lead was played by Sir Laurence Olivier, but the critics made up for it when reviewing his third play *The World of Paul Slickey*, a satire on gossip-column journalism, and Osborne was even chased down Charing Cross Road by infuriated members of the audience.

All of which helps to explain how the late Humphrey Carpenter could write a book in which what was, after all, an influential literary movement, was dismissed as a 'comedy' of the fifties.

My objection to this has nothing to do with irritation at being included in the dismissal. It is that Carpenter's book was lightweight and unobjective.

In the following pages I shall tell the story of the Angry Young Man movement from the viewpoint of one who is now virtually its last survivor.

1   Getting Launched

When I came to London in 1951, determined to become a writer, the literary landscape looked oddly bleak. The war had been over for six years, but there was still no sign of the kind of new generation that had emerged after the First World War. Critical mandarins like Cyril Connolly and Philip Toynbee were inclined to blame Joyce, because *Ulysses* was an impossible act to follow, and I was more than half convinced they were right.

At the end of the 1914–18 war, of course, it had all been quite different. English writing had taken that fascinating step into the 1920s, and it was obvious that a new era had arrived. The major figures of the previous generation – Shaw, Wells, Bennett, Galsworthy, and the rest – were still around and continuing to write. But the really exciting figures were D H Lawrence, T S Eliot, James Joyce, Aldous Huxley, Lytton Strachey and Virginia Woolf, who all had the effect of making their predecessors seem out of date.

When I went to London, most of that generation were dead or dying. Of their successors, Auden and Isherwood had moved to America, Graham Greene lived in France, and Stephen Spender, Louis MacNiece and Dylan Thomas no longer seemed to be producing important work. Two years later, Thomas was also dead. The 'younger generation' had failed to arrive, and the silence seemed ominous.

I left my home town, Leicester, because I suspected I would never become a writer in that environment, which was about as exciting as Clacton-on-Sea. Besides, I had married my girlfriend, a nurse named Betty, because she was pregnant, and wanted to find us a home nearer to the British Museum Reading Room, where Carlyle, Shaw and Wells had worked in their early days, and where I hoped to finish my first novel.

I had already made my first attempt to escape into a more interesting world when I hitchhiked to Paris at the age of nineteen, but failure to find work had driven me back to England within months.

London still had its share of bomb sites, many turned into car parks, and the area I chose, Camden Town, (because I liked the sound of it) looked oddly rundown, just like Paris when I had drifted there two years earlier. But even in working-class north London, I soon noticed that the rooms advertised on cards in shop windows carried the warning: No children or pets.

I found myself a labouring job on a building site, spent my evenings in telephone booths calling prospective landlords, and taking buses to remote places like Willesden or Tottenham in search of rooms – whose landladies flinched when I admitted my wife was pregnant.

We ended in a room in East Finchley, whose landlady stipulated that we should move before the baby arrived. There I often went to early mass – I was flirting with the idea of becoming a Catholic – and spent hours in the East Finchley Public Library. It was here I found Camus's *The Plague*, which had been recommended on some radio programme as one of the best novels published since the war. Its opening pages, with the rats dying of plague in Oran, gripped me, but I soon felt that it degenerated into talk. At all events, I learned that Camus was part of the new generation of French writers who called themselves existentialists. That was better than in London where, a year after my arrival, the literary scene was as blank as ever.

In a few months our landlady became nervous in case the baby arrived early, and gave us notice. Fortunately, the foreman at work – I had found a job in a plastics factory – offered us a room, and we were there when the baby arrived. It was a boy, and we called him Roderick.

It was also in this room that I listened to the complete Ring cycle on our small Bakelite radio, identifying the leitmotifs with a library copy of Newman's *Wagner Nights*. I also happened to switch on a programme with Dylan Thomas as some sort of guest commentator, and was surprised by his rich, booming English voice, and his amazing vocabulary as he answered one question by reeling off a list of synonyms.

On Saturdays I cycled to the British Museum, where I had obtained a Reading Room ticket, claiming I needed to access the library because I wanted to study the Egyptian *Book of the Dead*. This was not entirely untrue. For the past two years I had been writing the novel that became *Ritual in the Dark*, for which I was using the Egyptian myths of death and rebirth as a basic structure, as Joyce used the *Odyssey* in *Ulysses*. But it had finally dawned on me that *Ulysses* was a bad model, since even I had to admit that it moves too slowly, and decided instead to devise a plot based on the crimes of Jack the Ripper, which has interested me since childhood. After studying accounts of the murders in *The Times* for 1888 in the North Library, I would cycle over to Whitechapel and make sketches of the murder sites. I felt that the best way to give a novel authenticity is to base it, as Joyce did, on real places and events.

Soon we had to move again, since the crying of the baby kept our landlord and landlady awake in the next bedroom. And during the course of the next year, 1952, we moved twice more, until at the beginning of 1953, the marriage split apart. It was not yet over, but we were both sick of the instability, and it never came back together again.

In July 1952 I had learned from a full-page review in the *Times Literary Supplement* of the arrival of a novelist named Angus Wilson. His book was called *Hemlock and After*, and the anonymous reviewer described it as 'a novel of remarkable power and literary skill which deserves to be judged by the highest standards', adding that it was one of the wittiest novels since Oscar Wilde. I could almost sense the relief of the critic that a new writer had at last arrived on the scene.

I lost no time ordering it from the local library – 12s. 6d. was well beyond my resources – and began to read it on the way home. It was a disappointment, nothing like *The Picture of Dorian Gray*, and even less like *Vile Bodies,* to which another reviewer compared it. It was about a celebrated writer who, in middle age, discovers he is not only homosexual, but also has sadistic tendencies, and since he is a kindly, decent liberal, this wrecks his health and finally destroys him. The plot was absorbing, but there was something stiff and almost amateurish about the writing. In a sense, my disappointment was a relief. I had no wish to be left behind by the arrival of the new generation, particularly by a writer with my own surname.

But then, Wilson was apparently in his mid-forties, so belonged to the same generation as Spender, Auden and Isherwood. So I could relax for the time being.

Separated from Betty after January 1953, I took a job as a hospital porter at the Western Fever Hospital in Fulham. It was not taxing work, and that was its drawback. Our job was to sit in the porter's room and wait for admissions, then take the patients on trolleys down to the wards. Meanwhile, there was little to do but make tea and read. The radio played all the time, although in those days before the advent of rock 'n roll, it was mostly sport, sentimental songs and tunes from musicals like *Guys and Dolls.* When the feeling of stagnation became too overpowering, I sneaked off to one of the empty wards, full of old beds and damp mattresses, and sat there cross legged doing meditation exercises I had taught myself by reading Hindu scriptures.

Betty and I had every intention of continuing the marriage, although every time I went to see her we seemed to end up quarrelling. The final break came after I had found a flat in east London, and she came down to see it. Her mother had agreed to lend the money they wanted for 'furniture and fittings' (an excuse for collecting a premium forbidden by law). But after she returned to Leicester, Betty suddenly became suspicious of the landlady, and sent me a telegram asking me to cancel the whole deal. I was so disgusted that I decided to give in my notice at the hospital and go back to Paris. So, technically speaking, it was I who left my wife.

But before that happened, I spent much of that hot summer of 1953 in London coffee houses, and in one of them near Trafalgar Square, I met a teenager named Laura Del Rivo, who told me she wanted to be a writer. She was three years my junior (I was 22), came from a middle-class family in Cheam, and had a sweet childish voice. I found her charming, and was attracted by the thought of playing Henry Higgins to her Eliza. But Laura, it seemed, was already infatuated with someone else – a poet whose name she declined to tell me, and who apparently did not return her affection. I finally discovered that this was Bill Hopkins, and that he was the youngest child of a theatrical family from Cardiff.

Curious to discover why she preferred him to me, I sought him out in his favourite taxi-driver's café in St Giles, and found him impressive, with a natural dominance and Welsh fluency of speech. He worked as a sub-editor on the London edition of the *New York Times*, and had published some remarkable poems in small literary magazines, notably *The Watchman* edited by the poetess Iris Orton. He had decided to launch his own magazine, to be called *The Saturday Critic*, which would concentrate on castigating the inadequacies of the current literary establishment (like Stephen Spender, editor of *Encounter*, and John Lehmann, editor of *The London Magazine*). I lent him the first chapters of my ongoing novel, and one day when I went to the café, I found my typescript waiting for me with a note that read: 'You are a man of genius! Welcome to our ranks!'

I was pleased but, to tell the truth, not especially flattered, for I had taken it for granted that I was a man of genius since I was about thirteen.

And here I must establish a point that is of central importance to this book.

The sons of upper- and middle-class families are inclined to take a modest view of themselves because they mix with boys who are dominant and intelligent from the time they go to school. But in working-class schools, natural dominance and intelligence are less obvious. If their fathers work in factories, the sons are inclined to accept that they will do the same, and probably live in much the same kind of houses, and send their own children to the same kind of schools. There is no natural expectation of going into the Foreign Office or managerial training. Their horizons are limited because their expectations are low.

Now a few centuries ago, that would have been the end of it; the 'lower classes' expected to remain in the same station in life until they died. But the advent of universal education changed all that, and to learn to read was also to learn to dream.

This applied to women even more than men, for novels and women's magazines made them dream of handsome and dominant males and, for sensitive working-class women – for example, D H Lawrence's mother – the aspiration was often passed on to their children. I have long suspected that imaginative working-class women are the evolutionary spearhead of society, since the narrowness of their lives imparts an intensity to their daydreams that middle- and upper-class women, lacking the desperation, find it harder to achieve.

My father was a boot and shoe worker, and long before I left school (at sixteen) I felt stifled in the working-class environment of southeast Leicester. Daydreaming was as important as breathing oxygen. And since I knew that only my intelligence could save me from ending in a factory, a kind of desperate self-belief was a tool of survival. Besides, I had bought the new one-volume Shakespeare that had been published immediately after the war, and was delighted by the self-confidence about his own genius that he expresses in the sonnets.

So Bill's 'welcome to our ranks' only demonstrated that he and I had reacted in the same way. But Bill had arrived at the conclusion by a slightly different route. His parents had been on the stage, and were famous all over Wales as a double act. Bill was very young when his father died, and remembers seeing newspaper billboards announcing: 'Ted Hopkins dead'. He had concluded that all men receive the same treatment when they die, and this created a sense of his own uniqueness. When he finally discovered that most men's death goes unnoticed, it made him all the more determined to achieve something that would make his own death a notable event.

Soon he and I had established a relationship built upon a friendly rivalry about who could become famous first.

So in the autumn of 1953 I hitchhiked to Paris again, stayed in a room lent me by a friend I had made last time I was there, and looked around for work. Chance directed me to the office of a new magazine called *The Paris Review*, edited by a wealthy young American named George Plimpton. He took me to dinner and agreed to give me a job selling subscriptions to Americans living in Paris; I was allowed to keep a generous percentage of the money. I set out the next morning with a list of the Americans living in Paris and a street guide, but it proved to be hard and discouraging work that failed to bring the flood of customers George had forecast.

That evening, in a café called the Tournon in the rue Tournon, I met a group of expatriate writers connected with a small magazine called *Merlin*. This was edited by an American, Richard Seaver, who talked to me enthusiastically about a new writer called Samuel Beckett, whose play *En Attendant Godot* had been the hit of last winter's season. Beckett, he said, was pathologically shy and anti-social, and his work was all about loneliness and frustration. Seaver had inquired about publishing some of Beckett's work in *Merlin*, but had failed to make contact with him. Then one day there had been a knock on the door of his room, and he had opened it to find a tall, gaunt man peering at him through thick lenses. Without saying a word, the man had handed him a bundle wrapped in sacking and then turned and vanished down the stairs. It proved to be the manuscript of an unpublished Beckett novel called *Watt,* and Seaver lost no time in printing a chapter in *Merlin.* Now he was proposing to publish the whole novel.

Others present in the Tournon were a pretty American girl called Alice Jane Lougee, who financed *Merlin,* an American writer called Austryn Wainhouse, who was translating the works of the Marquis de Sade for the pornographic publisher Maurice Girodias, and an English poet named Christopher Logue. The latter had a strange, harsh voice and irregular teeth, and told me he proposed launching a magazine called *The Pillory,* that would reveal the corruption and nepotism of the literary establishment; every issue would show the face of a different victim in the pillory. (Herbert Read, I seemed to recall, was to be the first.)

This was the first time I had actually been among real writers, engaged in the production of literature. In London, and even in Leicester, I had met plenty of 'wannabees' who talked about books they intended to write and even produced manuscripts. But the *Merlin* crowd not only had ideas, but were reaching an audience with them. As I sat there on that first evening, I made a decision to stay on in Paris and try to establish myself as a writer of ideas.

It did not take much persuasion to get Seaver to agree to let me try to sell subscriptions to *Merlin,* and I was told to call at the nearby office and collect some copies to show as samples. But even with two magazines to offer, sales were slow. I managed to make enough to eat and pay my bus fares only by selling copies of *Merlin* or *The Paris Review* to people who were unwilling to purchase a year's subscription but glad enough to appease their conscience by buying a single copy.

At this point, Bill Hopkins turned up unexpectedly at my room near the Étoile. He had come to France to find out whether French printers would be cheaper than those in England, and I took him down to the Tournon to consult Dick Seaver. We found only Christopher Logue there, who explained that Dick's fellow editor, Alex Trocchi, was now in Spain on precisely the same errand – because French printers were proving too expensive. It looked as if Bill's trip to Paris had been a waste of money. Nevertheless, we spent a pleasant evening talking and drinking, and Bill and Chris Logue, both poets, seemed to enjoy one another's company. That night, Bill slept on a mattress on my floor.

I was delighted see him in Paris. I am basically introverted, and found the strangeness of a foreign city a drain on the energies. Bill is an extravert who is always full of optimism; he was convinced that a little fast sales talk was all that was needed to provide us with an income. So the next morning we set out with an armful of both magazines, and called at the address of every American expatriate living in the Champs-Élysées. Sales were less buoyant than expected, and we sold only a few subscriptions, but at least we had the pleasure of talking about literature and ideas as we plodded between addresses.

One thing was obvious: the literary scene in France was far livelier than in England. Sartre and Camus, whose view of human destiny is basically gloomy, nevertheless believed that man has freedom of choice, and can exercise it even in the face of death. Whereas the British saw the war as an exhausting struggle that had drained their energies and finally lost them an empire, the French still felt the sheer relief of being rid of the Nazis. Sartre had remarked that he had never felt so free as when he was in the Resistance, and might be arrested and shot at any moment. This excited me, for ever since I had started reading Dostoevsky at the age of sixteen, I had been obsessed by that story of how he had been condemned to death by firing squad, and had been reprieved at the last minute. It had taught him that, compared to the prospect of death, most of our human anxieties are trivial. And although the war had been over for eight years, there was still a flavour of freedom in the air.

Bill and I could sense this as we drank a glass of wine outside a café, or walked along the empty boulevards at night, talking about our lives and the techniques of the novel.

We were both looking forward to meeting Alex Trocchi, who was obviously the intellectual driving force behind *Merlin*. I was fascinated by the stories of the social and sexual rebel who wanted to create a new morality and politics, while Bill wanted to talk about the mechanics of launching a magazine. In fact, Trocchi and Bill obviously had much in common: both wanted to make a clean sweep of current standards. The title of Trocchi's essay 'Invisible Insurrection of a Million Minds', in his book of the same title, encapsulates his basic vision, as Bill's would be summarised in the title of an essay he wrote for *Declaration*: 'Ways Without a Precedent'.

But I have to admit that both of us were soon feeling doubts about the whole *Merlin* project. Most of them were making a living writing pornography for Maurice Girodias, whose father had been the original publisher of Henry Miller. Chris Logue had written a novel called *Lust*, and Alex Trocchi had written a 'fifth volume' of Frank Harris's *My Life and Loves*, and an interesting autobiographical novel called *Young Adam*, which he had adapted for Girodias's Olympia Press by simply inserting slabs of sex. He was also translating Apollinaire's sadistic fantasy *Eleven Thousand Virgins*, which ends with the hero violating and strangling a little girl. Austryn Wainhouse and Dick Seaver had embarked upon a complete translation of the Marquis de Sade, whom I had never read, although a glance at it convinced me that it could be absolved of being pornography on the grounds that the violence was too nauseating to be sexually exciting.

I also felt that their enthusiasm about Beckett was misplaced. The chapter of *Watt* in *Merlin* made it easy to see why he had failed to find a publisher. The flat, repetitive prose moves forward with incredible slowness, and the humour – for it is clearly meant to be funny – depends upon the grotesqueness of things seen in slow motion. Like a record played at a fraction of its proper speed, this gives normal events, such as conversation, an offbeat flavour which is oddly surreal.

Waiting for Godot, which had brought him celebrity, had depended upon this same trick of slow motion, as two tramps who stand under a tree for several hours, exchanging inconsequential remarks, and waiting for a man who fails to arrive. It is as if the author is saying: 'This is the kind of absurdity you take for real life. Is it as real as you think?' I was not surprised when Dick Seaver told me that Beckett often stayed in bed all day because he could see no reason for getting up.

As I talked to Dick, the idea of writing pornography for Olympia Press crossed my mind as a solution to the problem of staying alive, but soon evaporated when I looked at some of Girodias's publications in the English bookshop. I had an instinctive feeling that it is impossible to play with pitch without getting your hands dirty.

Moreover, my attempt to live the *vie bohème* had made me aware that I shared Thomas Mann's feeling that the true artist contains a streak of the bourgeois, with his craving for stability. So after a few weeks, when it became clear that Trocchi would not be returning yet, Bill and I borrowed our fares back to England from the British Consulate, for which we surrendered our passports. And since it was late November and Christmas was approaching, I decided to return to my family in Leicester.

There I decided to take a temporary job in a big store called Lewis's that was in need of Christmas staff. They assigned me to the carpet department. And within half an hour of arriving I was sent with two other beginners to a classroom on the top floor to learn the cash register. The girl who took us up in the lift was tall and slim, and her oval face would have been pretty but for a somewhat Roman nose. I expected her to speak with a guttural Leicester accent, which I hated, but when she stood in front of the 'class', I was pleasantly surprised that she had an educated voice. Moreover, she had the most sweet, good-tempered smile I had ever seen, and when she smiled at us, it made my heart sink, for I could see that unless I took myself in hand I could become hopelessly infatuated.

Her name was Joy Stewart, a name I also liked. One of my fellow recruits – a young ex-Sandhurst type named Flax Halliday – told me she was a management trainee and engaged to a fellow student from Trinity College, Dublin, intending to join him in Canada to get married. I took this stoically, for I had already regained control of my emotions by telling myself there was no point in wanting something that I couldn't have.

Flax and I became friends and drinking companions. His father was a book dealer who specialised in rare books, which he also bound, and he allowed Flax to live in the empty house next door. Flax had left the army because he saw no future in peace time, but was obviously dissatisfied and frustrated with civilian life. He was intelligent and strong-minded, but aware of the irony of possessing strength with no idea of what to do with it. He regarded my 'bohemian' tendencies with disapproval.

At the time we met he had just ended a love affair, and had already set his sights on another pretty managerial trainee named Pat. And this proved to be my good fortune, for Pat was a friend of Joy, and Flax's plan of seduction involved inviting Joy and myself to spend a weekend at his house to make up a foursome. Joy, who was also beginning to be bored with Leicester, was glad of the diversion; so she and Pat cooked our supper, after which she and I slept together on the rug, fully clothed, while Flax and Pat occupied the bed. When I tried to raise Joy's skirt, she firmly pushed my hand away.

Pat's seduction now accomplished, Flax had no further need of chaperones, and I had to find some excuse for seeing Joy regularly. I solved this by asking the manager of the store if I could present a Christmas show. He agreed, although he turned down my first suggestion – my play *The Metal Flower Blossom*, that I had based on an artist I knew in London – on the grounds that it would shock the older counter assistants. But he saw no objection to the first act of Shaw's *Man and Superman*, with myself as John Tanner and Joy as Anne Whitefield.

It had already dawned on me that Joy's air of self-possession was a cover for shyness and, as we began rehearsing, it became clear that this made her a poor actress. But that seemed unimportant compared to the pleasure of being able to see her as often as I liked. Soon she was allowing me to kiss her goodnight, although she remained otherwise as cool and unencouraging as ever.

The Christmas show was a success, although I have to admit that this was largely due to two excellent amateur comedians who worked in the carpet department. After that, Joy went home for the holiday, then to see off her fiancé at Southampton. When she returned to Leicester, I thought she seemed rather quiet and reserved, which I suspected was due to a feeling of guilt about her fiancé.

I had given up my job at Lewis's. But I soon found an opportunity to see more of Joy when Flax offered her a flat in his house. Since the room was bare and needed redecorating, I offered to do the job, and Joy would join me after work and cook me a meal. Then, on New Year's Eve, we went to a party at the flat of a friend, and I succeeded in persuading Joy to stay the night. And although we again slept fully clothed, I was beginning to sense that she was experiencing a certain self-division about her impending marriage.

Finally, two nights later, after eating supper in the sparsely furnished room, which still smelt of newly applied distemper, I again succeeded in persuading her to stay the night instead of returning to her lodgings. She agreed after much resistance and, since she had to wear it for work the following morning, proceeded to remove her skirt. As I climbed into the bed with her, I experienced a marvellous sense of enchantment; it seemed impossible to believe I could be so lucky. And although we spent another chaste night – since she was a virgin – I was happy enough just to feel her warmth and softness pressed against me; in fact, since a male is never free of inhibitions, was rather relieved that I was not called upon to prove my virility.

The next morning I cycled with her to Lewis's. And as I looked at her, and reflected that a month ago she had seemed unattainable, I found it incredible that we had just spent the night together. What is more, I had an odd intuitive certainty that we now belonged together.

So in early 1954 I returned to London; I took a room in Highgate, and found myself a job in a laundry. Joy gave in her notice at Lewis's, and joined me a month later, taking a room in Chalk Farm, and a job at a big store in Oxford Circus. But her parents were understandably baffled that she should decide to move to London when she was due to sail for Canada in a few months, and searched through some letters she had left behind in a suitcase. They were horrified to discover that she been 'seduced' by a dubious bohemian with no future prospects, and had visions of her being forced to return home pregnant and abandoned. One Sunday afternoon I was summoned to the front door to find a grim-looking middle-aged man who announced: 'My name is Stewart, sir.' And when I invited him in, he said he would rather talk in the car. When we were seated side by side, his first words were: 'Get out of town, Wilson.' I said what I was expected to say: that I was in love with her (not entirely truthful, perhaps, since what I felt was an overpowering attraction) and that she seemed to feel the same. He said that he was not going to allow her life to be ruined, and that unless I agreed to stop seeing her, he would take her back home. He told me that I would end in the gutter, and I pointed out that he did not know me and had no right to make such assumptions.

When, after half an hour, it was obvious that the conversation was going in circles, I got out of the car and went indoors. Besides, my hair was wet from a bath, and I knew this was an infallible recipe for catching an appalling cold (I proved to be right).

Her father then went on to Joy's lodging, and told her she had to stop seeing me. When Joy said she could not promise that, he said that at least she must promise never to come to my room, and to this she finally agreed.

I tried hard to persuade her to break her promise and was so furious when she refused that our relationship very nearly ended there and then. But it so happened that my landlord gave me notice – due to a misunderstanding about a gas fire – and when I had found myself another room a few miles away, I went to the store where she worked, told her I had now changed my room, and asked her to come and visit me there. We had not seen one another for a week, and I think she was missing me as much as I was missing her. So when she reminded me of her promise to her father, I pointed out that it was not the same room, and she allowed herself to be convinced by this piece of casuistry.

Our troubles were not quite over. When, a month or so later, her parents found out we were still seeing one another, I was summoned up to their home near Peterborough. There I explained that I had married at nineteen because my girlfriend was pregnant. When I told them she was a nurse who was nine years my senior, they immediately assumed that I had been inveigled into marriage by a schemer (which was not true). Joy's mother, a white-haired woman with a firm manner – she might have been the headmistress of a girls' school – announced that in that case we had to get engaged, and when I agreed, seemed to regard the problem as solved. (But I suspect she still had her doubts about a working-class son-in-law who had not been to a university.)

Since returning to London I had worked at a series of jobs – in a laundry, a garage (where I was a stock clerk), a wine company, and a plastics factory. The problem was that I hated this kind of work, which left me too tired and disgruntled to work on my novel. Then one day a friend told me that he had decided to wander around the Middle East, and had bought himself a tent and a sleeping bag. Suddenly I saw the solution – buy myself a tent, and sleep outdoors, thus saving myself having to pay rent. I moved out, leaving a friend to take over my room, and spent my first night outdoors sleeping on the edge of a golf course at Whetstone. But I was awake well before dawn, aware that the tent would be too conspicuous in daylight. Then I saw the answer: buy a waterproof cover for the sleeping bag, so I would be invisible unless someone fell over me.

I had saved enough money to live frugally for a few weeks. I left most of my books with Joy – such essentials as Shaw's collected plays, Lawrence's *Seven Pillars of Wisdom*, the Everyman *Thus Spake Zarathustra,* and the Nonesuch works of William Blake – and began to spend my nights sleeping on Hampstead Heath, which was within twenty minutes of Joy's lodgings. Every morning I would awake around eight o'clock, pack up my sleeping bag on the back of my bicycle, and freewheel down Haverstock Hill to a workman's café where I could get two large rounds of bread and dripping and a cup of tea for sevenpence, then cycle down to the British Museum.

There I left my haversack in the cloakroom, and spent the day working on *Ritual in the Dark*.

The deputy superintendent of the Reading Room was the writer Angus Wilson, whose *Hemlock and After* I had read two years ago. He had a mop of white hair, a prominent nose, and an amusingly high voice that could be heard all over the Reading Room when he was on the telephone. He was the first published novelist I had ever clapped eyes on, and I stared at him with fascination.

I already had an acquaintance in the Reading Room, although he worked behind the scenes as an assistant keeper in the Department of Printed Books; his name was Ian Willison, and he occasionally invited me for a cup of coffee in the staff restaurant. It was Ian who told me about the new literary movement that had sprung up in the past two years.

They were known as the Red Brick University writers, or simply as the Movement, and the best known were the poets Philip Larkin, John Wain and Kingsley Amis. Their aim, it seemed, was to write in a tough, unsentimental diction that was a reaction against the rhetoric and romanticism of poets like Dylan Thomas and W R Rodgers, whom they regarded as 'phoneys'. It was not unlike the kind of thing Hemingway tried to do for the novel in the 1920s.

It seemed that Wain and Amis also wrote novels, but quite unlike Hemingway's. Wain had achieved a certain celebrity in 1953 with *Hurry on Down,* a picaresque narrative whose discontented hero is determined to avoid being trapped in bourgeois values, and takes a series of labouring jobs to avoid settling for a respectable middle-class profession. In the following year, Amis had been even more successful with *Lucky Jim,* whose hero, a lecturer in a provincial university (based on Leicester) is revolted and enraged by anything he regards as highbrow, such as folk dancing and classical music. The book was obviously driven by a genuine disgust about what Amis considered 'phoneys', and Somerset Maugham had attacked this new type of rebel as 'scum'.

I was only mildly sympathetic. It all struck me as a kind of over-reaction, like Lawrence's obsession with class. I was far more interested in the problem of 'the outsider', men like Nietzsche, Van Gogh and Dostoevsky, who were tormented by the question of why we are alive and what we are supposed to do now we are here. I had been through a crisis of pessimism in my teens when I had come close to committing suicide, so all this preoccupation with 'phoneys' struck me as rather trivial. I suspected they took it so seriously because their middle-class backgrounds had cushioned them against more serious problems.

It was through the Reading Room that I made another interesting acquaintance. I fell into conversation with a young Canadian musician named Alan Detweiler, who invited me to the flat he shared with a Jewish-

Hungarian intellectual named Alfred Reynolds, who had fled from Germany to escape the Nazis. He proved to be an excellent cook and a music lover and, after an evening of eating veal *gulyas* with sour cream, listening to Beethoven quartets, and discussing Thomas Mann and Hermann Hesse, I readily agreed to become a member of a political discussion group that he called Bridge *(die Brücke)*, devoted to promoting liberal ideals. It consisted of a dozen or so enthusiastic young men who regarded Alfred as a guru.

It was there that I met a good-looking young man named Stuart Holroyd, who wrote articles about poetry for a small magazine; his dazzlingly pretty wife Anne, whom he had known since they were children, worked as a secretary. Unlike most of the Bridge group, Stuart was well read, with a special interest in the Metaphysical poets.

I soon concluded that Alfred's political doctrines were simplistic, amounting to a vague desire for universal peace, coupled with contempt for religion. Since I agreed with Shaw that man needs a religion as a matter of life and death, Alfred and I soon recognised we were intellectually incompatible, and I ceased to attend the meetings.

But Stuart and I remained friendly – even more so as he became aware of the inadequacies of Alfred's old-fashioned rationalism, and at my suggestion began to read works like William James's *Varieties of Religious Experience,* Aldous Huxley's *Perennial Philosophy,* and T E Hulme's *Speculations.* And it was when Stuart told me that he intended writing a book arguing that – as Jung put it – 'the soul has a religious function' that I began to feel that it was about time that I wrote my own non-fiction book.

By September 1954, the autumn rains had driven me back indoors, and I took a room in the auspiciously named Endwell Road in New Cross, and found a job in the Lyons Corner House in Leicester Square. Joy had now become a librarian in Stanmore, and we were so far apart that I saw her only at weekends – having convinced my landlady – a kindly soul named Mrs Harris – that we were married and obliged to live apart until Joy passed her librarianship exams. A few weeks before Christmas I took a better paid job sorting mail in the Central Post Office at St Martin le Grand. And since the Reading Room was more than an hour's cycle ride away, I went to the Museum less often.

I made Angus Wilson's acquaintance one day when I was trying to track down T S Eliot's essay on *Ulysses,* in which he talks about Joyce's 'mythological method'. I inquired at the central desk, and the assistant passed the query on to Angus, who an hour later, brought me a book containing the essay. He glanced down at the pile of manuscript in front of me and asked me what I was writing, and when I said it was a novel, offered to read it and, if he liked it, show it to his publisher. When I learned that he intended to take a long holiday at Christmas, this provided the incentive to work frantically and try to finish the first part of *Ritual in the Dark* so he could take it with him. I was able to hand it to him on Christmas Eve just before he left.

Joy went home for Christmas, but I had no money, and spent Christmas Day in my room dining on egg, bacon and tinned tomatoes. I felt oddly at a loose end without my novel, and that afternoon headed a page in my journal: 'Notes for a book *The Outsider in Literature*', followed by the words: 'To show that the "outsider" is evidence of a particular type of moral development that has its finest fruit in the Christian tradition.' (This last phrase betrays Eliot's influence.) In the local library I had discovered an excellent section on the mystics, and I had been reading Jacob Boehme and Saint John of the Cross. Within an hour I had sketched out the whole book.

I cycled to the Museum as soon as it opened again on New Year's Day. On the way, I recollected the Everyman Introduction to Henri Barbusse's war novel *Under Fire (Le Feu)*, with its description of Barbusse's first success, *Hell (L'Enfer)*, about a man in a boarding house who finds a small hole in the wall of his room, and spends all his days peering though it at the life that comes and goes in the next room. This struck me as the perfect symbol of the 'Outsider', and as soon as I got to the Reading Room, I ordered the book. It arrived at eleven, and I read it through in about five hours. Then, just before closing time, I copied into my notebook a quotation from it: 'In the air on top of a tram, a girl is sitting. Her dress, lifted a little, blows out. But a block in the traffic separates us . . .' And during the following weeks, I wrote the first chapter of *The Outsider*.

I read it aloud to a group of friends at the house of the Biblical scholar Hugh Schonfield, who lived in Highgate, and was pleased by their comments. The book flowed easily, and I had an odd intuition that this was going to be my breakthrough.

When Angus came back from his Christmas holiday, he returned the unfinished typescript of my novel with encouraging comments, but I told him I had started another book, and would probably finish it before I went back to the novel.

Meanwhile, I had found myself a job at a new coffee house that had opened in the Haymarket. Compared to the factories and laundries I had been working in, it seemed like paradise – pleasant surroundings and young and intelligent fellow employees, mostly drama students. I started work at five in the evening, so was able to spend my days in the Reading Room writing *The Outsider*. Because New Cross was too far away, I found myself a room near Baker Street, with a landlady who was a friend of our bohemian manageress Gabrielle Graham-King at the Coffee House.

The progress of the book was very satisfying. I had taught myself to write by keeping a journal since the age of sixteen, so this was almost like a continuation of the journal. I was writing about people who feel alienated from a materialistic society, and my original starting point had been those romantics of the nineteenth century who had experienced moments of ecstatic vision, then woke up to find themselves stranded in a world they hated. This, I felt, explained the high suicide rate among the poets and artists of the nineteenth century, and the number of deaths from alcoholism and tuberculosis. In the twentieth century, the despair had given way to a grim stoicism, and the resultant philosophy had called itself existentialism. Hemingway expressed it in the statement: 'A man can be destroyed but not defeated.'

Yet my natural optimism made me feel that it is not necessary to be either defeated or destroyed. There ought to be some other solution: the way glimpsed by the mystics and saints. My 'Outsiders' felt alienated in modern society – very well, let them try to create a society in which they *would* feel at home. Nietzsche, perhaps the greatest of them, had been defeated by the challenge and died insane, but that was because he was living and working alone, and because during his lifetime this whole problem was new and strange. But if enough Outsiders could learn to understand their problem, they might also learn to come to terms with it and fight back. The Outsider, I was convinced, was a kind of evolutionary 'throw-forward' – the opposite of a throw-back – to a more evolved form of man. And that, I felt, was why I was writing the book: to enable Outsiders to understand themselves.

It flowed faster than I had expected. It was as if I had been preparing to write this book for the past ten years, reading everyone from Goethe to Pirandello, Rousseau to Hemingway. At no point did I have any hesitation about what to write next; I felt almost as if it was being dictated.

One Sunday in spring, when I had already written a third of the book, Joy and I decided to hitchhike down to Canterbury cathedral. We stopped in Rochester at a secondhand bookshop and, as I browsed through the books on the sixpenny shelf outside, I saw one called *A Year of Grace* by the publisher Victor Gollancz. It was an anthology of mysticism, and as I looked through it I said to Joy: 'You know, I think Gollancz might be interested in the Outsider book.'

Over the next few days I typed up the Introduction and the chapter I was working on, which was about T E Lawrence, Van Gogh and the dancer Nijinsky. Then I sent them, with a covering letter, to Gollancz's office in Covent Garden.

Within ten days he had replied, saying he was interested, and would like to see the whole book.

I was breathless with delight. I immediately settled down to rereading what I had sent, trying to put myself behind Gollancz's eyes as he read it. It seemed twice as good as before. I wished Joy was there to hear the news, and cycled over to her room in Ealing – where she was at a librarian school – to tell her that it looked as if I might soon be a published author. She seemed to take it coolly – she was never a girl of strong reactions – but I could tell she was delighted.

For the next two months I worked hard, typing up what I had written in the North Library of the Museum, where I was allowed to use a typewriter, and after that going on to write a chapter about Nietzsche, and then one about Tolstoy's 'madman', who is overwhelmed by a sense of meaninglessness when he wakes in the night, a feeling he calls 'the horror'. I was now dealing with what William James calls 'the sick soul'. Then on to Dostoevsky and his 'underground man', who protests that in a world dominated by reason and logic, people would go insane to avoid losing their freedom.

At this point I heard that my mother was dangerously ill. A grumbling appendix had exploded and caused peritonitis. I decided to go to Leicester immediately, and on the way to St Pancras station, called in at Gollancz's office in Covent Garden, and asked the girl in reception if I could leave an unfinished typescript for Mr Gollancz. She said firmly No, he never looked at unfinished books. I pleaded with her, telling her that I had to catch a train, and that if Mr Gollancz refused to read it, I would collect it on my way back. Reluctantly, she agreed.

For a while it looked as if my mother would die. An operation to remove the suppurating mess failed, and a second, then a third was required, while she grew steadily weaker. She told me later that she thought she *had* died, and experienced a marvellous sense of peace. Then she saw an old man in white robes who told her: 'It's not your time yet – you'll have to go back.' I was immensely relieved to see her recovering; it would have seemed a brutal irony if she died before she could see my first book in print.

Back in London I found a parcel waiting for me. My heart sank for a moment until I found a letter saying that Gollancz would accept the book, and asking me to go and see him. So I cycled to Covent Garden, and was shown into the office of a big man with a bald head and a booming voice, who took me out to lunch, and asked me how on earth I had read so much by the age of 23. I replied: 'Boredom.'

As we shook hands outside his office, Gollancz said gravely: 'I think it possible you may be a man of genius.' As soon as I got home, I wrote and told my mother what he'd said.

Gollancz gave me an advance of £25 on the unfinished book, and I decided to give up my job in the Coffee House to concentrate on writing. He wanted it by the end of August, and I even tried dictating the next chapter – on *The Brothers Karamazov* – to a girl from the Coffee House who could take shorthand; when this proved too difficult, I began to type it straight on to the typewriter to save time.

In August Joy and I took a holiday in Cornwall, and it was made euphoric by a sense of excitement and hope. A few weeks later, when I delivered the typescript on time, Gollancz advanced me another £50. I had earned four months' wages with my pen.

Even so, I had to work in the Post Office again for Christmas. Because I was trying to make Gollancz's £25 spin out as long as possible, I now found my room near Baker Street too expensive (at £2. 10s. a week), and decided to try to find somewhere cheaper. Notting Hill was then inexpensive, and I went and looked in one of those glass-covered boards outside a newsagent's shop that advertised rooms and the services of prostitutes. ('Doris and Judy, erection and demolition experts.') One of them mentioned a house where the landlady was willing to charge a low rent in exchange for help with decorating.

I found it on the wrong side of Chepstow Villas – once a fashionable Edwardian property but now dilapidated and grimy – where the landlady agreed to charge me a pound a week for a completely bare bathroom that was not connected to the water main. Anne Nichols was a painter, bohemian and highly disorganised, whose property-owning mother had given her the place as a means of making a living. Dylan Thomas had once stayed in the basement, and two drunken Scottish painters named Colquhoun and MacBride occupied a top flat. So I moved into my cheerless bathroom, with a one-bar electric fire to keep warm, and spent days plastering and distempering crumbling walls. When Joy stayed with me for weekends we slept in a double sleeping bag on the bare floorboards.

I had told Angus Wilson that Gollancz was considering *The Outsider*, and he immediately suggested that I should show it to his own publisher Fred Warburg, of Secker and Warburg. He proved to be a less impressive character than Gollancz, striking me as a smooth businessman, but he liked the book, and offered to give me a contract. But since he also wanted me to lengthen the chapter on Lawrence, Van Gogh and Nijinsky, and I had no desire to start rewriting, I decided to accept Gollancz's offer. It seemed incredible that two publishers were bidding for me.

After Christmas, Angus offered to lend me his cottage near Bury St Edmunds to finish the novel, and I cycled there in February 1956 with a portable typewriter (borrowed from Laura Del Rivo) and the typescript in my haversack. The cottage was in the middle of a field, and it snowed heavily soon after I arrived, trapping me there. But it seemed exciting to work by the light of gas jets while the windows were dark with piled-up snow.

I returned to London with the finished typescript of *Ritual in the Dark,* and immediately submitted it to Gollancz. But he hated it and turned it down – he said he found it too sordid and depressing. But Angus liked it, although he agreed that it still needed some work, and on his offer to act as final arbiter, Warburg agreed to advance me £50.

Soon after that I went to my first literary party. A lady named Gwenda David, whose husband worked on *The Times*, was a talent spotter for the American publisher Viking, and was about to offer them *The Outsider*. She was giving a launching party for another new writer, Iris Murdoch, who had made her reputation with a novel called *Under the Net,* and whose second novel *Flight from the Enchanter* was about to be published. (In fact, the novels were written in reverse order.) She and I took an immediate liking to one another. Iris had a round, rather homely face that made her look more like a milkmaid than a philosopher (she had written a book on Sartre), and when she learned that I had not been to a university, offered to get me a scholarship at Oxford, a suggestion I gratefully declined.

At the same party, I met a young Scottish poet called James Burns Singer, who astonished me by telling me that he had read *The Outsider* in proof, and would be reviewing it for the *Times Literary Supplement*. He invited me to meet him the next day in the Haymarket, and accompany him to the offices of the magazine *Encounter* to collect a cheque they owed him for an article about the Scots poet Hugh M'Diarmid. The very idea of going to the office of an eminent literary journal impressed me.

The next morning, I met Burns Singer – he told me to call him Jimmy – and watched with awe as the cashier at *Encounter* gave him a cheque for £40, more than half the advance I had received for a whole book. Then we went to the bank to cash it, and to the nearest pub to drink it. During that afternoon I had my first experience of pub crawling, and of observing the incredible amount of whisky that a determined Scot can consume. The more he drank, the more fluently he talked; he seemed to know all his own poetry by heart, as well as most of Hugh M'Diarmid and W S Graham.

I had been invited that evening to the flat of a member of the editorial board of a magazine called *The Twentieth Century* to discuss contributing to an issue devoted to young writers. John Wain was also expected, and since Burns Singer wanted to meet him, I took him along. By the time we got there, he was hardly able to stand, and a large whisky provided by our host – a colleague of Ian Willison's from the British Museum – sent him into a deep sleep.

Wain arrived wearing a duffle coat and a cap, and looking completely unlike a writer which (I learned later), was part of the intention – as a founding member of the Movement, he believed a writer should regard himself as a kind of workman. Wain had an aggressive manner and a tight mouth, and as he talked about his admiration for Arnold Bennett and George Orwell, I got the feeling that he was prickly, possibly with a touch of paranoia. He glanced contemptuously at the recumbent Burns Singer (he would tell me later how much he detested drunken Scots) as the poet slept on peacefully, looking rather like Shelley with his long blond hair and girlish features. But I finally had to leave Jimmy behind.

Two weeks later, *The Outsider* was due to be published. A few days before that, Gollancz sent me to be interviewed by a journalist who lived in a mews in Kensington. His name was David Wainwright, and he struck me as too shy and quiet to be a real journalist. He seemed surprised that I looked so young (although Gollancz had concluded the blurb: 'The author of this remarkable book is only 24') and asked me questions about my background and education; when I told him about sleeping on Hampstead Heath, he became suddenly more attentive, pressed me for details, and began to scribble twice as fast. When the article appeared the following Saturday, my waterproof sleeping bag occupied a central place. So did a photograph of me wearing a polo-neck sweater, an item of clothing I had adopted a year or two earlier because it saved washing shirts.

David had told me that there would also be a review of my book in the *Evening News*, and Joy and I rushed out to buy it, but were unable to find it. But we did find an advertisement for next day's *Observer*, promising a review discussing whether men of genius were Outsiders.

The following morning, a Sunday, Joy and I were up early, and hurried down to the newspaper seller on the corner of Westbourne Grove; we looked through the *Observer* and *Sunday Times* as we walked back.

Both contained reviews by their lead reviewers, Philip Toynbee and Cyril Connolly, perhaps the most influential critics in the country. Both were full of praise. In the *Observer*, Toynbee called the book 'truly astounding', 'an exhaustive and luminously intelligent study of a representative theme of our time', and said it was a contribution to an understanding of our deepest predicament. He compared me to Sartre, and said that on the whole he preferred me.

In the *Sunday Times*, Cyril Connolly said I had a 'quick, dry intelligence which he applies to those states of consciousness which generally defy it', and said it was one of the most remarkable books he had read in a long time. He concluded by advising readers to 'keep an eye on Mr Wilson, and hope his sanity, vitality and typewriter are spared'.

We had only just finished reading them when another tenant asked if we had seen the review in the *Evening News*. This time we found it – at the bottom of a page – with a headline: 'He's a Major Writer – and He's only 24', followed by another glowing review by the book critic John Connell.

The tenant from the basement called to say I was wanted on his telephone (naturally, we had none of our own, and he allowed us to take calls in emergencies). It was my editor, John Rosenberg, ringing to congratulate me. What delighted me most was when he said: 'You'll probably make a great deal of money from this book.'

The phone went on ringing for the rest of the day; newspapers wanting to interview me, requests to appear on radio and television, and friends ringing to congratulate me. And it went on for day after day. *Life* magazine wanted to do a picture story with a photograph of me in my sleeping bag on Hampstead Heath. The *Sunday Times* asked if I would like to become a regular book reviewer at £40 a time.

During the following weeks *The Outsider* went into a second, a third, a fourth printing. It was soon taken by an American publisher (Viking had turned it down), and became a bestseller there too. Within a year it had been translated into a dozen languages.

What had happened? As I look back on it now, it seems clear. It had been more than ten years since the end of the war, and no 'new generation' of writers had appeared. The reputations of Wain, Amis, Iris Murdoch and Angus Wilson had never reached down to the level of the tabloid press, but now the penny-a-liners had a prodigy, a genius, to write about. Since they had no idea of what the book was really about, the picture they painted bore only a passing resemblance to what I had written. All they knew was that it was 'highbrow', and therefore above their heads. Then as time went by, and the absurd publicity reached a kind of frenzy, the 'serious' critics began to qualify their original enthusiasm; they were delighted to feel that it could now be dismissed as the product of a working-class autodidact.

There was another factor involved in the media frenzy that summer. I am sure that if I had been the only newcomer on the literary scene it would certainly never have reached such a pitch of hysteria. But two weeks before *The Outsider* was reviewed, a combative young drama critic with a craving for celebrity had acclaimed a play called *Look Back in Anger,* and launched its author on the path to fame. Within days, John Osborne and I were being bracketed together as 'Angry Young Men'.

I very much doubt whether a philosophical book about Outsiders would have aroused wide attention in the tabloids, with or without the sleeping bag. But with a second literary sensation in the same month, and a catchy phrase that seemed made for the convenience of gossip columnists, the story was irresistible.

I have no doubt that the Svengali behind the Angry Young Men was the combative drama critic with a taste for celebrity, Kenneth Tynan.

2   He That Plays the King

Kenneth Peacock Tynan seemed the last person in the world to bring a new realism to the British theatre, for he spent his whole life wrapped in a cocoon of fantasy. Paul Johnson describes, in *Intellectuals*, witnessing his arrival at Magdalen for the start of his second year at Oxford:

> I stared in astonishment at this tall, beautiful, epicene youth, with pale yellow locks, Beardsley cheekbones, fashionable stammer, plum-coloured suit, lavender tie and ruby signet-ring . . . He seemed to fill the lodge with his possessions and servitors whom he ordered about with calm and imperious authority. One sentence particularly struck me: 'Have a care for that box, my man – it is freighted with golden shirts.'

The elegant young man was not the son of a peer, but of a well-to-do Birmingham shopkeeper named Peter Tynan. At least, he thought he was until his last year at Oxford, when his father was carried off by bronchitis, and he discovered that he was actually the illegitimate son of Sir Peter Peacock, alias Tynan, former mayor of Warrington, who had been leading a double life for the past quarter of a century, and spending half his time living in sin in Birmingham with an ex-post office employee named Letitia Rose Tynan.

Sir Peter, a self-made man, had made the mistake of marrying a sour, bad-tempered lady named Maria Timmins, the elder sister of his deceased wife, and had eventually left her (with five children) when, in the last year of the First World War, he met Rose Tynan at a whist drive. Although plain and bandy-legged, Rose had a sweet temperament, and they started an affair. Soon Peter Peacock bade his wife of a quarter of a century farewell, and moved to Birmingham with Letitia Rose. When, in 1918, he was knighted for his services to Warrington (he was mayor six times) it was Rose he took to Buckingham Palace with him.

When Kenneth Tynan was born nine years later, on 2 April 1927, his father was 54 and his mother 38. From the beginning the child was adored and spoilt by his mother, although treated with less indulgence by his father. At grammar school he was naturally brilliant, taking a dozen school prizes, and in spite of a stammer, becoming secretary of the debating society and a fluent speaker. His father wanted to send him away to a public school, but his doting mother resisted and, as usual, won.

He was also a devoted filmgoer, and in 1942, when he was fifteen, was so enthralled with *Citizen Kane* that he saw it five times, and wrote admiringly to Orson Welles, who replied amiably, and would eventually become a lifelong acquaintance. When his mother took him to see Donald Wolfit in *Macbeth*, Tynan became an instant admirer of the old, heroic school of acting.

Like most literate schoolboys he also became an admirer of Oscar Wilde, and set out to imitate Wilde's dress sense by wearing a ladies' check raincoat and carrying an umbrella with a red silk ribbon. But Tynan was far too subtle to admit to anything as obvious as being influenced by Wilde, just as in later years he would avoid acknowledging his enormous debt to Shaw's drama criticisms. Neither did he share Wilde's sexual preferences, his own taste running to sado-masochism, with a preference for rounded female posteriors. In a school debate about whether the younger generation had lost the ability to entertain itself, Tynan's contribution was to advocate masturbation. (In later life he would describe himself as one of the last survivors of the species *Tynanosaurus homo masturbans*.) He was – in spite of a weak chest inherited from his father – smoking by this time, preferring Brazilian cigarettes in a very long cigarette holder.

An older schoolfriend, Julian Holland, had moved on to London and the BBC, and Tynan began spending weekends with him there, and devoting much time to the theatre, which also led him to practise the art of reviewing for his own private satisfaction. When he was seventeen, Wolfit's *Lear* became the talk of the London season, confirming Tynan's earlier admiration for the heroic school of acting.

In the following year Tynan became a member of a new drama group at school, and set out to persuade them to allow him to play Hamlet in his own shortened version. At first they declined, until Tynan gave a brilliant lecture on *Hamlet* to the school literary society and ended by delivering the soliloquies and explaining how he would edit the play; this won them over, and in due course Tynan's *Hamlet* was a remarkable success. He even managed to persuade the *Sunday Times* drama critic, James Agate, to come and see it. In the taxicab from the station Agate placed his hand on Tynan's knee and asked if he was homosexual. 'I'm af-f-fraid not.' 'Oh well, I thought we'd get that out of the way,' said Agate equably.

In the same year Tynan was granted a scholarship to Magdalen College, Oxford, of £50 a year. He hardly needed the money, but being granted the only scholarship that Magdalen dispensed that year speaks for his ability to charm and impress.

Hamlet had brought him another success; he had persuaded his leading lady, Pauline Whittle, to abandon her boyfriend and get engaged to him.

He also lost his virginity at this time, but this was to a girl named Enid, who was six years his senior. A week later he was convinced he was in love with yet another girl named Joy. Tynan was already practising the part of the dedicated Don Juan.

The *Hamlet* production had demonstrated his ability to organise, to make things happen. At Oxford he directed *Samson Agonistes* and Maxwell Anderson's *Winterset*, and played Holofernes in *Love's Labour's Lost*. He went to London productions and wrote reviews of them, one of which persuaded James Agate that he was 'a great critic in the making'. And his flamboyant lifestyle and colourful attire soon made him one of the best known characters in Oxford, recognisable from afar by his cloak lined with red silk, his bottle-green suits and gold shirts. (This was still a time of clothes rationing, but after all, his father owned several drapery shops.) He also got rid of the encumbrance of the engagement to take advantage of the bounteous supply of female undergraduates, and persuaded each of his conquests to donate a pair of her panties, with which he adorned the walls of his rooms.

He had also amassed an impressive collection of pornography. His devotion to the lash was openly proclaimed – he told an audience at the Oxford Union: 'My theme is: just a thong at twilight.' But he seems to have been less interested in being punished than in spanking bottoms, finding a kind of aesthetic satisfaction in the sight of little brown anuses peeping from between spread buttocks.

He gave wonderful parties, attended by London showbiz personalities, (and charging entrants ten shillings at the door) and was burnt in effigy by the young bloods. No one had made such an impact on Oxford since the days of Brian Howard and Harold Acton (whose ability to outrage the older generation is captured in Evelyn Waugh's *Brideshead Revisited* in the characters of Sebastian Flyte and Anthony Blanche).

The death of his father and the discovery of his illegitimacy came as a blow, for although he had no liking for his father, the idea of being a bastard hardly fitted in with his self-image as a young aristocrat, but he soon added the announcement of his status to his repertoire of shock tactics. He told an attractive young American actress whose stage name was Elaine Dundy: 'I am the illegitimate son of Sir Peter Peacock. I have an annual income. I'm twenty-three, and I will either die or kill myself when I reach thirty because by then I will have said everything I have to say. Will you marry me?' Elaine said yes, and this time he actually went through with it, marrying her in January 1951. She was the daughter of a wealthy New Yorker, who immediately raised her allowance.

When they returned from their honeymoon he took up an appointment to direct Cocteau's *Les Parents Terribles* at the Arts Theatre Club in the West End, but soon clashed with one of his leading ladies, Fay Compton.

The famous actress was the sister of the novelist Compton Mackenzie, and took badly to Tynan's innovations. When she threatened to leave the show, actor-manager Alec Clunes had to choose between a brilliant young rebel and a famous actress whose presence was essential to filling seats. It was Tynan who had to leave. This defeat put an end to his hopes of a career as a director, and the humiliation rankled for years.

In other ways, his career was prospering. On the recommendation of the theatre critic Harold Hobson, Longman's had accepted Tynan's book *He That Plays the King*, for which Tynan had obtained a foreword from Orson Welles by telling the actor that the book would not otherwise be published. It was an impressive first book, containing many of the theatrical reviews he had written since those early visits to London, and the title reveals that the virtue he most looked for in a production was heroic acting of the kind epitomised in Wolfit. Welles was the ideal person to introduce it, for he had once said that, for better or worse, he was a 'king actor'; this was not self-praise, but a recognition that his style of acting was at its best when playing the king. The book made Tynan's reputation as an authority on the theatre, and led to an invitation to write occasional criticism for the *Spectator*.

Then a minor disaster led to his first regular appointment. The year 1951 was Britain's Festival year, the centenary of Queen Victoria's Great Exhibition of 1851. The eminent actor Alec Guinness decided to produce *Hamlet* in a modern-dress production, and asked Tynan to undertake the role of Player King. Its first night was catastrophic, due almost entirely to the pranks of the lighting system, which behaved as if it was independent of the action on stage, so the ghost scene looked like a midsummer day while others were performed in unaccountable gloom. Later performances were free of these surreal effects, but that first night and its reviews were enough to guarantee a half empty theatre for the rest of its short run.

The *Evening Standard* theatre critic, Beverley Baxter MP, panned it in a review headed 'The Worst *Hamlet* I Have Ever Seen', and reserved particular acerbity for Tynan, 'who would not get a chance in a village hall . . . unless he was related to the vicar', then describing his performance as 'quite dreadful'. (Apparently he was under the misapprehension that certain critical remarks about himself in an anonymous review had been made by Tynan.) Tynan replied in a letter to the *Evening Standard*: 'I am quite a good enough critic to know that my performance in *Hamlet* was not "quite dreadful"; it is, in fact, only slightly less than mediocre', thereby confirming the already favourable opinion of himself conceived by the features editor, who asked him to contribute a series of theatre profiles.

Tynan set out to attract attention. According to Paul Johnson, he pinned on his desk a note with the words: 'Rouse tempers, goad and lacerate, raise whirlwinds.' A less than favourable profile of Danny Kaye – which drew angry criticisms from readers – was followed by an acidic 're-evaluation' of Vivien Leigh, implying that the limit of her ability was to be 'pert, sly and spankable, and fill out a small personality', and went on to observe ungallantly that at 40 she was well past her prime. As Laurence Olivier's wife she had recently received ecstatic reviews when the two of them had played *Antony and Cleopatra* and Shaw's *Caesar and Cleopatra* on alternate evenings at the St James's Theatre and Tynan, who venerated Olivier as England's greatest 'heroic' actor, suspected that her 'kittenish' qualities were causing Olivier to lower his sights and subdue his powers to meet her halfway. 'A cat, in fact, can do more than look at a king: she can hypnotise him.'

This profile aroused as much indignation as Tynan had hoped, and six days later he was invited to dine with the newspaper's proprietor Lord Beaverbrook.

Soon after that he went to New York to meet his wife's parents, and was asked to write an article for the *New York Times* on the Broadway scene, and monthly profiles for *Harper's Bazaar*. When he returned to London he was appointed the *Evening Standard*'s regular theatre critic in place of Beverley Baxter.

In 1952 the British theatre was not in as healthy a state as the critics liked to believe. It was still dominated by the essentially middle-class drama of Noël Coward and Terence Rattigan. The only British playwright of note to have emerged since the war was Christopher Fry, who had reintroduced poetic drama which had a captivating verbal ebullience, although T S Eliot was also pleading for a new poetic drama, and practising it with works like *The Cocktail Party*. Otherwise, when Londoners felt like a more serious evening, they went to a revival of Chekhov, or a play by Jean Anouilh, whose seventh play in four years was running.

When Tynan came along, the only eminent critic who was disturbed by this state of affairs was Harold Hobson, who wrote for the *Sunday Times*. Brought up as a Christian Scientist, he wanted to see more moral seriousness in the theatre. In 1952, after a trip to Paris, he was complaining that the theatre seemed to be cut off by soundproof walls from the real world of Cold War politics and industrial unrest. But Hobson lacked Tynan's desire to shock his contemporaries into attention.

Tynan, England's best theatre critic since Bernard Shaw, was determined to 'cut his way into the theatre at the point of his pen', and learned from Shaw the trick of jauntily introducing himself and his personality into his reviews. Like Shaw he was also cheerfully prepared to make enemies. A review of Ralph Richardson's production of *Macbeth* with Gielgud in the title role begins: 'Last Tuesday night at the Stratford Memorial Theatre Macbeth walked the plank, leaving me, I am afraid, unmoved to the point of paralysis', and both Gielgud's acting and Richardson's directing are shredded. A review of a play called *Héloïse* by James Forsyth begins: 'I was in some doubt, when the curtain fell, whether I should give way to rage or compromise on boredom.' Of *Timon of Athens*: 'Watching *Timon* was, I found, rather like going to some scandalously sophisticated party at which, halfway through, the host suddenly falls down drunk and begins to rave from under the piano.' Of a play called *Sweet Peril* acted by the husband and wife team Michael Denison and Dulcie Gray: 'The repulsively false reconciliation between the Denisons in the last act cannot be said to be trumped up, because the authors hold no trumps in their hand.' Of *A Day by the Sea*, 'To say that the cast rise above their material is an understatement: except by collapsing flat on their faces they could scarcely fall below it.'

Gielgud remarked on the 'wonderful-when-it-isn't-you' feeling of members of his profession when reading Tynan.

Tynan had turned against his old idol Wolfit, beginning a review 'Mr Wolfit's present supporting company explores new horizons of inadequacy.' But when he damned Wolfit's revival of the old warhorse *The Wandering Jew* by E Temple Thurston, remarking that Wolfit's style of acting should not be in a theatre but in a large field, and ended 'his beacon light is mediocrity', the enraged Wolfit threatened to sue, and to Tynan's disgust the *Evening Standard* decided not to stand and fight, but to settle out of court.

Tynan's own downfall came through threatening legal action. In May 1953, delighted with the furore that was being caused by his drama critic, the features editor, Charles Curran, decided to garner further publicity by asking the opinion of readers about whether they preferred Tynan or his predecessor Beverley Baxter. Typical of the replies was a lady who complained 'When, oh when, can we have Mr Baxter back as your dramatic critic? I can no longer stomach Mr Tynan's impertinences.' There were many more in this vein, compared to the few pro-Tynan letters.

But it was a letter from his fellow critic Ivor Brown that really stung him, ending with 'Young though he is, he is probably now too old to acquire other desirable, if not indispensable, attributes of the craft such as tact, good taste, good manners, the sense of fair play, and the subtler kinds of sensibility.' Enraged at what he saw as the editor's lack of loyalty, he wrote to say that if the *Evening Standard* printed another critical letter like that he would be compelled to sue for slander and libel. The editor, Percy Elland, rose to the challenge by sacking him. And although Tynan tried hard to get himself reinstated, even co-opting his wife – whom Beaverbrook fancied – to write to the newspaper's proprietor, it was all a waste of time and, by July 1953 Tynan was out of a job. The *Standard* agreed to pretend that this was by mutual agreement, but there must have been much chortling and back-slapping in Fleet Street and London's theatreland.

The humiliation turned out to be a blessing in the long run. Tynan found himself another position on the tabloid *Daily Sketch* in October, but decided to put out feelers towards the *Observer*, a serious Sunday newspaper that had experienced a revival under David Astor, son of the famous parliamentarian Nancy Astor. He had put together a powerful team that included Arthur Koestler, Philip Toynbee and Sir Harold Nicolson, and the literary pages were soon acknowledged as the best in Fleet Street.

At first the aristocratic Astor was unenthusiastic about Tynan, feeling that he had achieved celebrity by the un-English method of offending everybody, and that he was 'all flash and no substance'. Elaine Tynan sent him *He That Plays the King*, and he began to waver. What swung the balance was the simultaneous publication of two more books, *Persona Grata,* a volume of photographs with Cecil Beaton, and a short book on Alec Guinness. These convinced Astor that after all Tynan had enough *gravitas* to join the *Observer* team, and Tynan lost no time in giving in his notice to the *Daily Sketch*.

Sadly, this improvement in his career prospects was accompanied by a deterioration in his marriage. Tynan's interest in S/M had not diminished, and Elaine objected to being beaten on her bare bottom with a headmaster's cane, as well as the role-playing games he enjoyed, which included him dressing as a woman and wanting her to play the part of a man. To say Tynan's sexuality was immature may be unduly harsh, but what is clear is that it was intensely subjective, based upon introversion and masturbation fantasies. In his book on bullfighting Tynan quotes Geoffrey Gorer's comment that de Sade's philosophy is based on 'pleasure in the ego's modification of the outside world', i.e., the ability to impose one's will. To make a woman bare her bottom and endure smacks or strokes of the cane implies total dominance. The need to drag this dominance into the light of consciousness, so to speak, by this display of mastery argues an inadequate self-image – the kind of inadequacy that most teenagers accept as normal, but strive to put behind them through the process of growing up. The fact that Tynan never outgrew this inadequacy, but continued to play sexual games to the end of his life, indicates a soft underbelly to his personality that was easily damaged. This probably explains a curious comment made by Elaine in a letter to a newspaper after her separation from her husband, to the effect that she regarded Elvis Presley as the far greater man, a remark whose apparent irrelevancy implies that she saw Presley as a wholly masculine male and that Tynan was not.

There was another problem, indicated by Paul Johnson's comment that 'Tynan, while reserving the unqualified right to be unfaithful himself, expected loyalty from his spouse.' The science fiction writer A E Van Vogt has identified males of this type as 'Right Men', meaning that they are so addicted to being 'in the right' that it would take wild horses to make them admit they are wrong. Such men need to feel a sense of total mastery over their wives and families, and so they create a kind of miniature dictator state. But this craving for an autocratic self-image means that if the wife demonstrates her independence by leaving him, he plunges into total moral collapse which may even result in suicide – the foundation of the castle of illusion has been dynamited. Tynan's odd sexual games seem to confirm this notion of him as a Right Man balancing precariously on a teetering pinnacle of self-esteem.

His position as the *Observer*'s drama critic should certainly have soothed away any shreds of self-doubt. It made him one of the most influential critics in London. He used his new position to crusade for the kind of serious theatre he wanted to see and to attack the commercial theatre dominated by impresarios like Binkie Beaumont. 'The results of our culpable indulgence surround us,' he declared in this third *Observer* article in September 1954. 'No playwright rises above his audience's expectations for very long; why should he do his best work when *Dry Rot* and *The Love Match* are delighting the public with their worthlessness?'

A few weeks later he invented a useful characterisation of all he disliked in an *Observer* review entitled 'West End Apathy'. After describing the contemporary graveyard he goes on:

> If you seek a tombstone, look about you; survey the peculiar nullity of the drama's prevalent *genre*, the Loamshire play.
>
> Its setting is a country house in what used to be called Loamshire . . . Except when someone must sneeze, or be murdered, the sun invariably shines. The inhabitants belong to a social class derived partly from romantic novels and partly from the playwright's vision of the leisured life he will lead after the play is a success – this being the only effort of imagination he is called on to make. Joys and sorrows are giggles and whimpers: the crash of denunciation dwindles into 'Oh stuff, Mummy!' and 'Oh really, Daddy!' And so grim is the continuity of these things that the foregoing paragraph might have been written at any time during the last thirty years.
>
> Loamshire is a glibly codified fairy-tale world of no more use to the student of life than a doll's house would be to the student of town planning. Its vice is to have engulfed the theatre, thereby expelling better minds . . .

Here Tynan's mastery of the Shavian style (as in that penultimate sentence) can be savoured – he has absorbed it to such an extent that when he occasionally quotes Shaw in *Curtains,* his collection of dramatic criticisms, they are almost indistinguishable from one another.

Like Shaw, he also campaigned against the Lord Chamberlain, the member of the royal household who had the right to ban plays on grounds of sex or bad taste. Tynan's objection was that the Lord Chamberlain deprived the British theatre of the chance to grow up. For example, in the mid-fifties homosexuality was a major issue. In 1954, Lord Montague of Beaulieu, Michael Pitt-Rivers and Peter Wildeblood were charged with indecency between males, and Wildeblood sent to prison for eighteen months. In the following year Wildeblood wrote a book called *Against the Law* protesting about the laws prohibiting homosexuality, which stirred up a protest that led to the law being changed. But the theatre was not allowed to contribute to the debate because the Lord Chamberlain would not permit it.

In America homosexuality had long been openly discussed on stage, and in many of the plays of Tennessee Williams it plays a central role. In 1949, his *Streetcar Named Desire* had only just succeeded in scraping past the Lord Chamberlain, and the furore it had created guaranteed that it would not be allowed to happen again. Tynan was one of those largely responsible for the abolition of the Lord Chamberlain's office in 1968.

But Tynan's problem as an advocate of change was that he had no one to point to as an example of what theatre should be doing. Shaw launched his writing career with a book on Ibsen, but where was his modern equivalent?

Then, on 1 January 1955, Tynan found him, and wondered why it had taken so long. He and Elaine were in Paris, and Tynan went alone to see Brecht's *Mother Courage*. Five years earlier he had heard the American critic, Eric Bentley, lecture on Brecht, but had not been deeply impressed, since what he heard was basically theory – the theory of the so-called alienation effect, keeping the audience aware that this is a play, not real life.

But seeing this on stage was a different matter. Brecht was, of course, a dedicated Communist; he had moved to East Berlin in 1948 and formed the Berliner Ensemble, a company so highly disciplined that even for an audience with no German, the sheer vitality of its performance was mesmerising. (Anyone who wishes to experience that impact without the trouble of going to the theatre should listen to the Lotte Lenya American 1950s recording of *The Threepenny Opera*.)

The vitality was essential, for what Brecht was doing in *Mother Courage* was not presenting a drama so much as a history lesson, and history lessons can be dull. As a Marxist he believed in the economic motivation of history, in which human beings are moved by forces they do not understand; they think they act out of personal motives, but it is history that is pulling the strings. In the Brechtian theatre, the puppets have to dance with a vitality that makes them seem alive. The drama must have the impersonal force of a storm.

Which is why Tynan left the theatre that evening in a state of exaltation akin to religious conversion. When Elaine returned to the hotel that evening, he told her he was now a Marxist.

For a former devotee of Oscar Wilde and *fin de siècle* aestheticism, this sounds preposterous – from art for art's sake to the dictatorship of the proletariat. Neither is it easy to imagine an anti-authoritarian like Tynan knuckling under to dogmatic Communist ideology. But then, we have to try and understand what Tynan gained from this marriage of convenience. He said he stood for intellectual seriousness against Loamshire triviality, but this was too amorphous and indefinite to be more than a talking point. What he needed was a credo, a rock to stand on, a big stick to slash at his opponents, and this is what Marxism provided.

His wife Elaine was also pleased, for (as she comments in her autobiography *Life Itself)* she thought that his newfound humanitarianism might cause him to 'drop his desire to inflict physical pain and mental pain on another member of the human race. Specifically, me.' What she failed to grasp was that his Marxism was essentially a theatrical creed, and that caning a girl's bare bottom while she bent submissively was also, in its way, a piece of theatre.

This and other problems were destroying the marriage. Elaine had been an actress and had the reasonable expectation that marriage to a theatre critic might forward her career. She was disappointed, for Tynan's controversial fame did not predispose managers in her favour. In November 1954 she had auditioned for a play at the Arts Theatre, so had been unwilling to leave for Paris. Tynan used a method he had employed when she was unwilling to agree to sado-masochistic sex – he stood on the window ledge and threatened to jump until she gave way. But when they returned from Paris, she learned that she had been chosen for the part but dropped because they were unable to get hold of her. She was understandably frustrated and unhappy, and her drinking – a lifelong problem – increased.

Tynan took care to make no open declaration of his new Communist faith, and in a review of a Paris production of Brecht's *Caucasian Chalk Circle* in June 1955 seemed to wilfully mislead when he said: 'if I was unmoved by what Brecht had to say, I was overwhelmed by the way in which he said it.' But the welcome he gave to the first British production of *Mother Courage* by Joan Littlewood's Theatre Workshop makes clear – in spite of doubts about the production – that he was in the grip of a new enthusiasm.

For Tynan, the most exciting event of 1955 occurred in August, when a new theatre company held auditions in the Royal Court Theatre in Sloane Square. The moving forces behind it were an actor-manager called George Devine and a Devon poet and playwright named Ronald Duncan. The latter had combined with Benjamin Britten and Lord Harewood to launch the Taw and Torridge Festival in Devon in 1953, and they formed a group called the English Stage Company.

When they were seeking a London base, the Royal Court Theatre was proposed, and Devine, who was also trying to form a modern theatre company, met Duncan, and they agreed that Devine should be its director. The Royal Court was the theatre that had launched Bernard Shaw to fame half a century earlier with productions of *Man and Superman* and *John Bull's Other Island*.

Angus Wilson was approached and asked to write a play – for one of Duncan's basic ideas was to persuade novelists to write plays. When I first began to know Angus well, in that summer of 1955, he was working on *The Mulberry Bush*, about an Oxford professor and his wife, ageing liberals who have lost touch with the younger generation, to whom they seem too earnest and old fashioned. Their deceased son Robert, idealised by the Fabian Society, proves to have had a sexual skeleton in the cupboard, which is in due course revealed to everyone's discomfort. It was, in a sense, an old-fashioned well-made play, but too intelligent to be called Loamshire.

The Mulberry Bush launched the first Royal Court season on 2 April 1956. Its reception was friendly but not enthusiastic, most critics agreeing that it contained too many characters and was not sufficiently dramatic – in fact, that it should have been a novel rather than a play. These lukewarm reviews had the predictable effect on the box office.

The second play, Arthur Miller's *The Crucible*, about the Salem witchcraft persecutions of 1692, was clearly inspired by the Senator McCarthy anti-Communist witch hunts of the early 1950s, but British theatregoers were not much interested in American politics, and the play failed to attract audiences – the auditorium remained less than half full.

On 8 May 1956, the first night of a play called *Look Back in Anger* seemed as inauspicious as the first two. When the curtain went up on a cramped suburban attic bedsit with a housewife slaving at the ironing board, one member of the audience wondered why she had gone to the theatre to find herself back at home, while another said he expected to see himself walk in through the door at any moment.

Worse was to come as two working-class young men, obviously bored with a dull Sunday evening, lounged in armchairs and read the Sunday papers. One of them asks the other if the 'posh' Sundays (i.e., the *Sunday Times* and *Observer)* make him feel ignorant. When the reply is 'Not 'arf', he addresses the same question to his wife Alison, who comes out of a trance to ask: 'What's that?' After the question is repeated she says she hasn't read them yet. 'That's not what I asked you,' says the young man, 'I said . . .' His mild-mannered friend interrupts to say, 'Leave the poor girl alone. She's busy.' To which the aggressive one replies: 'Well, she can talk, can't she?' then asks her: 'You can talk, can't you? You can express an opinion. Or does the White Woman's Burden make it impossible to think?'

At which point it becomes clear that the disagreeable person – Jimmy Porter – is determined to pick a quarrel. Fortunately both his wife and his friend Cliff are so used to his outbursts that neither rises to the occasion. So Jimmy goes on directing his anger at the Sunday papers – specifically at the bishop of Bromley, who has called upon all Christians to support the manufacture of the H-bomb, and denies that he supports the rich against the poor when in fact he denies the difference of class distinctions. Then Jimmy refers irritably to J B Priestley for casting well-fed glances back to the Edwardian twilight, but nevertheless admits that he can understand nostalgia for the Edwardians. 'The old Edwardian brigade do make their brief little world look very tempting.'

After that there are reminiscences about his ex-mistress Madeline, who was ten years his senior, and made all life seem adventurous. Then after more pleas from Cliff to shut up, he goes on to attack Alison's mother and father, 'militant, arrogant and full of malice', and her brother Nigel, 'the platitude from Outer Space', who invited Jimmy to step outside when the latter called his mother evil minded. At this point the stage instructions read: *He's been cheated of his response, but he's got to draw blood somehow.* So he turns on his wife and tells her that the right word to describe her is 'pusillanimous', and elaborates on this until she says if he doesn't stop she'll go mad, at which he retorts: 'Why don't you? That would be something anyway.' They try listening to a Vaughan Williams symphony on the radio, but Jimmy claims that Alison's ironing is causing interference, and switches off.

This is the signal for an attack on Alison for her clumsiness and noisiness, and on women in general. Cliff tries to interrupt him with some horseplay, but Jimmy pushes him into the ironing board, which collapses, and the iron burns Alison's arm. Whereupon, Jimmy, his anger temporarily sated, goes off to read in his bedroom, and there is a scene in which Alison tells Cliff she is pregnant. When Jimmy comes back he is rather chastened, and apologises. But he still has enough combativeness left in him to say he wishes he was homosexual, to free him from the need for women. Then the news that Helena, an old friend of Alison's, is coming to stay makes him explode again, and tell Alison that he wishes something would happen to her that would make her grow up – such as having a child and losing it. Alison is so stunned by this piece of brutality that she moves upstage, and

Jimmy stands alone, soliloquising to the audience, explaining that Alison devours him as a python devours a rabbit every time they have sex, and that the bulge around her navel is himself, suffocating inside her. 'She'll go on sleeping and devouring until there's nothing left of me.' As he exits the curtain comes down.

I have dwelt so long on this first act because I want to convey just what that first-night audience found themselves confronted with (as I was about three weeks later). The impresario Binkie Beaumont walked out after the first act, and Terence Rattigan was only persuaded to stay by the critic T C Worsley, to whom he remarked ironically that the playwright seemed to be saying: 'Look, Ma, I'm not Terence Rattigan.' Osborne's mother, who went to the second night, was told by the barmaid upstairs, 'They don't like this one, do they dear? They don't like it at all. Never mind, it won't be much longer.'

The remainder of the play made this prediction seem plausible enough. In the second act, while Jimmy is away at the deathbed of an old charlady (thereby demonstrating that, no matter how disagreeable his manners, his heart is in the right place), Alison's father, alerted by her friend Helen to the domestic woes of his daughter, comes to take her home. Helen stays on, quarrels with Jimmy, slaps his face, and then unexpectedly takes him in her arms, a turn of events that leaves the audience slightly incredulous.

In the last act, Alison returns, having lost the baby, and Helen takes her leave, after which Jimmy resumes his attack on Alison, telling her she will 'never make it as a human being', and reproaching her for not attending the old charlady's funeral. But when he tells her, 'I may be a lost cause, but I thought if you loved me it needn't matter', she suddenly breaks down, and tells him that losing the baby has turned her into the kind of person he always wanted. 'Don't you see, I'm in the mud at last. I'm grovelling! I'm crawling!' and she collapses at his feet. And Jimmy, now the winner, looks down at her 'with tender irony', and suggests that they can now resume their favourite nursery game of pretending to be bears and squirrels.

Predictably, the reviews the next day were, for the most part, appalling, only tempered by the obvious feeling of some critics that a first play, no matter how bad, deserved a sporting chance. In the *Daily Telegraph* Patrick Gibbs said that Jimmy Porter needed to see a psychiatrist, Milton Schulman in the *Evening Standard* called the play a self-pitying snivel while, in the *Financial Times*, Derek Granger said that watching it was as uncomfortable as watching friends having a row. Devine and the rest of the company had no doubt it had been a flop. After Osborne had read the unsympathetic reviews the next morning, he arrived at the theatre to find general gloom, Devine comforting but obviously disappointed, and the director Tony Richardson saying: 'But what did you expect? You didn't expect them to *like* it, did you?' But they agreed that the sensible thing would be to wait until Sunday and see what Tynan and Hobson had to say.

So on Sunday Osborne walked off the boat on which he was living at Mortlake, and bought the *Sunday Times* and *Observer*. Hobson in the former started promisingly:

'Mr John Osborne, the author of *Look Back in Anger*, is a writer who at present does not know what he is doing. He seems to think that he is crashing through the world with deadly right uppercuts, whereas all the time it is his unguarded left that is doing the damage.' What he seems to mean is that while Jimmy pours out his scorn on the bishop of Bromley, complacent Conservatives and backward-looking Edwardians, the real damage is to the person who is closest to him, his wife.

Hobson went on: 'Though the blinkers still obscure his vision, he is a writer of outstanding promise, and the English Stage Company are to be congratulated on having discovered him.' He went on to say that the most moving moment of the play was Alison's 'heart-broken, grovelling yet peace-securing submission' that finally draws them together again.

But it was Tynan's review that brought rescue to the beleaguered English Stage Company as he unhesitatingly went overboard for Osborne:

'They are scum' was Mr Maugham's famous verdict on the class of State-aided university students to which Kingsley Amis's Lucky Jim belongs; and since Mr Maugham seldom says anything controversial or uncertain of wide acceptance, his opinion must clearly be that of many. Those who share it had better stay well away from John Osborne's *Look Back in Anger*, which is all scum and a mile wide.

Its hero, a provincial graduate who runs a sweet-stall, has already been summed up in print as 'a young pup', and it is not hard to see why. What with his flair for introspection, his gift for ribald parody, his excoriating candour, his contempt for 'phoney-ness', his weakness for soliloquy, and his desperate conviction that the time is out of joint, Jimmy Porter is the completest young pup in our literature since Hamlet, Prince of Denmark. His wife, whose Anglo-Indian parents resent him, is persuaded by an actress friend to leave him; Jimmy's prompt response is to go to bed with the actress. Mr Osborne's picture of a certain kind of modern marriage is hilariously accurate: he shows us two attractive young animals engaged in competitive martyrdom, each with its teeth sunk deep in the other's neck, and each reluctant to break the clinch for fear of bleeding to death.

The fact that he writes with charity has led many critics into the trap of supposing that Mr Osborne's sympathies are wholly with

Jimmy. Nothing could be more false. Jimmy is simply and abundantly alive; that rarest of dramatic phenomena, the act of original creation, has taken place; and those who carp were better silent. Is Jimmy's anger justified? Why doesn't he do something? These questions might be relevant if the character had failed to come to life; in the presence of such evident and blazing vitality, I marvel at the pedantry that could ask them. Why don't Chekhov's people do something? Is the sun justified in scorching us? There will be time enough to debate Mr Osborne's moral position when he has written a few more plays. In the present one he certainly goes off the deep end, but I cannot regard this as a vice in a theatre that seldom ventures more than a toe into the water.

Look Back in Anger presents post-war youth as it really is, with special emphasis on the non-U intelligentsia who live in bed-sitters and divide the Sunday papers into two groups, 'posh' and 'wet'. To have done this at all would be a signal achievement; to have done it in a first play is a minor miracle. All the qualities are there, qualities one had despaired of ever seeing on the stage – the drift towards anarchy, the instinctive leftishness, the automatic rejection of 'official' attitudes, the surrealist sense of humour (Jimmy describes a pansy friend as 'a female Emily Brontë'), the casual promiscuity, the sense of lacking a crusade worth fighting for, and, underlying all these, the determination that no one who dies shall go unmourned.

One cannot imagine Jimmy Porter listening with a straight face to speeches about our inalienable right to flog Cypriot schoolboys. You could never mobilise him and his kind into a lynching mob, since the art he lives for, jazz, was invented by Negroes; and if you gave him a razor, he would do nothing with it but shave. The Porters of our time deplore the tyranny of 'good taste' and refuse to accept 'emotional' as a term of abuse; they are classless, and they are also leaderless. Mr Osborne is their first spokesman in the London theatre. He has been lucky in his sponsors (the English Stage Company), his director (Tony Richardson), and his interpreters: Mary Ure, Helena Hughes, and Alan Bates give fresh and unforced performances, and in the taxing central role Kenneth Haigh never puts a foot wrong.

That the play needs changes I do not deny: it is twenty minutes too long, and not even Mr Haigh's bravura could blind me to the painful whimsey of the final reconciliation scene. I agree that *Look Back in Anger* is likely to remain a minority taste. What matters, however, is the size of the minority. I estimate it at roughly 6,733,000, which is the number of people in this country between the ages of twenty and thirty. And this figure will doubtless be swelled by refugees from other age-groups who are curious to know precisely what the contemporary young pup is thinking and feeling. I doubt if I could love anyone who did not wish to see *Look Back in Anger*. It is the best young play of its decade.

Did Tynan really like it so much? Or did he seize upon it as a cudgel to beat the West End theatre and demonstrate his own powers as an arbiter of fashion? Hobson certainly thought so. In a television interview in 1976, in a programme to celebrate the twentieth anniversary of *Look Back in Anger* and *The Outsider*, he said ironically:

'The first performance did have an emotional effect on one person in the audience, but nobody who was there with him guessed this until the following Sunday. Tynan's breast was torn with passion and emotion at the play, which he regarded as a tremendous political statement.'

On the same programme Tynan said:

One began to respond within ten minutes to this blazing figure on stage, who was spraying out all the ideas and thoughts that one had half-articulated in the previous ten years. One began to hear splendid grunts around one, the grunts of the affronted began to be heard, in the second half I think I heard a few seats clang, and I think I heard the exit doors go bang a couple of times, which at that time was a very good sign in the theatre. And by the end of it, one walked out serenely glowing, surrounded by disgruntled middle-aged faces, knowing that something very heart-warming had happened, and that one was dying to be on the street with the news.

Having digested these reviews, Osborne went off for a celebratory drink with George Devine and Tony Richardson. Then he had the experience I was to have two weeks later. His phone began to ring, with people wanting to ask him for interviews or invite him to dinner.

Oddly enough, all this had no effect on the box office; houses remained only half full. Then, two weeks later, the BBC was persuaded to present a 25-minute extract on television. Hobson was later to admit ruefully that this produced the effect that neither he nor Tynan had achieved, and *Look Back in Anger* was suddenly playing to packed houses.

It was apparently the Royal Court's press officer George Fearon who invented the phrase 'angry young man'. He disliked the play, and told Osborne grumpily: 'I suppose you're an angry young man.' And since *The Outsider* had been subtitled by its publisher 'An inquiry into the nature of the sickness of mankind in the mid-twentieth century', it seemed natural to group the two of us together as critics of modern civilisation. For a short time, the press wavered between calling the new rebels 'Outsiders' or 'Angry Young Men'. But the latter was undoubtedly the more catchy and explicit, and within days the gossip columns were full of references to the Angry Young Men.

Tynan's reaction to *The Outsider* and me was less welcoming; from the beginning he showed himself totally hostile. In a 1958 article on the Angry Young Men he describes me as 'a butterfly-theorist named Colin Wilson' and 'a brash young metaphysical', adding severely that although a playwright can get along without the disciplines of higher education, 'a philosopher cannot, as Wilson's book awfully proved'. This was not simply because, as a Communist, he bristled at my sympathy with the religious philosophy of T S Eliot and T E Hulme, but because it obviously irked him that a writer younger than himself had been launched to fame by the older generation of critics.

And what did I think of *Look Back in Anger?* My reaction can probably be gauged from the foregoing account of the plot. Jimmy Porter's determination to make his wife cry simply upset me, and I felt like telling him to shut up.

My reaction, of course, was due to the fact that I identified Alison with Joy, who was sitting beside me. If we had not been guests of a friend – the music critic Charles Osborne – I would have walked out after the first act, as Beaumont did and Rattigan meant to.

I could see that Jimmy was what I called an Outsider, an 'in-betweener' – that is, one who is too intelligent to feel satisfied with what life has to offer him, but not intelligent enough to impose his own terms. Even so, compared with the Outsiders I had been writing about – Nietzsche, Van Gogh, Dostoevsky – he seemed half-baked.

But even without making that comparison, I felt there was something wrong with the play itself. It was like a furious letter that someone writes to get pent-up anger and frustration off his chest – but then usually thinks better of sending, and throws in the fire. It was too personal, too vindictive, too undisciplined.

It was fairly obviously autobiographical, and I learned later that Osborne based Alison on his first wife, an actress called Pamela Lane, whom he'd met when he was acting in rep. They married secretly so that her parents would not find out, but they found out all the same and turned up at the wedding. Unfortunately, his wife's star rose as Osborne's sank, and she finally left him for a member of the committee of the theatre in which she was now the leading lady. Osborne was shattered and embittered. *Look Back in Anger* was clearly the result.

The problem of transferring this situation to the stage is that there is no way in which the audience can be made to see why Jimmy is so insulting to his wife. Alison seems a quiet, even-tempered girl who loves her husband so, as far as the audience is concerned, his anger seems the result of childish spoiltness and bad temper. As I watched it, I half expected people to start shouting abuse. The British would not stand for a play in which the central character keeps kicking his dog, so why should they stand for one in which he keeps kicking his wife?

There was another problem, which is pinpointed by the critic Ronald Hayman in his book, *John Osborne.*

> . . . anger has to be directed against something and if you're angry about everything, then you're not really angry. Jimmy Porter pours the same sulphuric energy into the attacks he launches on everything that surrounds him – Alison, Cliff, Helena, the Sunday papers, the social system, women in general, Conservative Members of Parliament, Sunday cinema audiences, Bill Graham, the H-bomb, people who don't like jazz, phoney politeness, nostalgia for the imperial past, Wordsworth, Alison's mother, people who have never watched anyone dying, the Church, and the apathy of everyone else in a generation that scarcely has anything to be positive about.

This is perhaps the most serious objection to *Look Back in Anger*. Doris Lessing, who would be classified among the 'Angries' when she shared a platform with us in *Declaration*, put it concisely when she wrote: 'It is not merely a question of preventing an evil, but of strengthening a vision of good which may defeat the evil.' Osborne had no such vision to offer, while Lessing, in her first novel *The Grass is Singing*, had provided a textbook example of how to target anger, to make it socially effective by directing it against the white attitude to blacks in Africa. The result of this ability to define her anger and its objects would make her, in due course, one of the few writers in *Declaration* who would develop beyond mere anger.

3   The First Wave

For some odd reason I never quite understood, I seemed to arouse in Kingsley Amis the same deep uneasiness I could sense in Tynan. It was John Wain who first made me aware of it when he told me how he and Amis had walked out on to the flat roof at a literary party, and seen me standing with Bill Hopkins leaning on the parapet with our backs towards them. Wain told me that Amis had said: 'Look, there's that bugger Wilson. I'm going to push him off,' and Wain had to grab him as he started towards me.

At the time I assumed that this was just the kind of buffoonery Amis was prone to when drunk. But after his death, when his *Letters* were published, I realised that the hostility towards me came close to paranoia. He tells a journalist, for example, that he suspected that a bottle of whisky I had taken to his home in Swansea – where Joy and I called when we were in flight after the 'horsewhipping incident' – was poisoned, and had left it on a shelf until a friend had 'guzzled it with no ill effects'. Since the bottle was sealed when I gave it to him, it is impossible that I could have poisoned it; this was simply the kind of thing Amis enjoyed making up to satisfy some odd little streak of malice in his fairly amiable, but also oddly unhappy, personality.

Like Tynan, Amis was the only child of middle-class parents. Born in April 1922, he spent his early life in Norbury, south of London. His father was a sales manager in the City. Both his parents were Nonconformists, having met at a Baptist chapel, and although they would later drift into an attitude of indifference to religion, his father retained enough of his Baptist attitudes to warn his son against masturbation on the grounds that it would induce insanity. The young Amis was not encouraged to read indoors, his father taking the view that he would be better in the fresh air, and that anyway, reading was 'anti-social'.

Amis senior was not entirely a kill-joy, since he possessed a remarkable talent for mimicry and clowning, with a gift for pulling faces 'that', says his son, 'made him one of the funniest men I have known . . . Every story called for a full deployment of facial, vocal and bodily resources.'

As an only child, Amis was obsessively fussed over by his mother; even when he was 24, and had been in the army, she tried to stop him from going on a camping holiday.

Amis's first two schools were fee-paying establishments, and at the age of twelve he was sent to the City of London School, where his father and two uncles had been educated. There, after a year, he obtained a scholarship, and after the outbreak of war in 1939, they were evacuated to Marlborough. In April 1941, after five terms as a public schoolboy he won a scholarship to St John's College, Oxford.

It was there that he met Philip Larkin, a fellow student who was to exercise an immense and crucial influence on his future, and would become the focus of his emotions to a remarkable extent – his son Martin going so far as to say, in his autobiography, *Experience*, that his father's feeling for Larkin 'was love, unquestionably love . . . He wanted to be with Larkin *all the time*'.

What Amis liked about him was Larkin's cutting sense of humour, sexual frankness (he admitted freely to masturbating), and free use of bad language which, for someone from Amis's sound Christian background, brought a sense of emancipation.

Larkin, a few months younger than Amis, was the son of a senior local government official, who admired Hitler and tried to run the Treasury Department of Coventry City Council as if it were the Third Reich, even exchanging letters with Hitler's finance minister Herr Schacht. By comparison, Larkin's mother was timid and completely under her husband's thumb, and seems to have had none of the obsessive mother-love of Amis's mother. On the contrary, Larkin would write in an early poem that he was brought up by his parents to associate love with filth:

> In our family
> Love was as disgusting as lavatory
> And not as necessary . . .

It becomes possible to understand how he came to write his most famous line: 'They fuck you up, your mum and dad.'

Fortunately, unlike Amis's father, Sydney Larkin's reading was wide and eclectic, and included the poetry of T S Eliot, Ezra Pound and W H Auden – the latter would become the most powerful influence on Larkin's early work.

Larkin, who had been at Oxford for two terms when Amis arrived, dressed in bohemian fashion with wine-coloured trousers and spotted bow ties, but was otherwise, Amis comments, 'aggressively normal'. Larkin was told about the newcomer by a fellow undergraduate, Norman Iles, according to his Introduction to *Required Writing*:

> 'I met him at Cambridge on a schol . . . He's the hell of a good man.'
> 'How is he?'

'He shoots guns.'

I did not understand this until later in the afternoon when we were crossing the dusty first quadrangle a fair-haired young man came down staircase three and paused on the bottom step. Norman instantly pointed his right hand at him in the semblance of a pistol and uttered a short coughing bark to signify a shot – a shot not as in reality, but as it would sound from a worn sound-track on Saturday afternoon in the ninepennies.

The young man's reaction was immediate. Clutching his chest in a rictus of agony, he threw one arm up against the archway and began slowly crumpling downwards, fingers scoring the stone-work. Just as he was about to collapse . . . he righted himself and trotted over to us. 'I've been working on this,' he said, as soon as introductions were completed. 'Listen. This is when you're firing in a ravine.'

We listened.

'And this when you're firing in a ravine and the bullet ricochets off a rock.'

We listened again. Norman's appreciative laughter skirled freely. I stood silent. For the first time I felt myself in the presence of a talent greater than my own.

One of the things Amis and Larkin had in common was a deep interest in sex. Larkin had had a homosexual phase at school, which had now given way to an intense interest in women – which, unfortunately, was not reciprocated. But he and Amis shared the cheerful assumption, common to most young men of nineteen, that a male's chief business in life should be to bed as many nubile girls as possible. Amis, having an engaging personality, wavy hair and a pleasant voice, soon succeeded in getting rid of his virginity with a girl comrade in the local Communist Party (which he joined in his first year). Larkin, who lacked his good looks, would remain a frustrated virgin for several years more, and contented himself with masturbation, which he regarded almost as a religion. (He remarked: 'I don't *want* to spend circa £5 [in taking a girl out] when I can toss off in five minutes, and have the rest of the evening to myself.')

Although Larkin failed to impress women, his fellow undergraduates found him fascinating. One of these, a brilliant and determined young man from Stoke-on-Trent named John Wain, wrote in *Sprightly Running*:

His literary self-training had already begun and had already borne some fruit; and this, combined with his quietness, his slight stammer, and (perhaps) the implication of giant intelligence produced by the fact of his having a large dome-like head and wearing very thick glasses, all helped to make him 'the college writer'.

And Wain speaks of Larkin's 'rock-like determination to do whatever it might be necessary to do in order to write well'. This aura of strength and determination is clearly what also impressed Amis, and produced a feeling that came close to adulation.

What impressed and delighted Amis most was Larkin's tendency to scathing intellectual judgements. When studying the college library copy of Spenser's *The Faerie Queene*, Amis found on its last page a note in Larkin's handwriting: 'First I thought Troilus and Creseyde was the most *boring* poem in English. Then I thought Beowulf was. Then I thought Paradise Lost was. Now I *know* that *The Faerie Queene* is the *dullest* thing out. Blast it.'

'I have no recollection of ever hearing Philip admit, or again be ready to tolerate, any author or book he studied, with the possible exception of Shakespeare,' Amis remarks in his *Memoirs*.

This attitude clearly struck him as marvellously liberating – more so since Larkin was widely read in modern literature, and could not be rejected as an illiterate oaf. Amis proceeded to imitate his wholesale dismissals, telling Larkin that when his tutor praised Chaucer's humour, 'I could hardly keep myself from breaking wind in his face.' Dryden is dismissed as 'a second-rate fucking journalist', and he claims that studying Wordsworth aroused in him a desire to put the whole Wordsworth circle 'in a big house, so they could not get out and be scalded to death with urine-steam'. For this kind of derogation of the literary great he invented the phrase 'horse-pissing'.

Larkin and Amis began to collaborate on what the latter described as a series of 'obscene and soft-porn stories', often involving schoolgirl lesbians. Larkin's own first semi-serious venture into fiction was a spoof school story set in a girl's boarding school called Willow Gables, and featuring a kind of lesbian alter-ego named Brunette Coleman. As he became increasingly absorbed in her, Larkin made her write a mini-autobiography, and even an essay called 'What Are We Writing For?', a serious study of early twentieth-century boarding-school fiction. It seems clear that Larkin had, to some extent, been taken over by his creation, transferring his own homosexual tendencies to a female character. *Trouble at Willow Gables* and *Michaelmas Term at St Brides* (both virtually full-length novels) seem to hint that, under different circumstances, he could easily have become a full-blown transvestite.

In the summer of 1942, Amis was called up to join the army, and became a second lieutenant. Larkin, who had been exempted because of poor eyesight, went on to take a first class degree, and in late 1943, after being turned down by the Civil Service, found a job as a librarian in the small town of Wellington, Shropshire, where he ran the library single-handed, and where (he told a friend) his main duty was 'handing out tripey novels to morons'. The job at least gave him time for writing, and he had soon completed the first draft of a novel called *Jill*.

This is not, as its title might suggest, about a girl, but about an Oxford undergraduate named John Kemp, lonely, shy and painfully unsure of himself, who is sexually attracted to his muscular room-mate Christopher. In a moment of pointless mendacity, he invents a younger sister named Jill, and goes on to fall in love with his fantasy. Then, improbably, he meets a real Jill who looks exactly as he had envisaged his imaginary sister. But when he nerves himself to steal a kiss from Jill, the outcome is disastrous; he is hit in the face by Christopher, then thrown in the fountain by a crowd of hearties. And as the battered and humiliated hero lies in bed with pneumonia he reflects sadly that love dies, whether fulfilled or unfulfilled – reflecting the depressive nihilism which would become one of Larkin's main characteristics as a mature writer. He seems to be saying that the gap between fantasy and reality is simply too wide to be bridged.

Jill makes the reader aware of another unbridgeable gap – between the Larkin on whom Amis was so fixated – 'aggressively normal', Rabelaisian, intellectually disciplined – and this hapless, embarrassment-prone self-portrait that reminds us of Aldous Huxley's early heroes. Can they actually be the same person?

The answer that suggests itself is that Amis was hardly aware of Larkin's vulnerability because his own, though disguised by his skill as a raconteur and mimic, was even greater. When he took a seventeen-year-old girl named Hilly out, he let her walk him home instead of vice versa because he was afraid of returning in the dark – a characteristic confirmed by his second wife Elizabeth Jane Howard. While his son Martin said he 'refused to drive and refused to fly, [and] couldn't easily be alone in a bus, a train or a lift'. His publisher Tom Maschler speaks of his fear of hailing taxis. And even when going to a chemist to buy his first packet of condoms, Amis had to persuade a friend to go with him. The inference seems to be that Amis was a bundle of guilt neuroses disguised by a bluff exterior.

After meeting Amis, Larkin's subsequent girlfriend Monica Jones made the perceptive comment: 'Kingsley wasn't just making faces all the time, he was actually trying them on. He didn't know who he was.' To such a person, Larkin's self-sufficiency and need for solitude must have seemed almost superhuman.

As to Larkin's failure with women, Amis himself had had too many affairs to overrate their importance in building up shaky self-esteem. (While in the army he had had several affairs, and contracted scabies from a Brussels waitress.) The crucial difference between Amis and Larkin seems to have been that Larkin was willing to face and analyse his own fears whereas Amis was too insecure even to attempt it. He preferred to pretend they didn't exist.

In Wellington, Larkin's craving to put his schoolgirl fantasies into practice led to less than satisfactory results. One of the schoolgirls who used the library was sixteen-year-old Ruth Bowman who (as Andrew Motion points out in his biography *Philip Larkin, A Writer's Life*) bore some physical resemblance to Larkin himself: 'her apprehensive, short-sighted face mirrored his own.' Larkin's stammer disappeared when he was with Ruth. She was enough of a bookworm to appreciate his wit and culture, even if, with her Methodist background, she was shocked by his language. She was certainly too innocent to be aware of the part schoolgirls like herself played in his masturbation fantasies.

It took two years for the fantasy to mature into reality, and for them both to lose their virginity simultaneously. Amis was informed, and wrote to congratulate him on having 'slipped a length on misruth'. Larkin did not record what he thought of the reality of sex, but it is probably safe to assume that, given his depressive temperament, he found it disappointing.

The affair was to drag on for another four years, during which time Ruth put up with his vacillations and depressions, and with her own guilt about fornication and fear of pregnancy. For a while they even became engaged. But Larkin's deep suspicion about marriage, and his fear of commitment, finally prevailed.

Amis, meanwhile, had been demobbed, and returned to Oxford, where in 1947 he also achieved a first. But the next step, a B. Litt, turned out to be a disaster. Amis's adviser was Lord David Cecil, whom he regarded 'as a prime dispenser of "horse piss",' and who represented everything Amis loathed about academia – Amis told Larkin that he regarded Cecil as a 'silly, unhelpful, posturing oaf'. Amis's thesis was on the decline of the Victorian audience for poetry, but when Cecil conducted the viva, it all seemed to go wrong, and it was turned down.

The problem lay in the fact that Cecil and Amis were polar opposites in every way – Cecil, the erudite don, and Amis, the reluctant student who was busy cultivating a contempt for culture as a bulwark against his lack of self-esteem. Cecil must have sensed how much Amis detested him – if, indeed, he was not aware that Amis's imitation of him had convulsed many an undergraduate audience.

But the failure was a serious blow that further eroded Amis's confidence. He could easily have revised the thesis and tried again; that he did not do so suggests that the prospect of further rejection worried him too much.

Instead he hardened his 'anti-culturism'. His letters to Larkin, full of invective about the writers he has to study ('Oh Christ, I've got to write a bleeding essay all about that sodding old bore Langla[n]d'), make it clear that Larkin's contempt for the classics had been fully absorbed into the Amis persona. Amis's mother and father could not have been more mistaken when they told him, after meeting Larkin: 'Whoever you've got your cynical views from, it isn't from him.'

Jill had been accepted by Fortune Press, a small concern run by a man named Caton, who never paid his authors. (Larkin suspected he made his money from pornography and published 'respectable' authors as a front.) Caton also asked Larkin for a volume of poems, the result being *The North Ship*. Neither book aroused the slightest interest.

Larkin then went on to write a second novel, *A Girl in Winter,* which shows a considerable technical advance on *Jill,* but clearly springs from the same depressive view of the world. Originally entitled *The Kingdom of Winter*, the main character, Katherine, is a central European exiled by the war to England. An assistant librarian in the provinces, she is as much a misfit as John Kemp in *Jill*. During a cold winter, she is looking forward to meeting again an ex-penfriend named Robin, to whom she was attracted during a brief summer interlude a few years earlier. Their affair never progressed further than an awkward and unsatisfactory kiss in a punt. The middle section of the novel is a flashback to the summer she spent with his family. But her hope that things will be better this time founders on the fact that he has become a drunken lecher. At the end of the book he persuades her to let him spend the night with her, although she objects that it would be meaningless. To which he replies with male logic, 'What does that matter?' But even he seems to feel that their sex has been a failure.

Even more than *Jill, A Girl in Winter* makes the reader aware of Larkin's self-division, which amounts almost to a split personality. One of his two selves is a superbly disciplined writer while the other is crippled by a sense of inadequacy and depression that is akin to what Sartre called 'nausea'.

This was based on his belief that women found him unattractive, which was based in turn on a conviction of his own ugliness. What he was failing to grasp was that any man with a dominant personality – which Larkin had – possesses the requisite quality for attracting women. If Larkin could have learned from Amis that sexual success depends on an attitude of mind, it would have transformed his self-image.

In fact, the writing of the two novels had caused him to move in the opposite direction, writing to Norman Iles, 'You aim at increased positiveness of character while I aim at increased negativeness, a kind of infinite recession in the face of the world.' This explains why his mature poetry seems to celebrate seediness and shabbiness in a manner reminiscent of Graham Greene's early novels.

Larkin recognised his 'dual personality'; writing to his friend Jim Sutton:

> The strongest feeling I have these days is a double one – personal sorrow and impersonal joy. Everything that my personality colours is a balls up – my own affairs and so on. But when I am being 'no more, no less than two weak eyes' everything is filled with a blessed light, bells, bugles, brightness and lord knows what. It's an odd feeling, and the split – which seems to widen day by day – is alarming.

But even Larkin recognised that 'living in a state of infinite recession in the face of the world' was not a practical way of organising his life. He began thinking about getting away from Wellington, and finding a publisher for *The Kingdom of Winter*. He found himself an agent, who succeeded in placing the book with Faber & Faber – they suggested changing the title to *A Girl in Winter* – and began taking a correspondence course in librarianship so that he could apply for jobs elsewhere. In June 1946, he applied for an assistant librarianship at University College, Leicester, and after an interview was accepted. He moved to Leicester in September.

It was there he met the second woman in his life, Monica Jones, who was a lecturer, known for her eccentric dress and forthright views. She and Larkin were attracted, but it was four year before they had sex. In due course she became Amis's model for the neurotic Margaret in *Lucky Jim*. In fact, she seems to have been its starting point, for in 1948 Amis was telling Larkin that he was going to begin a comic novel featuring Monica when he had finished his present novel *The Legacy*. The latter is about a young poet called Kingsley Amis, who has been left a fortune by his father, but can only qualify for it by entering the family business and marrying a certain girl; he rebels at first but ends by giving way – a conclusion that provides an insight into Amis's ineffective self-image at the time.

Amis's life had developed complications of its own. Soon after his return to Oxford in January 1946 he saw a pretty blonde in a tea room, and sent her a message via a woman friend asking her out. Her name was Hilary ('Hilly') Bardwell, and she was seventeen, and a model at Ruskin art college. Being a virgin she was difficult to persuade into bed, but eventually yielded. By July he had been to stay with her family in Harwell, Berkshire. The father, a civil servant, was interested in folk dancing (which Amis soon added to his list of detestations), while one brother played the recorder, had a baying voice and wore a corduroy jacket. They would, respectively, become the models for Professor Welch and his 'arty' son Bertrand in *Lucky Jim*.

When Larkin had succeeded in seducing 'misruth', Amis had urged upon him the efficacy of Durex, but in December 1947, just as he was beginning to tire of her, Hilly became pregnant. They were married in January 1948, two years after they had met. Having been forced into marriage, Amis made a mental vow to pursue women as if he was still single. Sexual conquest had become an addiction.

After trying several universities, he succeeded in gaining a lectureship at Swansea, where he began teaching in September 1949. But it seemed a dead end. They were short of money, and Hilly had to take a part time job washing up in a café. He saw his only salvation as writing his comic novel, and began working on *Dixon and Christine*, about a junior lecturer who detests academia. The setting for the novel was provided by a trip to see Larkin in Leicester. (After a visit to the senior common room he told Larkin, 'Someone ought to do something with this.') His notes on the novel included: 'Crappy culture. Fellow who doesn't fit in.' Jim Dixon was even named after the road Larkin lived in. Amis finished the first version in November 1951.

In 1950, after two years, Larkin had left Leicester for Belfast. Officially, he was still engaged to Ruth Bowman, but unofficially Monica Jones was now the woman in his life. Possibly it was to escape from both of them that he applied for the job at Queen's University. To prepare for sexual abstinence he took his now considerable collection of pornography, and his ongoing diary of masturbation fantasies. But abstinence was averted. He became friendly with a professor of philosophy, Colin Strang, and when he found that his wife Patsy was amenable to an affair, was glad to enter an arrangement in which he was safe from marriage.

It was while waiting for him in his room that Patsy read his masturbation diaries, and was mildly shocked. Larkin was upset. He was willing to be frank with Amis, whom he regarded as an equal, but his mistress was different. In spite of which, the couple began to use pornographic photographs as an aid to their love-making.

He also felt comfortable with an attractive student called Winifred Arnott, because she was engaged. His attempts to bed her were frustrated when she married, and he declined his invitation to the wedding. But this irritation led to one of the first of his mature poems, 'Lines on a Young Lady's Photograph Album'. For the reader who knows anything about Larkin, it is clear he wants to use it for his masturbation fantasies:

> My swivel eye hungers from pose to pose –
> In pigtails, clutching a reluctant cat;

and he wonders whether she would notice if he stole one of her in her bathing costume. Larkin was now 31, and at last hitting his stride as a poet.

Amis's literary career was still hanging fire. *Dixon and Christine* having been turned down by one publisher, Amis sent it to Larkin in Belfast, and began rewriting it under his direction with the new title of *Lucky Jim*. He resisted efforts to turn Dixon into a more dynamic character, his attitude, consistent with his passive self-image, being that 'I wanted to tell the reader that if chaps in the shit climb out of the shit, it's by good luck, not by their own efforts'.

Slowly, with many suggestions from Larkin, and even with some quotations from his letters, *Lucky Jim* began to take shape. One of the funniest scenes in the novel, Jim's anarchic lecture on Merrie England, was Larkin's idea, and Amis adopted it unwillingly, saying it 'would be awfully difficult to do'.

The acceptance of the book came about through a series of serendipitous events. In 1952, some of Amis's poems had appeared in a PEN anthology edited by one of his former professors, and in a biographical note, Amis had mentioned that he was writing a novel. This happened to be seen by Hilary Rubinstein, nephew of the publisher Victor Gollancz, who had known Amis slightly at Oxford, and who now wrote to ask if he could see it. So it was to Rubinstein that Amis sent the completed typescript in April 1953. The following day he was able to write again to tell Rubinstein that some of his novel would be read on a programme called *First Reading* on the BBC Third Programme.

It was John Wain who was responsible for this. He had been offered the job of presenting the programme because its previous presenter John Lehmann, who had edited *Penguin New Writing*, was felt to rely too heavily on the older generation of prewar writers. Wain decided to include a long extract from *Lucky Jim* at the beginning of the first programme – the passage in which Dixon wakes with a hangover and finds that his cigarette has burned a hole in the bedclothes. Hilary Rubinstein heard this, and when he went into the office, found several of the staff convulsed with merriment as they talked about it. This was the decisive factor in making up his mind. (He told me two years later that it was one of the few novels that had made him laugh out loud.) Victor Gollancz himself disliked it, regarding it as 'vulgar and anti-cultural', and was inclined to turn it down. Rubinstein's enthusiasm carried the day, and *Lucky Jim* was accepted.

John Wain had already progressed further than Amis or Larkin. While in his second year at Oxford he had launched a small magazine called *Mandrake*, in which both Amis and Tynan had appeared, Amis reviewing *A Girl in Winter*. After a first class degree, Wain had been given a junior fellowship at St John's, and a lectureship at Reading University. Amis envied him his success, and was to some extent inspired by it to begin writing his own first novel. Even there, Wain beat him to it. His picaresque *Hurry on Down*, named after a jazz lyric, was accepted by Secker and Warburg, and was due to be published in the autumn of 1953. Even his advance was bigger than Amis's – £250 as against £100. Then, when *Lucky Jim* was accepted by Doubleday in America (Gollancz acting as agent), Amis again vaulted past Wain, telling Larkin gleefully that his combined advances came to nearly twice Wain's. And this sense of rivalry would continue for many years until it turned into bitterness and mutual hostility.

Both *Hurry on Down* and *Lucky Jim* have central characters who are revolted by the idea of middle-class respectability. Wain's hero, Charles Lumley, lives in a rented room in a dreary Midland town, having just come down from Oxford with a poor degree in History, and with no idea what to do with his life. All he knows is that he loathes everything that his lower middle-class parents would like him to do.

His first step is to leave his lodging after lying to his landlady that he is a private detective who must pursue a swindler. Then he calls at the home of his fiancée, and encounters instead her disapproving sister and brother-in-law, whose reproaches cause him to react by insulting them, then seizing a bowl of greasy washing-up water and throwing it over them, after which he rushes out to get drunk at the nearest pub.

It is while in the pub, among working-class drinkers, that he realises that 'he was imprisoned in his class, not one of them, condemned to solitary confinement if once he strayed from his own kind', and thereupon determines to do something about it. Suddenly he is filled with determination to become 'classless' (which means to join the working class), and the rest of the novel chronicles his adventures as a window cleaner, a van driver, a drug smuggler, a night-club bouncer, a hospital orderly and a chauffeur, until, by luck rather than calculation, he ends by getting the girl and a job (as a comedy scriptwriter) that offers a promising future. He has ended by doing what he began by rejecting, but had an interesting time getting there.

The most striking thing about the novel is that it seems to embody the ideas that would later be regarded as typical of the Angry Young Men. Lumley's explosion in the first chapter about his girlfriend's petit bourgeois parents might have been put into the mouth of Osborne's Jimmy Porter. This also applies to his tirade against the standards and values of a crowd of right-wing ex-rugby types he encounters at a party thrown by one of the junior doctors, from which he is forcibly ejected.

The novel has a hectic forward movement and an air of inspired improvisation that keeps the reader chuckling and turning the pages. There is no subtlety of characterisation – the effects are laid on in poster paints applied with a whitewash brush. Its publication in October 1953 was greeted with some excellent reviews, most of which acknowledged its faults – its slapdash construction and lack of plausibility – but praised its enormous vitality. J B Priestley recognised it as a work in the same picaresque tradition as his own early novels.

Amis wrote to Wain to congratulate him on the novel, adding: 'It is very funny in parts and does succeed above all in getting across a grotesque and twisted view of life' – to which he hastens to add, in case this sounds critical 'which is what I try to do, though it's not the same view'.

It was certainly not. If *Hurry on Down* was driven by irritation with postwar England and its outdated values, the origin of *Lucky Jim* was rather more personal – intense dislike of certain people, including Monica Jones, and Hilly's father and brother. In the case of Leonard Bardwell, the model for the pedantic Professor Neddy Welch, the dislike soon became obsessive and slightly paranoid. Amis wrote to Larkin on 12 July 1949:

> I hate him; I hate him; I HATE the old APE'S BASTARD. I have almost stopped being amused by hating him, too . . . I shall swing for the old cockchafer unless I put him in a book, recognizably, so that he will feel hurt and bewildered at being so bated.

It is not easy to understand why Amis was so enraged by his father-in-law. Leonard Bardwell was something of an eccentric scholar. He had learned Swedish, Welsh and Romanish (spoken only in the Swiss canton of Grisons), which he believed to be the tongue of the tinkers, and was interested in Esperanto. He was a medievalist and loved morris dancing – he seems to have been a fairly well-known figure in folk-dance circles.

Martin Amis says in *Experience*: 'I loved him, and was always amazed by the amount of energy he devoted to me . . . I would notice as he showed me some stunt of a drawing on a folded piece of paper, that he was even more excited than I was.' He explains his father's hostility by saying: 'the truth is that he was irritated by Daddy B's innocence.'

Clearly, then, Bardwell senior was no status-obsessed egoist, like Professor Welch ('No other Professor in Great Britain . . . set such store by being called Professor'), but an almost childlike enthusiast. So why did Amis find him so unbearable?

The reason slowly emerges in the early pages of *Lucky Jim*, where Jim Dixon is driven to the Welch's home for tea. Welch is also an innocent. It never strikes him that anyone could be less interested in early music and the Welsh language than he is himself. For Amis, now set in his pose as an anti-intellectual, all this was unforgivable. So Welch induces in Dixon the same impatience and intolerance that Leonard Bardwell induced in his son-in-law.

Dixon is even more dissatisfied with his prospects in postwar Britain that Wain's Charles Lumley – in fact, it is more than dissatisfaction: it is boredom, disgruntlement and utter disaffection. He has another reason for feeling depressed; at the Welches he will see Margaret Peel, a neurotic colleague who is staying there while recovering from a suicide attempt. (Monica Jones's middle names were Margaret Beale.) And he cannot afford to offend her, since he needs to stay on the good side of Professor Welch, on whom depends the security of tenure he is hoping for.

This is also the reason he feels obliged to accept an invitation to a music weekend at the Welches, where he can only express his apathy and disgust by calling upon his repertory of faces – his Chinese Mandarin face, his Eskimo face, his Edith Sitwell face. But even those are insufficient to express his loathing of the Welch's son Bertrand, a bearded painter with a baying voice, who is soon threatening to punch him on the nose.

Jim escapes to a pub and gets drunk, then falls asleep in the guest bed with a lighted cigarette that ruins the bedside table and burns a hole in the bedclothes. Bertrand's girlfriend Christine helps him to conceal the damage. She is the kind of girl Jim has always dreamed about, blonde, pretty and unaffected, and his inferiority complex is eased when he notes that she has a slight trace of a cockney accent. Their mutual attraction does not escape Bertrand and leads to a fight, which Dixon succeeds in winning by luck rather than skill.

Larkin's suggestion that Dixon should lecture on Merrie England provided the novel with its climax. Dixon prepares for it by taking two large swigs out of a whisky flask proffered by Christine's rich uncle. Then he begins the lecture by unintentionally imitating the mannerisms of Welch and the principal, and ends by informing his stunned audience that 'Merrie England was about the most un-Merrie period in our history. It's only the home-made pottery crowd, the organic husbandry crowd, the recorder-playing crowd, the Esperanto . . .' – at which point he collapses.

Predictably, he is sacked. Then Christine's rich uncle comes to the rescue with an offer of a job as his private secretary – a job Bertrand has been angling for. And the book ends as Dixon walks off with Christine to catch the London train.

Published three months after *Hurry on Down*, in early 1954 *Lucky Jim* was an even greater success, and won the Somerset Maugham Award (to the disgust of Maugham who had described Dixon and his kind as 'scum'). From then on, Amis and Wain were bracketed together.

This seems a fair-enough comparison until we look more closely. Wain's novel is in many ways an anticipation of *Look Back in Anger*, and expresses the same feeling of social frustration and desire for change. *Lucky Jim* has no wider target, just individuals. Charles Lumley wants to see the last of the class system; Jim Dixon just wants to see the last of Neddy Welch, his son Bertrand, and Margaret Peel. So the novel has no message about British society; it simply tells us what Amis likes and doesn't like. The reader could hardly be blamed for shrugging his shoulders and asking so what?

This was my own reaction when I read *Lucky Jim* in 1956. What right had Dixon to look down on people who enjoy morris dancing and

Elizabethan music and sing madrigals? In what way is he their superior? Does his overdeveloped sense of boredom give him the right to dismiss them as pretentious? In the final analysis, all that Amis seemed to be saying was that he was bored by many cultural activities that other people enjoyed. Which is a comment on Amis rather than on the activity.

Of course, everyone is boredom-prone. But then, most of us are also aware that when we find something boring, this is partly our own fault. A child is bored by classical music because he does not yet understand it. If he later comes to enjoy it, this is because he has learned that making a certain effort of comprehension brings rewards. A spoilt child is less likely to make that discovery than one who is prepared to make the effort.

Reading the Amis–Larkin correspondence underlines that their relationship was a kind of training in schoolboy irreverence. When Amis discovered Larkin's notes at the end of *The Faerie Queene* declaring it the dullest poem ever written, it seems to have burst upon him as a kind of revelation. He no longer had to feel inferior in the face of things that he found hard to appreciate. He merely had to dismiss them as boring, and the kind of people who enjoyed them as pseudo-intellectuals. Larkin had granted him total absolution for intellectual laziness. He could now accept it upon Larkin's authority that anything he found boring was, in fact, not worth any effort, and could be condemned without a pang of self-doubt, just as he could stop being ashamed of masturbation because Larkin admitted to it so frankly.

Larkin eventually came to have reservations about his disciple's wholesale dismissals, writing to Monica:

> I sought his company because it gave me a wonderful sense of relief – I've always needed this 'fourth form friend', with whom I can pretend things are not as I know they are . . . Now I don't feel like pretending any longer . . . He doesn't *like* books. He doesn't *like* reading. And I wouldn't take his opinion on anything, books, people, places . . .

To be rigidly fair to Amis, an objective look at his career reveals that the success of *Lucky Jim* trapped him in a negative stance from which it was virtually impossible to escape. Even the 'filthy Mozart' comment in *Lucky Jim* expressed Larkin's attitude rather than his own. (In his biography, Motion records that Larkin read a newspaper throughout a Mozart concert.) So after *Lucky Jim* Amis was typecast as a cultural saboteur, and got into playing this role with a certain sullen defiance.

In *The Angry Decade* (1958) Kenneth Allsop comments on 'the stubborn disenchantment and the insistent lowbrowism that runs through all Amis's work', and adds:

Certainly one of the freshest and sharpest critical minds now writing, he can undermine his own authority with a silly piece of bravado such as the introduction to the page review in the *Spectator* of *The Outsider*. 'Here they come,' he wrote, 'tramp, tramp, tramp – all those characters you thought were discredited, or had never read, or (if you are like me) had never heard of: Barbusse, Sartre, Camus, Kierkegaard, Nietzsche, Hermann Hesse, Hemingway, Van Gogh, Nijinsky, Tolstoy, Dostoevsky, George Fox, Blake, Sri Ramakrishna, George Gurdjieff, T. E. Hulme and a large number of bit players . . .'

In fact, after this fatuous start (what university lecturer has never heard of Sartre or Camus or Hemingway?) Amis went on to offer a workmanlike account of *The Outsider* in the *Spectator*:

With admirable clarity and unpretentiousness, Mr Colin Wilson shows that all his legionnaires, miscellaneous as they may seem, were animated by the same kind of distress and took up similar attitudes to it. The Outsider – their collective label – is the man who has awakened to the chaos of existence, to the unreality of what the literal-minded take to be reality. He does not accept the conditions of human life, and finds release from its prison only in moments of terror or ecstasy. He tries to solve the problem of his identity, to discover which of his many I's is his true 'I', but reason, logic, any kind of thought is no help here, or indeed anywhere. He is anti-humanist ('humanism', Mr Wilson tells us, 'is only another name for spiritual laziness', anyway), but he is not, or preferably not, a man of action. He wants to get out of his predicament, and mysticism of some sort is perhaps his only route; if he is lucky he may end up as a saint.

This makes it clear why the book would put Amis on the defensive. I cannot be dismissed as a pseudo-intellectual like Bertrand Welch ('admirable clarity and unpretentiousness'), but if 'the Outsider does not accept the conditions of human life', while Amis clearly does, then I must somehow be criticising people like Amis, 'insiders'. He goes on to defend himself: 'At the risk of being written off as a spiritual wakey-wakey man, it is worth asserting that to tear one's fascinated gaze away from the raree-show of one's own dilemmas, to value Mr Pickwick higher than Raskolnikov, to try to be a bit pleasant occasionally, are aims worth making an effort for.'

After that he goes on the attack:

> The Outsider's most untenable and annoying claim . . . is that of possessing a large share, if not a monopoly, of depth and honesty and sensitivity . . . But are these 'Outsider questions' real? Admittedly, to ask oneself 'How am I to live?' is to ask something real . . . But it would be hard to attach any meaning, except as an expression of lunacy or amnesia, to 'Who am I?'

Here Amis's aim is to portray himself as the sort of normal chap who has never experienced a moment's self-doubt in his life. But he, like everyone else, had been a teenager, and every teenager has experienced the insecurity that lies behind the question, for his sense of himself is still fluid and evolving. In fact, most human beings have at some time felt a certain dissatisfaction with themselves because they have not become the person they would like to be. To ignore it or pretend otherwise is a sign of insecurity – or dishonesty.

I felt this instinctively as I read *Lucky Jim*, but did not know Amis well enough to know that I was treading close to very sensitive ground. Even so, reading *Lucky Jim* made me dissatisfied with the lowbrowism that Amis was peddling as honesty. Having no desire to read beyond the first 50 pages – the bed-burning episode made me feel uncomfortable – I asked Joy to read it. She enjoyed it, but her comment was 'Not much gilt left on the gingerbread', by which I understood her to mean that, having dismissed so much modern culture as 'phoney', Amis had left himself standing in a rather bleak landscape.

The kind of comments that incensed me were: 'Nijinsky with his pitiful ravings, Granville-Barker with his pretentious "idealistic" twaddle, and Arabian Lawrence, who, whatever his claims as a man, was surely a sonorous fake as a writer.' These struck me as downright aggressive stupidity that aroused in me a desire to kick him in the crotch and beat him up.

I wrote Amis a letter, not intended to be hostile, but trying to explain what I found unacceptable about his attitudes. I kept no copy, but a letter to Robert Conquest from Amis's records his reaction, with quotation from me. 'This anti-culture stuff gets you nowhere', and 'I have a lot of things I want to establish – vital things for the course of modern history – and knocking you and other misplaced figures off their pedestals will be the first step.' (I had in mind Wain and Osborne as his intellectual cohorts.) Amis comments: 'Good stuff, eh? I give him 2 years before paranoia closes over his head.'

A few weeks later, the journalist Dan Farson asked me to meet Amis. He had been writing a newspaper series on the Angry Young Men, and had interviewed both of us. Joy and I met Amis in a pub in the Charing Cross Road. He was good-looking, and his voice had a pleasant timbre. We got on well and I liked him instantly.

As a result of the meeting I could then see that he had been caught in the same snare I had. The success of *Lucky Jim* and *The Outsider* had made us both fair game for gossip columnists who, almost by definition, are people who never read. They had quickly reduced *The Outsider* to a book about social rebels like James Dean, and *Lucky Jim* to an approving portrait of a young man who hates Mozart. I could see that nothing Amis ever wrote in future would allow him to escape the 'lowbrow' label, just as nothing I could say or do would allow me to escape being called an Angry Young Man.

Amis's review of *The Outsider* showed that he had decided to make the best of his own label. But that was not before he had made an attempt to escape it in his second novel.

It was Dan Farson who advised me to read *That Uncertain Feeling* (1955). I did, and was impressed. This is a bleak and realistic tale about adultery, and the first-person narrative gives it a sense of honesty that has immediate appeal. There was no aggressive lowbrowism, and the book apparently has a moral theme. John Lewis, a South Wales librarian, who lives in cramped lodgings with his wife and two small children, meets an attractive socialite, Elizabeth Gruffydd-Williams, who is a member of the local amateur dramatic society. He attends one of her parties and allows himself to drift into an affair – which is soon suspected by his overworked wife. Elizabeth's husband is on the library committee and has the power to offer him promotion. But just as his adultery seems about to break up the marriage, Lewis and his wife decide to try again, and move to a mining village, where he takes an office job, and turns his back on adultery and promotion.

The novel was praised by critics, who were obviously caught off guard by the fact that it was so unlike *Lucky Jim*. What none were aware of was that it was basically autobiographical, and that its dedication to his wife Hilly was a kind of apology. Mrs Gruffydd-Williams stood-in for many women with whom Amis had had affairs in Swansea.

It had started soon after his marriage, but the success of *Lucky* Jim had presented Amis with endless opportunities for extending his range. As long ago as July 1949, he was telling Larkin: 'Nick and his girl and my wife and my girl (ssh!) and me went to a carnival here.' This was eighteen months after his marriage to Hilly, and less than a year after the birth of their first child. In October of that year, he was telling Larkin: 'On Friday I am giving a little coffee-party for six of my students . . . I am inviting the one I want to bugger and the two I most want to fuck.'

When, inevitably, Hilly found out, and realised that many of his casual affairs were with women she regarded as friends, she reacted by having affairs of her own. In 1956 one of these, with Henry Fairlie of the *Spectator*, came close to breaking up their marriage as Hilly considered leaving him. Amis was dismayed: 'Having one's wife fucked is one thing; having her taken away from you, plus your children, is another.' Moreover, another mistress 'whom I was rather attached to . . . has decided to give me up'. To Amis's relief, both women changed their minds. And the marital reconciliation (though not the reconciliation with the mistress) provided the slightly improbable climax of *That Uncertain Feeling*.

It would not last. A few years later, as Amis lay sunbathing on a Yugoslav beach, his wife wrote on his back the inscription '1 FAT ENGLISHMAN I FUCK ANYTHING'. Shortly after this they split up.

Wain was to be less fortunate with his own second novel in 1955. With *Living in the Present,* it suddenly became clear that he had one major shortcoming as a novelist: that he seems to dislike most of his characters. This gives his books a tinge of bitterness that spoils them as surely as a bitter flavour would ruin a bottle of wine.

Living in the Present is about a man who is so disgusted with the futility of life that he resolves on suicide, but decides to take with him the person he most detests. The hero, Edgar Banks, is a schoolteacher; his chosen victim a neo-fascist named Philipson-Smith. Banks follows him to Switzerland, then Italy, but all his attempts to kill him turn into farce. Finally, Banks falls in love and marries the girl, and is suddenly amazed that he ever contemplated suicide. This climax, like most of the book, is slightly unconvincing. It is as if Wain's mind works on an abstract level that is slightly out of touch with reality.

For the reader, incredulity creeps in on the first page, when a cadging neighbour comes to borrow glasses, and Edgar tells him, 'I want to tell you how much I detest you', and goes on to be extremely rude. Even the most insensitive sponger would feel offended and make for the door, but this one cheerfully goes on helping himself to the glasses and records. Wain seems totally unaware of how real people behave.

In 1960, five years later, the novel was published in America, and Wain wrote a preface that makes clear why it was such a disaster. He wrote it, he says, according to a strict plan. 'Today . . . I can see the point at which I ought to have torn up my plan. Instead, I wrote doggedly on.' That is to say, Wain started to write it with willpower instead of enjoyment, and it shows.

Unfortunately, this would remain true throughout a career that would span fourteen novels. This was a pity, for Wain was, in many ways, one of the most serious writers of his generation, and a critic who is always worth reading. But the aggression and paranoia of his personality shows through in the novels and makes them hard to enjoy.

By 1956, Larkin had joined Amis and Wain as a literary celebrity. November 1955 saw the publication of *The Less Deceived*, which included his lines on Winifred Arnott's photograph album. Only 300 copies were printed, and that seemed justified by the silence that greeted it. But at Christmas *The Times* included it among its books of the year, and a reviewer in the *Spectator* said it was probably one of the best books of poetry published since the war. *The Times Literary Supplement* described Larkin as a 'poet of exceptional importance', and suddenly the book has sold 1,300 copies, and reached its fifth reprint. Overnight, Larkin was in demand as a book reviewer and broadcaster.

His attitude to his success was slightly ambivalent. Until the publication of *Lucky Jim* he had seen himself as a novelist, and had made two attempts to write his third novel. *No For An Answer* was based on his ambiguous feelings for Ruth Bowman, and was abandoned as their relationship guttered out. But *A New World Symphony,* which was started in 1950 in response to Amis's comment in the Leicester common room 'Something ought to be done about this', was to be about a university lecturer based on Monica Jones. Several chapters were written, but it was abandoned when Amis started to rewrite *Dixon and Christine* as *Lucky Jim.* In spite of his massive editorial efforts, Larkin was relatively sure that Amis's novel would remain unpublished ('I refuse to believe he can write a book on his own'). So the acceptance of *Lucky Jim*, and its subsequent success, came as something of a shock.

Larkin's view was that *Lucky Jim* had destroyed the prospects for *A New World Symphony*, and therefore his own possible future as a novelist. And since it was on becoming a novelist that he pinned his main hopes of escaping the drudgery of librarianship, this was painful. 'Why,' he asks in a poem of March 1954, 'should I let the toad *work*/ Squat on my life?'

> Six days of the week it soils
> With its sickening poison –
> Just for paying a few bills!
> That's out of proportion

The shattering of his hopes of making a career as a novelist was among the reasons that, after five years in Belfast, he decided to apply for a librarian's job at the University of Hull.

What happened as a result of this decision would be a total change in the direction of his career, and a startling reversal of his attitude to 'the toad work'.

On 25 November 1955, Larkin presented himself at the University of Hull, to find seven other candidates ahead of him. When his turn came, the panel was impressed. One of them wrote:

. . . a tall, shy, serious-looking young man with thick-lensed glasses and a slight stammer. But all this seemed unimportant as he outlined his work in Belfast. There was a quiet authority in the way he described, of all things, the work on the issue desk in the library there. One could hardly imagine a less promising subject to impress the committee, but he made it intensely interesting, with a wealth of detail which never approached the tedious. Above all, I remember the exact and lucid sentences formed without hesitation and the incisive mind.

Later that afternoon, Larkin was appointed.

Before leaving, he had told Patsy Strang that he wanted the job because it would 'mean harder work and more responsibility', a curious statement from one who regarded work as a poisonous amphibian. What Larkin would discover in the years at Hull was that he had outgrown his early romanticism, and the fundamental strength of character, inherited from his father, was beginning to show through,

Larkin became the librarian at the University of Hull in March 1955.

4 Court Intrigues

I met John Osborne soon after we both became 'famous'. George Devine wrote to me asking me if I was interested in writing a play for the Royal Court, and inviting me to lunch. I found George very impressive, with his strong face and firm mouth, a pipe clamped between his teeth, and horn-rimmed glasses that gave him the look of a thinker. I was even more impressed when he remarked that he liked plays of ideas.

Devine also invited to lunch Nigel Dennis – thin, middle aged and very English – whose novel *Cards of Identity* had been the major success of the 1955 spring publishing season. At the request of the director Tony Richardson, Dennis had turned this into a play, and both Richardson and Devine had no doubt that it would be the hit of their first season, and would make up for the failure they expected from *Look Back in Anger*. In the event, it was *Cards of Identity* that flopped and *Look Back in Anger* that made the money. And now, undepressed by the failure – or perhaps simply elated by Osborne's success – Devine was preparing to ask Nigel Dennis to write another play, and to persuade me to do the same.

He did not have to try very hard. The prospect of having a play presented in the theatre that had launched Bernard Shaw was intoxicating. I had been addicted to Shaw ever since, at the age of fifteen, I had heard a radio performance of *Man and Superman* during the first week of the BBC's Third Programme. For the next few years my ambition was to be a playwright.

George Devine was very friendly and kind – I could see why the younger members of the English Stage Company looked up to him as a father figure. He told me to treat the Royal Court as a kind of playwright's workshop. If I had ideas I wanted to try out, to write them down in the form of dialogue, and then to listen as a group of actors read them aloud. That was how most major playwrights had learned their craft, from Molière to Ibsen – and on how to work with actors.

After lunch at a local restaurant, we went back to the theatre, and I was introduced to Osborne and Tony Richardson. Osborne both looked and sounded like an actor, with wavy hair, and a drawling accent. The length of his chin, which seemed disproportionate, prevented him from being good looking – that, and a sensuous mouth that looked as if it had acquired its shape from pouting. He was, at the time, acting in *Cards of*

Identity, disguised by a bald head and false teeth. But although he was the centre of attention at the Royal Court, I suspected that it was the tall, thin Tony Richardson who was the real power behind the throne and the person Devine regarded as his successor.

Not long after meeting Osborne, I asked him to a party that I was giving for *The Outsider.* My new prosperity meant I was able to move from my ground-floor room at Chepstow Villas to a two-room flat on the first floor – which was just as well, since there must have been fifty guests. John came with his leading lady Mary Ure, a beautiful Scots girl, whom he would marry. Unfortunately, Mary shared the temperament of so many of her countrymen, and was inclined to drink too much (a tendency that would kill her less than twenty years later). Assertively drunk on brandy, she told me that John was the greatest English playwright since Sheridan, and added that *The Outsider* was merely an anthology of other people's books. John stood there looking intensely embarrassed, obviously wishing she would shut up. (In the proof of his book on the Angry Young Men, Humphrey Carpenter had claimed that I had been equally rude to Osborne, telling him what I thought of *Look Back in Anger*, but when I pointed out that I would not have dreamed of being rude to a guest, he agreed to remove it.)

Soon after that exhilarating afternoon with Devine and Nigel Dennis, which made me feel that my dreams of the theatre were about to be realised, I went to see *Cards of Identity,* and was dazzled by it. In every way it seemed to me a better play than *Look Back in Anger.*

It was a farce that might have been a collaboration between Spike Milligan and Ivy Compton Burnett: its theme being that the British middle classes – to which Nigel himself belonged – have no real sense of identity, and that their inner vacuity has left them all with an unconscious craving to become somebody else.

It is this that makes Nigel's collection of middle-class ciphers an easy prey for the brainwashing techniques of three confidence tricksters who use some (undisclosed) form of hypnosis to transform them into servants and menials.

Why did it flop? Because when characters are standing on stage in front of you, it is hard to persuade you that they feel uncertain about their identity – they look too solid. It works in the novel because a novel takes place inside the reader's head, so that tricks of style can make the implausible seem plausible. On stage it was too obviously a piece of intellectual sleight of hand. But simply as farce, it was as hectic and funny as the Marx Brothers.

Before I could settle down to writing – or even thinking about – my own play, my life had undergone a seismic disruption that drove me out of London.

Because of the success of *Look Back in Anger* and *The Outsider*, the tabloid press had discovered that the Angry Young Men made good gossip-column material. As the endless fatuous publicity dragged on from 1956 into 1957, given a new lease of life by the tremendous success of John Braine's novel *Room at the Top* in March 1957, the phenomenon thoroughly outstayed its welcome, and created in the British press an atmosphere of irritable hostility like an approaching storm. Before long, almost every reference to Angry Young Men was dyspeptically hostile.

Where *The Outsider* was concerned, this usually took the form of dismissing it (as Mary Ure had done) as an anthology of quotations. My publisher Victor Gollancz watched with dismay my plunge within months from intellectual stardom to relegation as some kind of imposter.

Friends like Angus Wilson and Stephen Spender advised me to keep my head down and avoid journalists, and I thought I was doing fairly well until that evening in February 1957 when Joy's father burst into my room shouting 'Wilson, the game is up', and announced to Joy I was a homosexual and had six mistresses.

It so happened that we were giving supper to a villainous old queer called Gerald Hamilton – the model for Christopher Isherwood's Arthur Norris in *Mr Norris Changes Trains* – when the door burst open and Joy's father marched into the room, followed by her mother, brother and sister, and waving a horsewhip. It seemed Joy's sister had got hold of a diary of mine when I was visiting Joy in hospital, and garnered some lurid and bizarre ideas from my notes for my Jack the Ripper novel *Ritual in the Dark*. Her father had no opportunity to use the horsewhip, for other tenants came in to investigate the shouting, and prevented Joy from being dragged off by the arms, while I was ringing the local police. After ascertaining that Joy was over 21, an embarrassed policeman told her parents they would have to leave my flat.

Gerald Hamilton had meanwhile disappeared, which was soon explained when a crowd of journalists and photographers arrived at the front door. We let them in and told them what had happened; but when a second wave arrived ten minutes later, decided to escape out of the back door, and spent the night at the flat of a young editor named Tom Maschler, who was in the process of putting together an anthology of 'Angry Young Men' called *Declaration*. The next morning we decided to leave for Devon, where we stayed with a writer named Negley Farson, until the press caught up with us once more, and we fled on to Dublin, where Joy had been at Trinity. For over a week the scandal filled the popular press – it was the 'silly season' when there was no other news – but when *Time* magazine published a photograph of us both, we decided that anonymity was impossible, and returned to London, where my publisher Gollancz begged me to move to the country.

Which is how we came to live in a farm cottage near Mevagissey, in Cornwall. There I wrote a sequel to *The Outsider,* which was finished in mid-June and published as *Religion and the Rebel* (of which I shall speak later).

Soon after the move to Cornwall, I was asked by the *Daily Express* to go to London to review the first night of Osborne's new play *The Entertainer* at the Royal Court.

I came to London a week earlier, in early April 1957, to see the first night of Beckett's *Fin de Partie* (later called *Endgame*) at the Royal Court. I had enjoyed *Godot,* which I had seen at the Criterion Theatre in 1955, even though I felt that it was twice as long as it should be. But it was at least funny, with a distinct influence of Laurel and Hardy.

Fin de Partie carefully eschewed anything that might amuse, or even interest, the audience. A despotic, blind man sits in an armchair, flanked by his dying parents, who are in dustbins. He has a whistle to summon his servant, who is semi-crippled and walks with stiff legs like a Frankenstein monster. There is no plot – just rambling, fragmentary dialogue that gets nowhere. The servant's opening statement: 'Finished, it's finished, nearly finished, it must be nearly finished' is fairly typical. Later, the old woman dies, and the servant is asked what the old man is doing. 'He's crying.' 'Then he's alive,' says his son indifferently.

I felt paralysed with boredom and irritation. Why was the audience listening patiently to this depressing rubbish? It made me think of what the Russian Leonid Shestov had said about Chekhov: 'Stubbornly, despondently, monotonously, Chekhov did one thing only: in one way or another he killed human hopes.' But at least Chekhov had fought hard as he died of tuberculosis. The perfectly healthy Beckett merely moaned.

His short mime-play that followed, *Act Without Words*, seemed to me to give the game away and reduce this pretentious symbolism to sudden clarity. A man lies on an empty stage until wakened by a shrill whistle. A carafe is then lowered from the ceiling on a string, and he tries to take it. The carafe rises out of reach. He takes a box and stands on it; the carafe again rises out of reach. He balances a second box on the first, but the carafe rises yet again. He tries a third box, with the same result. Finally, he lies down in disgust, and refuses to move even when the carafe is dangled within an inch of his nose. Curtain.

So Beckett was not complaining about the metaphysical meaninglessness of life, but about the fact that some malicious destiny seems to enjoy frustrating our efforts. Fate, Beckett is saying, is not merely indifferent, but vindictive – the complaint of every pessimist in history.

I met Beckett at about this time at the Royal Court, and had every intention of asking him what the devil he thought he was achieving by writing this dreary rubbish; but he was such an obviously decent and gentle sort of person that I didn't have the heart.

The following Sunday in the *Observer* I was delighted to find that Tynan and I were in unexpected agreement, and that he accused Becket of facile pessimism, and of projecting a merely personal violence. But in the face of Beckett's increasing reputation, he gradually backed down.

A week later I went again to the Royal Court to see Osborne's new play *The Entertainer*.

I was rather looking forward to this, for I had gathered from the publicity that Laurence Olivier was playing a music-hall entertainer. One of the few parts of *Look Back in Anger* that I had enjoyed was the music-hall sketch in Act Three, when Jimmy and Cliff do a song and dance routine.

Within minutes my optimism had evaporated. Osborne was determined to make his entertainer as unentertaining as possible. Archie Rice is a second rate comedian in a rock 'n roll nude show in a seaside town, living with his family in rundown lodgings. If he ever possessed the knack of being funny he forgot it years ago. But he still has a jaunty manner, a flashing smile that fails to reach his eyes, and an unabated lust for the girls in the company. His wife Phoebe works in Woolworths and his younger son as a hospital stoker, while another son is in the army in Egypt. The daughter Jean is an art teacher with a social conscience, who marches to protest against the Bomb and attends rallies in Trafalgar Square. Archie's father Billy is an old-time Edwardian comedian of the kind who used to sing songs about breaking the bank at Monte Carlo; now all he can do is dream of the England of his youth and snarl grumpily about the bad manners of the younger generation.

Although Archie and his father have (implausibly) been to public schools, and Archie's brother is a rich barrister, this branch of the Rice family consists of what Shaw called 'downstarts'. Archie has financed the nude show on borrowed money, and it is unmistakably heading for bankruptcy. Osborne seems to be implying that the Rices are symbolic of an England that has fallen into gloom and decay.

By this time, so had I. But I perked up momentarily when Olivier stood in the spotlight on a darkened stage and began his patter:

I've played in front of them all! 'The Queen', 'The Duke of Edinburgh', 'The Prince of Wales', and the – what was the name of that other pub? Blimey, that went better first house [pause]. I've taken my glasses off. I don't want to see you suffering. What about these crooners, eh? What about these crooners? I don't know what we're coming to. I don't, honest. Look at the stuff they sing! 'The Dark Town Strutters' Ball', 'The Woodchoppers' Ball', 'The Basin Street Ball' – it's a lot of nonsense, isn't it? Don't clap too loud – it's an old building.

And after more of this he goes on to sing a song, 'We're all out for good old number one, number one's the only one for me'.

Clearly, it was all intended to show us that the Archie was a boring and depressing has-been, but Osborne seemed to feel that the best way to do that was by boring and depressing his audience. Possibly for the middle-class drama critics, and for West End audiences from more affluent parts of the capital, it may have seemed a richly evocative slice of life in mean streets. But for me it was all too reminiscent of the dreary provincialism I grew up in, with its endless clichés and petty selfishness, and the sense of being trapped for ever in second-rateness.

Of plot there was virtually none. The son in the army is kidnapped by Arabs, held for ransom, then predictably murdered. All this drew on recent events when Egypt's President Nasser had thrown the British out of the Suez Canal; a kidnapped British sergeant had been held for weeks, then murdered. For me, Osborne's use of a current event only demonstrated his lack of invention and the bankruptcy of his creative talent.

Archie is finally driven to persuade his father to come out of retire-ment to try and save the show. Jean says indignantly: 'Are you going to destroy him too? He's the only one of us who has any dignity and respect for himself . . . and your going to murder him.' Which is, of course, what happens, and when Billy dies, his coffin is draped with a Union Jack.

Before that tragedy the play seems to be mainly bad-tempered bickering. Phoebe has bought a thirty-shilling cake to welcome her son home; the old grandfather helps himself to a slice, and Phoebe bursts into howls of squalid fury. 'That bloody *greedy* old pig – the old pig, as if he hadn't had enough of everything already – he has to go and get his great fingers into it!'

I could feel the audience cringing and trying not to listen.

What was Osborne trying to say? That there was an England somewhere out there that was full of things he hated: hypocrisy and boredom and lies and self-deceptions, and bogus symbols like a gloved hand waving from a golden coach? But the play failed to convey this because it lacked coherence and any kind of underlying unity. It was like listening to a drunk telling you how badly life has treated him. It seemed to me that Osborne was trying to make me feel emotions that I rejected with distaste, like asking me to take a bath in dirty water.

In the final scene Archie stands on a bare stage and sings:

Why should I care
Why should I let it touch me,
Why shouldn't I sit down and cry
To let it pass over me?

Then his wife appears holding his raincoat and hat, and with a final gesture of bravado he says: 'You've been a good audience . . . Let me know where you're working tomorrow – and I'll come and see YOU,' and he walks offstage with the orchestra still playing 'Why should I care?'

It was Beckett all over again.

But I couldn't go to the pub next door and forget my weariness over a bottle of wine, for I had to take a taxi to Fleet Street and write about it.

Clearly, it would be impossible to tell the truth – that Osborne seemed to me utterly without talent. It would look as if I was indulging in a personal vendetta. And I did not dislike Osborne personally – on the contrary. One evening only a few months earlier, after taking an ex-girlfriend for a meal in Chelsea, we had knocked on John's door in Woodfall Street, near Sloane Square, and he had invited us in, given us a brandy, and been kind and sympathetic (although with a flash of the old pungency when he described an actress we both knew as being the kind of girl who 'needed to be fucked by a syphilitic gorilla').

So in the *Daily Express* office at eleven o'clock at night, on an old typewriter whose keys had to be attacked as if hammering nails, I wrote an article whose main point was that this was the end of the absurd myth of the Angry Young Men, which had been invented by Fleet Street. Osborne was not angry – just full of sadness and nostalgia for an England that ceased to exist in 1913, and whose play was like a valedictory blown over a silent battlefield . . .

I almost convinced myself that *The Entertainer* was a moving elegy for the old music hall. Then I remembered how atrocious it had really been, and went out to El Vino's with some *Express* journalists, and made up for my earlier restraint.

I was fairly certain that Osborne was going to receive the full brunt of the press's savagery the next day, and was staggered when, after Bill Hopkins and I had been out to buy the newspapers, I found nothing but praise for Olivier's 'faultless' performance, and his versatility in turning from *Henry V* to a broken-down comedian.

Clearly, Osborne had escaped a roasting because his leading man was the undisputed head of the theatrical profession. But how much longer could he escape?

Watching *The Entertainer* also made me aware of my own feelings about England, and why I rejected the 'angry' label. I hated this British preoccupation with class that had been hanging around like the smell of a greasy kitchen since D H Lawrence. As far as I could see, it didn't matter a damn which class you were born into. Since *The Outsider* came out I had met many members of the 'aristocracy' and could see clearly that in the twentieth century, social position had become irrelevant. Human beings are all in the same boat. The only important question is what they do with their lives.

But then, the only British contemporary for whom I felt sympathy was Iris Murdoch. Iris, like myself, regarded herself as part of a continental rather than British tradition. We had nothing whatever in common with Wain, Amis, Osborne or John Braine.

Which is why, when I returned from reviewing *The Entertainer*, I settled down at last to work on my own play' in a thoroughly disgruntled state of mind.

My head still full of saints and mystics after writing *The Outsider* sequel, I wanted to do a play that would develop Shaw's remark that civilisation cannot survive without religion.

At about this time I saw a review of Nigel Dennis's second play, *The Making of Moo,* which had been presented two months after *The Entertainer*, and was surprised to see that it was a crude, rationalistic attack on religion. I liked Nigel, and assumed he was too intelligent for that kind of thing. But then, I had felt the same about my friend Alfred Reynolds, Stuart Holroyd's former mentor, who regarded religion as a confidence trick played on the gullible by cunning priests, and been disappointed. How could intelligent people fail to see that, on its most basic level, religion is a deep dissatisfaction with what Heidegger called 'the triviality of everydayness'?

By 'religion' I was not, of course, talking about what Bergson called the 'closed religion' of dogmas and prohibitions, but the 'open religion' of saints, mystics and poets. What was needed was not some new religious cult but some simple way of accessing religious or mystical *experience*, of the sort that must have been known to the monks and cathedral-builders of the Middle Ages. Aldous Huxley thought that mescalin might do it; as a method of experiencing the sheer reality of the world that lies outside the narrowness of our senses. But I was inclined to doubt this, and a later experience with mescalin confirmed my scepticism.

What I wanted to do was to write a play that would present the problem on stage.

Since what I called Outsiders were people who experienced a natural craving for something beyond 'everydayness', the play, which I decided to call *The Death of God*, would obviously have to be about the clash between an Outsider and an 'insider'. I decided to set it in a monastery at the foot of the Carpathians, which is shared by two monastic orders, one of which has been made homeless by a war that has dragged on for years. The abbot of the visitors is Father Dominic, young, impatient and sharp-tongued. The other abbot, Father Carleon, who by some medical miracle has reached the age of 135, I saw in my mind's eye as a kind of combination of Jung and Albert Schweitzer – which is why his colleague regards him as a doddering heretic.

As the play opens, the newly arrived Father Dominic is losing no time in revealing his hostility. Instead of talking theology, Carleon explains that there is a practical reason why they must co-operate. He summons a nurse, who is accompanied by her patient, a man in a monk's habit, who has undergone plastic surgery, so that his face is still encased in bandages. The abbot orders her to remove them, then asks Father Dominic if he recognises the man. But before allowing him to reply, the abbot tells the nurse to take her patient away. Then he repeats his question. After some hesitation, Dominic answers hesitantly: 'Eric Streicher?'

Streicher was the dictator of the southern hemisphere before he was reportedly killed in a plane crash three years earlier; his body was never recovered. Now the older man reveals that, in fact, Streicher was not killed, only badly injured and facially disfigured. Ever since then, he has been suffering from amnesia. The monks have nursed him back to health.

The abbot explains his plan. The dictator's mind, like his body, can be restored to health. And when that happens, Carleon believes, he will be a changed man – no longer paranoid and violent, but sane and benevolent. Hypnosis and psychological techniques of rehabilitation have guaranteed that. Now all that remain is to restore his memory. When that happens, his first concern will be to bring the war to an end.

Of course, the abbot proves to be wrong. With his memory restored prematurely – through the violence of killing his nurse's lover – the dictator proves to be as paranoid as ever. And it is his own second-in-command – the man who became his successor – who finally kills him and has the body burned.

I sent the play to George Devine in September 1957. Very soon it was returned to me with a brief note in which he said that he felt it was not 'dramatically alive', but thanking me for allowing him to see it first.

Understandably, I was furious. What had happened to his promises of working with me to improve it? At the very least, I deserved an apologetic letter explaining what was wrong with it. I wrote him a letter saying as much.

Now it so happened that Bill Hopkins was staying with us. And Bill's brother Ted worked on the *News Chronicle*. When Bill read my letter, he suggested that I should allow the *News Chronicle* to publish it as 'an open letter to George Devine'. Bill's brother Ted passed it on to several other newspapers, and most of them ran the story the next day.

One of them had also rung the Royal Court, and been put on to Ronald Duncan, the poet who had originally founded the English Stage Company. Asked what he thought of my play, he replied that it read like a child's TV serial, and that I ought to be a soap-advertisement salesman.

Ted Hopkins rang me to get my reaction. Who was Ronald Duncan? he asked me. I said I knew very little about him except that there were many letters to him in Ezra Pound's printed correspondence, and that Pound had said he would become a great poet. As far as I knew, this had not happened. Ted then asked me: 'Would you say that if you were a soap-advertisement salesman, you'd send him a packet to wash out his dirty mouth?' I said hastily: 'No!' for I had no desire to go in for this kind of abuse. Nevertheless, my comments on Duncan appeared the next day, together with some stinging retort from Duncan.

At this point I realised we were both being used by the press to provide the gossip columnists with material. So I wrote direct to Ronald Duncan, suggesting we should not allow this to happen. And to my surprise, I received a charming letter from him saying he quite agreed, and suggesting that I should call at his farm next time I was in North Devon. Some time later, Joy and I decided to stop there on our way back from a visit to our north Devon friend, Negley Farson.

Here I should say something about Duncan, for as well as being the founding father of the Royal Court, he was as 'angry' as John Osborne. Typically, Osborne (in his autobiography, *A Better Class of Person*) describes him as the 'Black Dwarf of North Devon', and refers to his capacity to 'spout bile'.

The 'black dwarf' was a reference to Duncan's stature and to the fact that his complexion was so dark that he might have taken for an Indian. One uncomplimentary acquaintance told me he looked like an Italian wine waiter. But the large, dark eyes had a touch of the lost child, and he had a considerable appeal for women. He also possessed that most beguiling of qualities, a wide-ranging and sharp intelligence.

His wife Rose Marie had been a film starlet, and when I first met her – when she was about 40 – she was still beautiful. But I soon gathered that all was not well with the marriage. The reason was simple – Ronnie could not resist other women. This is not to say he was a libertine. He was simply a romantic who found women so fascinating that he kept becoming emotionally involved with them without ceasing to be in love with his wife. He was, he said, a natural bigamist.

This had not always been so. As a young man he had studied at Cambridge under Dr Leavis, and imbibed his admiration for T S Eliot and his view that literature should have a moral foundation. He had become a pacifist, travelled to India to become a disciple of Gandhi and, when he returned, bought a farm in Devon and tried to set up a commune, with its own literary magazine and drama group. He wrote plays for the group, and it was one of these plays, *This Way to the Tomb*, that went on at the Mercury Theatre in Notting Hill Gate, where Eliot's *Murder in the Cathedral* has become the hit of an earlier season. Reviews were respectful but unenthusiastic, and everyone expected it to run for a fortnight. At which point, Beverley Baxter, the drama critic of the *Evening Standard* (and Kenneth Tynan's predecessor) performed for Duncan the same service that Tynan would perform for *Look Back in Anger*, and gave it a rave review that filled the theatre and caused the play to run for a year.

The music was written by Duncan's friend Benjamin Britten, whose *Peter Grimes* had just been the success of the opera season. Britten had asked Duncan to write him a libretto, and the result was *The Rape of Lucretia,* which also became a success. Then he was asked to translate and adapt a play by Cocteau, *The Eagle has Two Heads,* which achieved the same success. Duncan had scored the greatest hat-trick since the young Somerset Maugham had three plays running in the West End simultaneously.

All this had been achieved by the time he was 31. Since he was 26, he had run his farm and stayed faithful to his wife. And his life thus far had not been notable for sexual adventure. But for a poet with a romantic temperament, the eternal feminine was hard to resist. And women found his combination of fame and intelligence equally hard to resist. First came an affair with an art student named Petra, then with an Italian actress, then with his secretary Antonia, and several more liaisons which he describes with characteristic frankness in his autobiography *How To Make Enemies*. Most of these were carried on quite openly, and many of the women came and stayed at the farm and became friendly with Rose Marie.

And Rose Marie? I learned her side of this extraordinary story when, perhaps a year after I first met her, she and I were lying on a beach close to their farm, watching Benjamin Britten paddling in the sea with a young boy. I asked her casually whether she had ever had any homosexual experience, and she looked at me in astonishment and said: 'You mean to say you didn't know about Monica?'

Monica was an attractive woman with cropped grey hair who often stayed at the farm. I had assumed she was some kind of secretary or factotum. I said: 'Good God no! It didn't even occur to me!'

She then told me, with her usual astonishing frankness, a most remarkable story.

She had put up with Ronnie's affairs because this seemed the only alternative to divorce – which she had contemplated once or twice. But Ronnie was such a convincing talker, explaining that as a poet he was a natural bigamist, that she always allowed herself to be persuaded into changing her mind. Nevertheless, the knowledge that Ronnie was having affairs prevented her from enjoying sex, and she found herself becoming frigid.

Ronnie found this baffling, and sent her to see a psychiatrist. His advice was that if Ronnie failed to satisfy her, she should masturbate after he had reached a climax. So this is what she did. But Ronnie complained that this made him feel he was being 'used'.

One day, in the course of an argument, Ronnie asked her: 'What would really excite you sexually?' And after giving this some thought, Rose Marie admitted that she felt that watching another couple have sex would do it.

'That's easy,' said Ronnie, 'Antonia won't mind.' Antonia was Ronnie's secretary, whose seduction is described in *How To Make Enemies*.

The three of them decided that a town environment would be more suitable than their farm. Accordingly, they decided that their flat in Maida Vale should be the location for the experiment.

For some odd reason, they decided that the tripartite adultery should be preceded by an elaborate symbolic ritual. From the Portobello Road they obtained a number of tall vases made of crystal glass.

Then they went into the bedroom and stripped, after which all three ran downstairs and smashed the vases with high-heeled shoes. (Rose Marie said the carpet was full of glass crystals for months.) Then they went back to the bedroom where, lying on a huge double bed, Ronnie made love to Antonia while Rose Marie watched them and masturbated. She said it was the most powerful climax she had ever experienced.

When Ronnie and Rose Marie were discussing it later, Ronnie said: 'You realise this means that you're lesbian?' And he went on to tell Rose Marie that what had really excited her was not that she was identifying with Antonia being possessed by her husband, but with Ronnie possessing Antonia. 'You'd like to make love to her yourself.'

Rose Marie said she didn't honestly think so. But Ronnie told her he would prove it to her by finding her a lesbian partner. So Monica was co-opted, and while Ronnie went off to bed with his latest mistress, Rose Marie retired to the next room with Monica.

'And was he right?' I asked. 'Is that what you really wanted?'

She shook her head pathetically. 'No, I don't like it.'

But Ronnie remained so committed to his theory that he went on to write a play called *The Catalyst*, in which a couple's marriage is saved by the introduction of a lesbian third party . . .

It is a pity that I did not meet Ronnie sooner. If we had been friends before I submitted *The Death of God*, he might well have persuaded Devine to abide by his promise of a 'try out', and led me to writing more plays. As it was, the bitterness caused by Devine's abrupt rejection at least led to Duncan and I becoming close friends, and during the next two decades I was often the confidant of the woes occasioned by his subsequent love affairs. We remained close until his death in 1982 at the age of 68. Typically, he died of lung cancer from chain smoking.

James Joyce commented to his friend Frank Budgen that a man's character is not simply a matter of how he feels and what he does. Equally important is the question of whether he is lucky or unlucky. Do chimney pots fall on his head in a high wind or do people leave him legacies? I always felt that this helps to explain Ronnie's persistent bad luck. He once described his life as 'coffee, muddle and misery'. A person with that attitude is tempting fate, and in Ronnie's case, fate duly obliged by providing him with reasons for feeling that life is a series of disasters punctuated by treacheries.

Where the Court venture was concerned, that attitude was not entirely unjustified. In his book, *The Theatre of George Devine*, the drama critic Irving Wardle writes: 'There followed [a] lunch at which Devine gave Duncan the impression of being wholly in sympathy with all his theatrical attitudes and plans for the company.' But the accord was only superficial. What Devine had in mind was Brecht and Sartre, and while Ronnie had no strong political views, he felt the dislike that most poets feel for Stalinism. Wardle goes on:

> Devine had small regard for Duncan's work which he viewed as an irrelevant hangover of the club theatre decade. Duncan's high church attachments, his elitist attitudes and his literary bias stood for a tradition which Devine intended to supplant by establishing an alternative milieu for modern writing in the theatre. It is superbly ironic that the architect of the demotic writers' theatre should have received his brief from the high priest of the poetic drama movement. Each regarded himself as forward-looking; and as hostility built up between them at the Royal Court, each came to regard the other as a fossilized relic of the 1930s.

Ronnie was emphatically not a 'high churchman'; even in the days when he most admired Eliot he could hardly be described as religious, and by the time I knew him, even that was long behind him. But his purpose in forming the English Stage Company was to get his own plays performed, and he could hardly have chosen a worse partner than Devine.

The two Duncan plays scheduled for production at the Court were a poetic drama called *Don Juan*, and its sequel *The Death of Satan*. They went on immediately after *Look Back in Anger* and before *Cards of Identity*. The result is described in Osborne's *Almost a Gentleman*: '[George] put on two of Duncan's plays . . . in the opening season with the unconcealed intention of killing them off as soon as possible. Bile was soon to spurt from the Black Dwarf of North Devon as his work was ruthlessly cut up by George and Tony [Richardson] and turned into a triumphantly unpresentable evening.'

What Devine did was to hack both plays so they could be staged on the same evening, an expedient that obviously ran the risk of exhausting the audience. Wardle says: 'Duncan . . . felt that Devine poisoned rehearsals by instilling an atmosphere of wearisome contractual obligation.' The result, as its director intended, was that both plays were reviled by the critics.

The odd thing is that, as Wardle points out, Osborne and Duncan had much in common:

> . . . both elitist, both attracted to religious themes, both given to intemperate abuse, and in these two productions [*Look Back in Anger* and *Don Juan*], both saying much the same thing. Osborne got the credit for introducing the 'anti-hero', but he could well have shared it with Duncan. Don Juan and Jimmy Porter are both men of passion invading the territory of good manners. The message is the same: England has gone to sleep behind its mask of respectability; it would be better to wake up and feel something, even if that means treating your wife badly or being sent to hell.

Devine himself commented to a friend: 'Mr Duncan's play failed abjectly and rightly as it was completely out of date.' The truth is that it failed because Devine wanted it to fail. Presented separately, the two plays would have stood an excellent chance of success, as they had been at the Taw and Torridge Festival. And when I saw how ruthlessly and skilfully Devine got rid of the company's founder, I realised that I had got off fairly lightly with a mere rejection note.

The warmth that grew up between Duncan and myself was to some extent based on the fact that we agreed with Shaw that civilisation could not 'survive without a religion'. And we both felt that our careers had been derailed by this Angry Young Man nonsense. Ronnie's hope of reviving poetic drama in England foundered as the Royal Court became the home of 'kitchen-sink drama'.

What neither Duncan nor I realised was that Devine's increasing drift to the left was largely due to Kenneth Tynan, and that Tynan was the Macchiavelli behind this plotting and backstabbing. He had demonstrated his powers as a king-maker with *Look Back in Anger*, and was now consolidating his position as the new arbiter in the British theatre. For Devine, he was obviously a critic who had to be kept appeased. Lindsay Anderson, the documentary film director who was a member of the

Communist Party, became one of the Royal Court's directors in 1957, and other leftists followed.

By this time, Tynan had acquired himself an unexpected ally – my friend of the Café Tournon days, Christopher Logue.

5 The Paris Input

In his autobiography *Prince Charming*, Christopher Logue describes how he had returned to London in 1956, and how one morning in June, as he was walking through Soho, a friend from the Tournon called his name from an upper window, and invited him up. Logue found himself in the flat of the singer Annie Ross. 'Her other guest was a skinny, pale, long-legged, skull-faced man wearing a green suit, a pink bow-tie, and a frilly purple shirt.' Tynan was lying back in a chair, a cigarette between the third and fourth fingers of his right hand, and 'a stream of opinions, gossip and ambitious plans, broken by an occasional stutter, rushing from between his lips'.

Before they parted, Tynan had invited Logue to the Royal Court to see *Look Back in Anger* and, when Logue mentioned his admiration for a documentary film called *O Dreamland,* recommended him to ring its director, Lindsay Anderson, and introduce himself.

It was soon after this that I encountered Logue at a party given by Melvin Lasky, the associate editor of *Encounter*. I was delighted to see him because I had fond memories of his kindness to me in Paris, and I shook him warmly by the hand. 'Chris, how are you?' To my surprise he looked at me unsmilingly and said: 'Hello Wilson. My name is Christopher, if you please.' I was baffled by his coolness until it dawned on me that, like so many others, he resented the *succès fou* of *The Outsider*.

Tynan would undoubtedly have fanned the flames, for he lost no opportunity of describing me as a fascist. I have no idea how he reached this odd conclusion, for I regarded myself as a socialist, having been converted by the arguments of Bernard Shaw. But then, I was not deeply interested in politics anyway and, like most writers in the free world, hated Communism for regimenting its artists. Tynan was on the side of regimentation, if it could produce results like the Berliner Ensemble's *Mother Courage*. So for him any writer who was more interested in ideas qualified as a fascist.

Look Back in Anger was in its fourth week when Tynan took Logue to see it. Tynan was wearing a wolfskin overcoat, and Logue noticed how he preened through the foyer. He regarded himself – quite rightly – as the play's midwife, the man who had saved Osborne from being dismissed as a clumsy and undisciplined amateur.

Like me, Logue had cringed at the bears and squirrels scene, and admits that the play was monotonous and that Jimmy Porter went on and on.

Logue was not the only one of the *Merlin* crowd who had returned to London in time for the literary revival. He had been preceded by Alexander Trocchi, the writer Bill and I had been hoping to meet in Paris. Alex had arrived in December 1955 (six months before *Look Back in Anger* and *The Outsider*), and he and Logue met at a party in Kensington, and went off into a corner to smoke Trocchi's Gitanes. He told Logue: 'I'm going to live in New York, take heroin and write a textbook for dope fiends. I want to cut off my retreat.' He added quickly that he intended using heroin wisely for creative purposes.

By an extraordinary coincidence, Alex found himself a room in the bohemian household where I lived in Notting Hill. He was a tall, powerfully built man with a Scots accent, short hair, and craggy good looks – I could see why he was a magnet for women. After he had been there about a week, my landlady Anne confided with her charming naïvety: 'The moment I saw him I realised he was the type I always end in bed with. But he doesn't seem to show the slightest interest in me.' This may have been because she was in her thirties, while Alex's taste ran to younger women who could be dominated.

As we became friendly I learned that his life had been, in its way, as difficult as my own. He had been born in Glasgow in 1925 to middle-class parents, his father a piano player and second-generation Italian immigrant. But after the First World War his career as a manager of bands and orchestras flagged as public tastes in music changed, and when he could no longer support his family, his wife took over and ran a boarding house. She died of dysentery when Alex was sixteen. Two years later he joined the Fleet Air Arm – partly because a beautiful girl with whom he was in love said she would marry a pilot. He lost his virginity on a flight of steps with a ten-shilling whore who rubbed spit on his penis to facilitate entry.

At Glasgow University after the war, the 22-year-old struck the senior lecturer as being 'manifestly of genius'. He was studying literature and philosophy, and when he was introduced to the work of A J Ayer, decided he was a logical positivist. Betty Whyte, the beautiful girl he had been in love with since he was twelve, went to live with him in a cottage. She is reported as saying: 'He was impregnable, like a bright god.' He and Betty married secretly when he was 21, she 22. But laziness and overconfidence led to a second-class degree. Even so, no one doubted his brilliance, and he was granted a travelling scholarship, which enabled him to wander with Betty and their baby daughter all over Europe. They ended in Paris, where he proposed to study film at the Sorbonne. He began contributing 'Letter from Paris' to the *Scots Review*, and sold a long poem to a literary journal called *Botteghe Obscura,* which paid top rates (and to which Burns Singer also contributed). When Betty returned to England to see her dying father, Alex started an affair with a pretty married girl called Jane Lougee, who had an allowance of $100 a month, and who lost no time writing to Betty to tell her, explaining that he loved them both. She rushed back to Paris, where Alex persuaded her to separate, then he returned to Jane's studio apartment. Betty, now with two children, went to live in Madrid, with Jane's money paying their allowance. When Alex went to visit her she ended up pregnant with a third.

The first copy of the long-planned magazine *Merlin* (the title, chosen by Christopher Logue, a reference to Ezra Pound) came out in May 1952. In the following year, Logue fell in love with a Brazilian girl from a prominent family, but when the family took her away she stopped answering letters and Logue decided to commit suicide, travelling to Perpignan with that intention. Trocchi followed him, to find him, as he expected, on a lonely beach where Logue was struggling to open a tin of rat poison. Trocchi persuaded him to return to Paris.

Merlin went on from strength to strength, publishing Henry Miller, Genet, Sartre, and chunks of Sade, as well as Samuel Beckett, who came to regard Alex as a protégé. *Merlin* lasted for eleven issues and (as noted earlier) Bill Hopkins and I went around Paris selling copies from door to door.

To make money, Trocchi wrote pornographic books for the dubious French publisher, Maurice Girodias, who had launched a series of dark green paperbacks called the Travellers' Companion series – for English-speaking tourists – and translated two obscene novels by Apollinaire, while Logue wrote a novel called *Lust.* The Travellers' Companion series would eventually include Nabokov's *Lolita,* J P Donleavy's *The Ginger Man,* and Terry Southern's *Candy.* Trocchi even wrote a spurious fifth volume of Frank Harris's *My Life and Loves,* and spiced up a serious novel, *Young Adam,* with some raunchy sex scenes for the eager American traveller. It was Girodias's commissions that enabled the *Merlin* crowd to continue living in Paris for a year or so more.

But it was also a novel published by Girodias that led indirectly to the demise of *Merlin* and the return of Trocchi and Logue to London. This was *The Story of O,* published under the pseudonym Pauline Réage in February 1954.

The author was, in fact, a 47-year-old translator named Dominique Aury, who worked for the publisher Gallimard. The daughter of a middle-class family – her father was a teacher – she had always been a passionate lover of books, and had in due course drifted into magazine journalism. In the early years of the war she met the distinguished critic and editor Jean Paulhan, 23 years her senior. Both were in the Resistance, and became lovers, although he was married. Ten years later, feeling she was losing his interest – he had a roving eye – she tried to win him back by writing a book that would appeal to him. Paulhan was into domination (and had written the Introduction to a new edition of the works of Sade, which Austryn Wainhouse was translating into English). Aury recognised in herself a basic masochism, the desire to be her lover's slave. *The Story of O* was intended to excite his eroticism.

It created an instant sensation and would become a bestseller.

The book opens with two lovers taking a stroll in the park; then he hails a taxi. In the back he makes her take off her suspender belt and panties. She is told to sit on the leather seat with her bottom naked. They stop in front of a country mansion, and after he has cut off her bra, she is told to go and ring the doorbell. Inside she is introduced into a household where she is to learn to be the perfect slave to her lover. And she is made to submit to a series of ordeals of the kind that Sade's *Justine* has made familiar, the mildest of which is being raped anally and orally by the man to whom her lover has loaned her, Sir Stephen.

In effect, Aury was telling Paulhan: 'Do whatever you like with me. I am completely yours.' Apparently it worked, and they remained lovers until his death in 1968.

Trocchi was stunned by it, since his own sexuality responded powerfully to the notion of domination and submission, and he thereupon decided that, if he was to write more pornography for Girodias (who had brought out *The Story of O* in English), it would be necessary for him to conduct some research into the subject. First, he insisted on having sex with a prostitute in a hotel room with Jane looking on. 'He wanted,' says Andrew Murray Scott in *Alexander Trocchi: The Making of the Monster*, 'to show that love is stronger than sex.' Then he persuaded his friend and disciple, Baird Bryant, to loan him his wife Denny for a night. Trocchi proceeded to enrage Jane by bedding the attractive Mary Smith (a pretty English girl who had provided me with a camp bed for the night in Paris in 1953). Alex then decided they had to have an orgy, and a number of his male friends and their wives were enlisted. The idea was for Alex to watch and correct the males on their sexual techniques, and he held a long wooden ruler – he would have preferred a leather whip but was unable to afford one – to administer raps for defects in performance.

When Logue returned from a trip to Rome with the Scots poet W S Graham, and moved in with Jane and Alex, Jane decided it was time for her to move out and leave for America. With her went Betty Trocchi's income. Alex now divorced her.

According to Andrew Murray Scott – who was also in Paris – Trocchi was regarded as 'the most talented and prepossessing writer on the scene, the one who, had a straw poll been taken, would have been voted the most likely to become our generation's Joyce or Hemingway.' But, Scott detected, the experimentation with drugs and sex had left him 'confused, bruised and out of touch with reality'.

Unfortunately, his next step was hardly designed to improve this situation. In 1954, the year of his sexual experimentations, he had met a young revolutionary named Guy Debord, who was the founder of a group called Situation Internationale. A disciple of Rimbaud and Lautréamont, and of Céline's nihilistic novel *Journey to the End of Night,* Debord had characterised modern society as 'the Society of the Spectacle', arguing that, rather like ancient Rome with its bread and circuses, the aim of capitalism is to keep everyone drugged with television, cinema and advertisements so they fail to notice that they are being exploited. In fact, anyone who reads Andrew Hussey's biography of Debord, *The Game of War,* quickly divines that his basic drive was an enormous desire to be famous, fuelled by extremely high dominance, and the same kind of intolerance towards his followers as Karl Marx or Lenin. In short, he was a control freak.

It must have been interesting for Alex to encounter an ego even more assertive than his own. Debord would achieve his moment of glory as a leader in the students' revolt at the Sorbonne in 1968, when it looked for a while as if de Gaulle was about to be unseated by the rock-throwing rebels.

But all this was still to come when Trocchi met him in 1954. For Alex, the meeting came at exactly the right time, when he was feeling oddly deflated by his quest for the ultimate sexual experience, and had generated an appetite for something less demandingly carnal. As a logical positivist, he had already subscribed to a philosophy not all that remote from Marxism. Now he underwent a kind of conversion. Hussey says: 'according to Debord's strict instructions, [Trocchi] broke all contact with his former friends, abolished *Merlin*, and set about promoting the revolutionary avant-garde.'

So when I met Alex in Notting Hill in January 1956, he was a man with a secret mission – to carry the Situationist message across the world. Debord apparently wrote to congratulate him on carrying the revolution as far away as Mexico. Naturally, he gave me no hint of his revolutionary task – but then, I made no secret of my detestation of Marxism. Alex soon found a young and beautiful schoolteacher named Janet to share his bed.

Soon Janet discovered she was pregnant. Having no desire to add to his family, Alex recommended an abortion. We all knew a Soho character known as Arthur the Abortionist, a short, red-headed man who had been our landlady's lover, and on the evening he came to perform the operation, Alex decided to throw a party. I, like everyone else in 24 Chepstow Villas, attended, while Arthur was closeted with Janet in the bedroom.

Unfortunately, the abortion went wrong, and Janet nearly died of loss of blood, and had to be taken to St Mary's Hospital in Paddington.

Not long after this, only a few weeks before the publication of my *Outsider*, Alex left for New York, and embarked on the next stage of his curious and disastrous odyssey. Although he later returned to London fleeing from the American police on drug charges, by then I would be living in Cornwall, and we met only once more before his death 28 years later from drug addiction and lung cancer.

Back in Paris, Maurice Girodias was continuing to pursue his chequered career as a publisher of dirty books for his company, Olympia Press. And across the Atlantic, interesting things were happening, whose repercussions would soon reach Paris.

On 7 October 1955, at a San Francisco poetry reading chaired by Kenneth Rexroth, the 29-year-old poet Allen Ginsberg would read aloud a poem that began:

> I saw the best minds of my generation destroyed
>   by madness, starving hysterical naked,
> dragging themselves through the Negro streets at
>   dawn looking for an angry fix . . .

and his incantatory tone was emphasised as his novelist friend, Jack Kerouac, accompanied him by chanting aloud: 'Go, go, go, go' and beating on his wine jug. Soon the audience had joined in, snapping their fingers and tapping feet as if to a jazz set. Then the room exploded into applause.

What Ginsberg and Kerouac had done that evening was to launch the movement known as the Beat Generation.

Its more spectacular public launching would come about in March 1957, when 520 copies of *Howl and Other Poems*, published by Lawrence Ferlinghetti's City Lights Press, was seized by customs officials as obscene. The court case that followed received national publicity and, when in October 1957, Judge Clayton Horn found Ferlinghetti not guilty of publishing obscene writings, the book became an instant bestseller. So did Kerouac's second novel *On the Road*, which had been published a month earlier. His first, *The Town and the City,* had made little impact seven years earlier, but that was before he had learned to write in his new free style, hurling the words at the paper like an action painter flinging paint.

When the US customs had seized *Howl*, Ginsberg had been on his way to Paris. And it was shortly after the book's acquittal that Ginsberg walked into the office of Maurice Girodias in the rue de Nesle and dropped on his desk a dilapidated and – literally – rat-eaten typescript of a book called *The Naked Lunch* by a homosexual drug addict named William Burroughs.

Strangely enough, in view of his penchant for novels about sex, Girodias turned it down, remarking disapprovingly: 'There's no fucking in the book.'

The writer Terry Southern, who claims to have been present at this rejection, pointed out an example on page 17. Girodias read it and said: 'It's only a blow job.' And he went on to remark that the title was no good either. What was a naked lunch?

With a burst of inspiration, Southern declared that it was American slang for sex in the afternoon.

'Ah,' said Girodias, brightening, 'You mean like our five-till-seven.' In France the phrase refers to the time a man goes to bed with his mistress.

'This is more like an orgy,' said the quick-thinking Southern.

Girodias allowed himself to be convinced, with the result that *The Naked Lunch* would join Christopher Logue's *Lust* and Alex Trocchi's *Young Adam* (in its 'dirtied-up' version) in the Traveller's Companion series.

But Girodias was right; the first fuck *is* in chapter seven, and even that is a description of a Chinese boy being sodomised in a hammock, and it takes place in a surreal atmosphere of nightmare. In fact, most of the book seems designed to produce nausea rather than sexual arousal.

Burroughs, a tall, skinny figure whose grey suit looked as if it has been draped on a skeleton, was the heir of the adding-machine family, and was known to the American public largely because he had drilled his drug-addict wife through the temple with a .38 automatic when trying to shoot an apple off her head to demonstrate his marksmanship. The killing was ruled accidental. He had written a novel called *Junkie* about his drug addiction, and another called *Queer* about his homosexuality. A group of disconnected texts he had written in the fever-ridden delirium of heroin withdrawal, mainly about violence and sexual perversion, were edited by Ginsberg and Kerouac into *The Naked Lunch*. In due course, it would become the most famous – if unread – text of the Beat Generation.

But Girodias would have other claims to celebrity, one being the publication of another untidy typescript that had seen multiple rejections. *The Ginger Man* by James Patrick Donleavy may be regarded as Girodias's first important literary discovery, since it had arrived as early as the autumn of 1954, and might have been rejected if it had not been accompanied by a letter saying that it had been turned down by the American publisher Scribners on grounds of obscenity. But the obscenity, complained Donleavy, was an important part of the novel, and its removal would detract from it.

Donleavy, a good-looking Irish American, who had studied (like my wife Joy) at Trinity College, Dublin, had written the book, as he explained, out of 'the fist I shook and the rage I spent', and may therefore be classified as an Angry Young Man. But it was hardly accurate to describe it as obscene – it was simply scatological.

It opens in a Dublin bar with two Trinity students complaining about their lack of cash, and then going back to the flat of one of them, Sebastian Dangerfield, to get drunk. Having no money, Dangerfield goes out to a local grocer and opens an account which he has no intention of paying, then returns with liquor and food. When his friend has staggered off into the night, Dangerfield, who is prone to violence when drunk, attacks his pillow and mattress with an axe. The next morning, awakened amid the chaos by his wife, who wants to know why he didn't meet her off the train, he tells her to shut up and finally punches her in the face, after which, he tries to suffocate his screaming baby with a pillow.

Donleavy writes it all in a kind of sub-Joycean telegraphese that frequently makes it hard to work out what is going on. This is Dangerfield discovering that he has been sitting on a train with his penis (the 'ginger man' of the title) exposed:

'What's he doing? Pointing into his lap. Me? Lap? Good Christ. It's out. Every inch of it. Leaping for the door. Get out. Get out. Fast.'

And so Dangerfield rampages on, writing begging letters, sponging off his friends, hurling a bottle of whisky at a barman's head, and beating up a cab driver. In one memorably unpleasant scene, he forgets that the lavatory is disconnected and drenches his wife in the room below in ordure and wet toilet paper. When she finally walks out on him he has already seduced two Dublin working girls, and will seduce more.

In *The Angry Decade* Kenneth Allsop describes him as a 'rogue maladjust', and adds: 'Yet there is a distinct horror about this book, which is Dangerfield's frantic flight from anything that might mean continuity or responsibility. There is nothing wrong with Donleavy's character delineation: Dangerfield is as consistent and relevant as an epileptic fit.'

It was published in July 1955, and Donleavy was outraged when he received his two copies to see that it was in the Traveller's Companion series, and contained a list of its fellow dirty books in the back (*The Enormous Bed, Rape, School for Sin, The Libertine, Play This Love With Me, Tender Was My Flesh*) in which it was listed as number seven.

Donleavy suspected, probably correctly, that Girodias had published it in the Traveller's Companion series to prove to the French authorities – who were talking of closing him down – that he was publishing books of literary merit.

Donleavy swore revenge. So when someone recommended him to try an English publisher named Neville Spearman, he sent him *The Ginger Man*, which was promptly accepted. Now it was Girodias's turn to be outraged, as he pointed out that he held world rights.

But when both had gone to court, Donleavy found himself the winner by a technicality. Girodias had failed to assign himself British copyright by filling in an official form. (Girodias never had contracts with his porn writers, but relied on word of mouth.)

I myself had a chance to observe Donleavy's implacable fury about Girodias when I met him in at his flat in Broughton Road, Fulham, in 1958.

I made his acquaintance through a literary journalist, Bob Pitman, who had run a piece about him in the *Sunday Express*. He had relayed some of the stories about Donleavy: how he kept only one book in the house – *The Ginger Man* – and was usually to be found reading it; about how he once removed the back of his fireplace, because the neighbours' fireplace was on the other side of the wall, and their fires were large enough to heat both rooms.

After Bob's account of the plot of *The Ginger Man*, I expected to meet a hulking brute with bulging muscles and an uncertain temper, so was surprised to be introduced to a slim, quiet-voiced man with a D H Lawrence beard and a smile of considerable charm, who told me to call him Mike. His dark-haired wife Valerie was one of the most dazzlingly beautiful girls I have ever met, and I found myself hoping she was not the model for Dangerfield's wife Marion. (But she was.) There were so many toys, playpens and nappies around the place that I got the impression they had fourteen children.

When I mentioned that I had been in Paris in 1953 and had met the *Merlin* crowd when they were writing dirty books for Girodias, he made some comments about the latter's personal character that made it clear that he regarded him as a monster, and gave us a short account of the publication of *The Ginger Man* in which deceit and fraud figured largely.

Now, in retrospect, having read a full account of the story in John de St Jorre's marvellously funny *Venus Bound, The Erotic Voyage of Olympia Press and Its Writers* (1994), it seems to me that Donleavy was being more than a little paranoid about Girodias, who had at least launched him into print when no one else would risk it.

Donleavy and I liked one another, and Bob and I spent such a pleasant hour there that I determined to make another attempt to read *The Ginger Man*, which I had bought in Paris. My first attempt had stalled at the scene where Dangerfield punches his wife in the face and tries to suffocate the baby, which I found as upsetting as Jimmy Porter's beastliness to his wife in *Look Back in Anger* – in fact, more so since Jimmy Porter never actually hits her. But since I now regarded Donleavy as a friend, or at least a friendly acquaintance, I felt obliged to press on.

I still found it hard work, and could have wished he had been less influenced by *Ulysses,* and not been quite so wholesale about it. Joyce had at least interspersed his slabs of interior monologue with evocative descriptions of Dublin. Donleavy writes it all in a fractured prose that often defies interpretation, so the reader tries to grasp what is happening through a kind of impressionistic fog of language.

There was another problem with *The Ginger Man*. Much of it is clearly unrealistic. No man could really sit on a train unaware that his penis is dangling out. Neither would ordinary Catholic working-class girls perform oral sex on the hero and permit him to sodomise them.

When I wrote to Donleavy, I took care not to voice any such criticisms. But he never replied. This surprised me, since he had struck me as courteous, but when I mentioned it to Bob Pitman, he said: 'No, he doesn't answer letters – he says it saves time.'

This, it seemed to me, was an important clue to Donleavy. No sensible person can read *The Ginger Man* without feeling that he is trying to make a virtue of behaving like a spoilt child. To actually live like that would be to invite disaster. But in his dealings with Olympia Press, Donleavy continued to play his game of being 'the wild ginger man', with disastrous results to his own finances and those of Girodias. The legal battle between them would drag on for more than a decade until, in 1968, the bankrupt Olympia Press was bought by Donleavy – through his second wife Mary. Both combatants had by then spent a fortune on lawyers, and were exhausted.

Girodias's next major literary discovery in no way qualifies either as an angry young man or a member of the Beat Generation, but can hardly be left out of any account of literary scandal in the 1950s because he is so central to it.

In the spring of 1955, Girodias made his most remarkable literary discovery so far. A lady named Doussia Ergaz, a Russian émigrée living in Paris, came to see him to explain that another Russian émigré, a certain Professor Nabokov, who now taught at Cornell University in Ithaca, NY and had already published several novels, had now written a book that had horrified the four American publishers to whom he had shown it. It was called *Lolita*, and was about a middle-aged man's love affair with a twelve-year-old girl.

The typescript, in two volumes, arrived the next day, and a reading of the first two pages was enough to convince Girodias, 'This is it.'

Vladimir Vladimirovitch Nabokov had been born into an aristocratic family in St Petersburg in April 1899, the son of a distinguished politician. They left Russia after the defeat of the White Army in 1919, and moved to Berlin, where his father was assassinated in mistake for a Russian democratic leader. There Nabokov wrote his first novel *Masha*, predictably enough about Russian exiles in Berlin. Fleeing once more, this time from the Nazis, he went to America, and there became friendly with the critic

Edmund Wilson, who introduced his work to publishers – he had already written ten novels in Russian. His first novel written in English, *The Real Life of Sebastian Knight*, about a biographer's futile quest, was published in 1941. In the same year he became a lecturer in comparative literature at Wellesley College for Women, where he founded the Russian Department. (A biography of his wife Vera by Stacy Schiff makes it clear that he saw no moral objection to having affairs with his students.) He also became curator of Lepidoptery at Harvard – butterflies were a lifelong passion. He had become an American citizen in 1945, and in 1948 became head of the comparative literature department at Cornell.

This distinguished Russian *litterateur* was the author of the typescript Girodias was reading. It was wittily and charmingly written, and so obviously of literary merit that Girodias anticipated no problems with the law. In June 1955 he signed a contract agreeing to pay an advance of about $5,000, far above his usual. He made up for this generosity by awarding himself 33 per cent of translation rights. (Most publishers would have been – and still are – contented with ten.) In September 1955 it appeared in two volumes, under Nabokov's own name – the professor having finally dropped the original plan of using a pseudonym.

Nothing happened. No clamour, no recognition, no reviews.

Then, by pure chance, my friend Bob Pitman took a hand in the story. At that time, in late 1955, Bob was a schoolteacher who wrote for the small-circulation Labour newspaper *Tribune* and who, by a staggering piece of good luck, had been appointed literary editor of the Beaverbrook *Sunday Express* because (he told me) he and Beaverbrook were both asthmatic.

Bob and his wife Pat lived in a flat in Napier Road, Kensington, and Bob used to take his four-year-old son Jonathan to the newly opened Holland Park. Here Jonathan became friendly with another small boy called Philip, with whose father Bob fell into conversation. The latter introduced himself as Mike Donleavy, who mentioned that he had written a book that had been published in Paris. Hoping for a review, Donleavy asked his publisher to send Bob a copy, and in due course, a book parcel arrived containing *The Ginger Man,* as well as a two-volume novel entitled *Lolita*.

Bob, who had a year-old daughter named Katie, was horrified by *Lolita*, and not exactly enchanted by *The Ginger Man*, to which he reacted much as I had – feeling that its hero was a stupid and unpleasant oaf for whom it was hard for the reader to feel anything but a desire to see him knocked down and jumped on. Nevertheless, like myself, he made allowances for friends, and did an interview with Donleavy.

On Christmas Day, 1955, the *Sunday Times* published a page in which well-known writers chose their 'best books of the year'. One of Graham

Greene's choices was *Lolita,* of which no one had ever heard – except Bob Pitman. Bob lost no time in telling John Gordon, the editor-in-chief of the *Sunday Express*, what *Lolita* was about. And Gordon, a charming and easygoing Scot with a strong Presbyterian streak, denounced Greene and Nabokov in his weekly column.

It was one of those literary quarrels in which no one is too serious. Greene had once lost a job as a film critic by saying that the short skirt of nine-year-old Shirley Temple was intended to titillate dirty old men in grubby rain macs, and like Nabokov, he clearly had an eye for nymphets. He now reacted by announcing the formation of a John Gordon Society, whose purpose was to protect British parents from insidious works of child pornography that might place their daughters in peril; among others he enrolled Angus Wilson and Christopher Isherwood, and the joke enlivened Fleet Street for a few weeks, increasing the circulation of the *Sunday Express*.

For Nabokov and Girodias it was a heaven-sent windfall of publicity that increased the book's sales and brought the 56-year-old exile belated celebrity. Nabokov had never doubted that he was a man of literary genius whose works were unsuited to the taste of the century of Hemingway and Joyce. One may speculate that this, his twelfth published novel, was shrewdly designed to break the deafening silence, and explains why, after insisting that *Lolita* had to be published under a pseudonym, he was unable to resist the temptation to use his own name after all.

I finally bought *Lolita* in 1958, when I was on a lecture tour of German universities, and made a detour via Paris. In Left-bank bookshops I purchased banned works like *Lady Chatterley's Lover*, *The Ginger Man*, *Lolita* and volume 5 of *My Life and Loves*, whose author was now living on a barge in Flushing, NY and becoming a heroin addict.

Lolita interested me far more than Lady Chatterley or Frank Harris because I felt I understood what it was really about. In a sort of revelation, I recognised that the underlying subject of the book was *the feeling of sexual underprivilege that is bound to permeate a society like ours*. Its roots can be traced back to that original Angry Young Man Jean-Jacques Rousseau, in whom the feeling of sexual underprivilege and social revolution are inextricably bound together.

The prudery of the nineteenth century was designed to limit sexual licence as new techniques of communication made men and women more aware of their own sexuality. The novel in particular had seemed to be a vehicle of corruption since, from Richardson to Stendhal, seduction was one of its main preoccupations. Then the rise of big stores like Selfridges (owned by an American tycoon), intended to appeal to housewives, brought a new dimension to advertising, since it was hard to show pictures of women's clothes without showing the body inside them. By the beginning of the twentieth century, most newspapers carried sketches of flat-chested women in a state of 'unerotic undress'. Gordon Selfridge's first underwear advertisements in the *Daily Mail* in 1909 caused him to be attacked as a kind of pornographer.

So by about 1910, the sex-conscious young male on his way to work, accustomed to seeing women encased from head to foot in clothes that gave little hint of the body underneath, suddenly found himself bombarded with hints of the bedroom.

My first book *The Outsider* begins with the hero of a 1908 French novel describing his torment at the swaying skirts of women on the tops of buses. 'It is not a woman I want, it is *all* women.' And on the first page of *Ritual in the Dark*, the hero goes up the escalator of the London Underground, and finds that advertisements showing women in their underwear produce an effect like 'a match tossed against a petrol-soaked rag'. As a fairly highly-sexed teenager, I had found this kind of thing a nuisance, like being perpetually interrupted by the ringing of a telephone when you're trying to work.

And this, I felt, is what *Lolita* is really about: the sense of 'sexual under-privilege' experienced by any normal male in a society where he is bound to feel a continual sense of sexual frustration – the underprivilege which had been a revolutionary force since Rousseau's Julie yielded her virginity to her tutor.

Then why make Lolita a twelve-year-old 'nymphet'? Because she better symbolises the sense of the forbidden, the unattainable.

This also made me recognise the centrality of the role that sex played among the writers of my generation – Amis, Larkin, Wain, Iris Murdoch, Osborne, Braine, Donleavy, Trocchi and Tynan. Dickens had been obsessed by social underprivilege, but since about 1900, the great underlying theme of literature has been *sexual* underprivilege.

It was *Lolita* that finally provoked the French police to act against Olympia Press. In November 1956, a police inspector from the Vice Squad paid a visit to Girodias's office, and took away *The Story of O* and 25 volumes of the Traveller's Companion series, including *Lolita*. On 20 December the ministry of the interior issued an order banning all of them.

There was an element of absurdity in this ban, which had probably been engineered by the British government under the Repression of Obscene Publications Act. *The Ginger Man* was already out in England in a mildly censored version, under the Neville Spearman imprint, and *Lolita* was being translated into French for publication by Gallimard (and appeared in due course without hindrance). Moreover, in early 1957, copies of *Lolita* which had been seized by American customs were quietly released after a few weeks, and when Girodias asked why, he learned that they had been deemed harmless. This meant, in effect, that the book could be published in America without fear of prosecution.

Of course, the ban was not aimed primarily at *Lolita* – even if that was the book that had started the scandal – but at the other 24 genuinely pornographic works.

Girodias proceeded to sue the ministry of the interior on the grounds that the law they had invoked was supposed to be used against subversive political publications.

Early in 1958 he won, and the ban was withdrawn – only to be renewed on appeal a few months later after de Gaulle came to power.

Eventually, it was Dominique Aury, the author of *The Story of O,* and her influential lover Jean Paulhan, who got the ban lifted. The minister of justice was privately approached and was asked to a small luncheon party at his house at Croissy. Although nothing was said about the book, the next day the minister issued a decree ending the ban.

When *Lolita* was eventually published in America, then England, and was filmed by Stanley Kubrick, Nabokov became a rich man, and was able to give up teaching and move with his wife to Montreux, Switzerland, where they lived until his death in 1977.

Girodias also had nothing to complain about. He had reduced his original demand for 33 per cent of the royalties to 20 per cent, but even that was twice the normal rate and, as a percentage of a bestseller, was enough to satisfy his highly developed rapacity.

6 'As for Living . . .'

Before the lifting of the police ban in 1959, Girodias had become involved in the publication of another work that straddled the line between pornography and literature: a novel called *Candy*.

This had started as a short story by Terry Southern, a 32-year-old Texan who in 1956, after a stint in the army, was living with his wife Carol in Geneva, where she worked for the United Nations. They were short of money, so when Southern was visiting Paris, he decided to follow the example of his friend Mason Hoffenberg, and write a dirty book for Girodias.

Trocchi had given him the idea. He had seen Southern's story 'Candy Christian', about, in Southern's words: 'a fabulous, blue-eyes, pink-nippled, pert-derrière darling who was compassion incarnate, so filled with universal love that she gave herself – fully, joyfully – to Derek, a demented hunchback.' Southern turned down Trocchi's offer to publish it – for no payment – in *Merlin,* but in due course decided to take up his suggestion to turn it into a novel.

So, with 'hemp-maven extraordinaire' Mason Hoffenburg, author of *Sin for Breakfast* and *Until She Screams*, Southern went to the rue de Nesle to offer the idea to Girodias. The latter had, according to Southern, already seen some of it, which Alex Trocchi had copied for him. He offered Southern what sounded an immense sum – 10,000 francs a month for four months – to complete the book. However, since this was before the revaluation of the franc, when it was worth only a hundred to the dollar, this was a mere four hundred dollars or a hundred pounds.

Candy was to be a female version of Voltaire's *Candide*, a sweet simpleton who is soon parted from her virginity. Southern said that whenever he thought of her, he got a tremendous erection.

Girodias planned to publish in 1957, but in fact it was not even delivered until the summer of 1958. Southern was not, as far as writing was concerned, a long-distance runner, which is why he decided he needed a collaborator. But Hoffenberg was a druggie who was even more erratic. The result was that, even with Girodias's ability to rush a book into print, it took until October 1958.

It is an outrageously funny book. Dr Krankheit, the author of a work called *Masturbate Now!* is a superb comic invention, as is his doting Jewish mom who takes a job as a cleaner in the hospital so she can be near her baby. Girodias was a little concerned in case the humour had the effect of diluting the sexual impact of the porn, but need not have worried; as with *Lolita* the humour made it possible to take it seriously as something other than a dirty book, and which guaranteed its long-term survival.

Sales were slow but steady, and bootleg copies found a ready market in New York, where its reputation began to grow.

Girodias had given the authors a regular contract instead of the usual word-of-mouth deal that had sufficed for the *Merlin* crowd; but he continued to take a hefty share of foreign royalties – one-third. Even this did not save him from the usual mess of legal entanglements – all of which could have been avoided if he had merely taken the trouble to stick to the contract. Instead, Southern's New York agent had to remind Girodias in August 1963 that they were still waiting for a royalty statement for the first half of the year. Girodias would have done well to heed it, for he was sitting on a gold mine. Instead, he let things drift, with the consequence that, in November 1963, he received a letter stating that the agreement with his authors had been terminated due to failure to render reports of earnings.

In fact, the authors had accepted an offer from the American publisher Putnams and, in early 1964, it became an instant bestseller and sold over a million. Hollywood became interested. A paperback edition with Dell was delayed because the hardback was still selling. But another paperback company, Lancet, had got wind of the fact that the book was not legally protected in America since Girodias had ceased to own the rights, and launched a pirated edition. Dell hastened to bring out its own edition, which soon overtook the Lancet version, even though it cost twenty cents more – it sold two and a half million, compared to Lancet's million copies.

Putnams now saw the advantage of validating Girodias's 1961 contract to fight Lancet. They agreed to pay 100,000 dollars, to be divided between Girodias and his two authors.

All this litigation had finally bankrupted Girodias, which explains why Donleavy's new wife, Mary, was able to buy the Olympia operation in 1970. Meanwhile, taking advantage of the new climate of tolerance in publishing, Girodias moved to New York, and relaunched Olympia Press there in 1967. The deal with Girodias had also enabled Southern and Hoffenberg to sign the film-rights contract.

The film of *Candy* (1968) was panned by critics as atrocious – an unknown Swedish actress had been chosen to play the all-American teenager – but a star cast that included Marlon Brando, Richard Burton, James Coburn, John Huston and Ringo Starr assured its financial success.

Sadly, there was a sense in which, for Southern and Hoffenberg, all this success was a disaster. It provided Hoffenberg with money to feed his dope habit, and he died of lung cancer at the age of 63 in June 1986. Southern went on to became a highly paid Hollywood scriptwriter, whose most memorable successes were *Dr Strangelove* and *Easy Rider*, that classic evocation of the Beat Generation in the 1960s.

The Hollywood lifestyle led to his putting on a large amount of weight and, seemingly, to the death of his talent as a novelist. After *Blue Movie* (1970), a Hollywood satire in the tradition of Nathanael West's *Day of the Locust* – and which, like that novel, seems to end by sharing the boredom, stupidity and coarseness it is satirising – Southern published nothing more for 22 years until *Texas Summer,* a short elegiac novel about childhood, which was virtually ignored. He died of respiratory failure in 1995.

When Trocchi went to New York in 1956, he took a job as a scow captain on the canal in Flushing, NY (a scow is a long flat barge), on which he was virtually a caretaker with nothing much to do, and gave himself up to experimenting with heroin.

Why he did this I found at the time baffling, since it seemed – and indeed proved to be – a form of mental suicide. Then, in New York in the early sixties, I met a girl who told me she had sailed up and down the Hudson with Alex and shared his heroin fixes. I asked: 'Didn't you get addicted?' She shook her head. 'It takes some time before the body develops a chemical dependency on a drug. I just made sure I stopped before that happened.'

So this is probably the explanation of how Alex got hooked. He miscalculated how long he could take heroin without developing dependency. From then on, slowly but quite surely, it destroyed his life.

As a result of the months on a scow, he wrote a 'novel' – in fact a journal – *Cain's Book*, of which Barney Rossett, of Grove Press in New York, sent me a proof copy in 1959.

Although I obliged with some comment that could be used in advertising, I did not particularly like the book. It seemed to me virtually static, describing life on the scow and an endless series of 'fixes', enlivened with a few sexual encounters, two of them homosexual. (I still suspect the latter was thrown in out of bravado, to illustrate the catholicity of Alex's sexual tastes, for he always struck me as totally heterosexual.)

What I could see clearly was that *Cain's Book* fitted into the thesis that Edmund Wilson had first outlined in *Axel's Castle* in 1931, and that I had expanded in *The Outsider*: that although modern writers, like Joyce, Eliot, Gertrude Stein and Proust, may seem to signal a radical break with the past, their lineage can be traced to nineteenth-century romanticism, with its longing to turn its back on the boredom of everyday reality – all encapsulated in that phrase of Villiers de Lisle-Adam's hero Axel: 'As for living, our servants can do that for us.'

Yeats also caught its essence in lines from 'The White Birds':

> I would that we were, my beloved, white birds on
>   the foam of the sea.
> We tire of the flame of the meteor, before it can
>   fade and flee;
> And the flame of the blue star of twilight, hung
>   low on the rim of the sky,
> Has awaked in our hearts, my beloved, a sadness
>   that may not die.

To tire of the flame of a meteor, which lasts for only a few seconds, must be some kind of record for ennui. A person steeped in this emotion, which is fundamentally lassitude, inevitably feels a weary melancholy.

We instantly recognise the same mood in the opening words of Proust's novel: 'For a long time I used to go to bed early', and the long meditation on childhood that follows.

Decadence ripened into decay and sheer exhaustion in the work of Samuel Beckett, whose trilogy *Molloy, Malone Dies* and *The Unnameable* was published by Girodias in 1959. More than any writer considered in this book so far, Beckett may be seen as a descendant of the *fin-de-siècle* romantics; he is almost unable to move under the burden of lassitude and discouragement.

Beckett himself virtually admitted that his fundamental problem was laziness when he called the hero of his first volume of stories, *More Pricks Than Kicks*, Bellecqua. The name is taken from a Florentine friend of Dante, a manufacturer of parts for musical instruments, who is described by a contemporary as 'the most indolent man who ever lived'.

No one who reads *More Pricks than Kicks* can doubt that it is auto-biographical, and that Bellacqua is Beckett's vision of himself.

Deirdre Bair's biography, *Samuel Beckett*, shows how this came about. As a youth in Dublin, living in a comfortable middle-class home, Beckett struggled against boredom – the inability to convince himself that anything is worth the effort. The feeling is dangerous because it is self-validating. The more you feel weary and depressed, the more obvious it is that the rest of our hectic society is made up of madmen who have not yet grasped the truth that nothing is worth doing, and that we had all better sit down and refuse to move.

We instantly recognise the futility syndrome in the opening of Beckett's first novel *Murphy* (1938), written in his twenties: 'The sun shone, having no alternative, on the nothing new.' For a long time during this period, Beckett lived at home, drank too much, and did nothing.

For decades Beckett suffered intense depressions that occasionally brought him to the point where he feared insanity. During the Second

World War he lived in Paris in poverty, and when the war was over, hastened back to Dublin in search of money. There, once more, he lived at home, drank too much, and drifted into the usual fatigue and self-disgust. It was then he received the insight that determined the future direction of his work.

One evening a long walk had taken him to Dunlaoghaire Pier, where a winter storm was in progress. There he had his 'revelation'. A television programme on Beckett expressed it: 'Where others had sought enrichment, he would keep impoverishment. It was like resolving to go naked . . .'

In *Krapp's Last Tape* the hero expresses it: 'What I saw then was that the assumption I had been going on all my life, namely . . . [Beckett's leader dots] clear to me at last that the dark I have been fighting off all this time is in reality . . . my most unshatterable association till my dying day.'

To anyone who has read Deirdre Bair's biography, it becomes plain that all Beckett's problems sprang from being born into a reasonably well-off family who could support him while he nursed his deep disinclination to choose any course of action. His kind of boredom is suffered by many teenagers, probably a majority, but being born into circumstances that allowed him to go on indulging it into his thirties meant that he wasted most of his early life in the state that theologians used to call *accidia*. And he would have undoubtedly continued to suffer from it for the rest of his days if the beginning of the Second World War had not turned his life upside down. But by that time Beckett was simply too old to change his outlook.

Back in Paris after the war he put into effect his decision to write about mental 'impoverishment', and began a novel called *Molloy,* which is a kind of Kafkaesque dream. It opens with monologue by a confused schizophrenic named Molloy, who says he is in his mother's room but doesn't know how he got there. All he wants, he says, is to finish dying. He then tells how he set out on a journey on a bicycle, with his crutches strapped to it. After a rambling and disconnected narrative in which nothing much happens, except that he runs over a dog, goes to live with the lady who rescues him from an angry crowd, then leaves her because he feels she is trying to take over his life, he collapses in a ditch, then finds himself in his mother's room.

In the second novel, *Malone Dies*, the narrator, a dying man, is for all practical purposes the Molloy who was so confused in the previous book, and he lives in a room like the inside of a skull. Again, nothing much happens, except that the old woman who brings him soup and empties his pot stops coming, so he will presumably starve to death, and a stranger (the undertaker?) comes to stare at him.

Dying, he tells a disjointed story about a poor couple whose main hope is that their son will become a doctor; however, he becomes a tramp and ends in an asylum. One feels that Beckett is saying 'Serve them right' for wasting their time on hope.

Exhausted, Beckett decided on a change of pace, and began a play. Inevitably, its subject was the meaninglessness of life. In a bleak landscape, with nothing in sight but a tree, two tramps stand in the dusk, waiting for a man called Godot to arrive. They are not sure when he will arrive, or even if they are in the right place. When one of them comments: 'Nothing to be done,' the other replies: 'I am beginning to come around to that opinion.' The judiciousness of the reply signals that, as in *Watt*, the humour will spring from the contrast of the formality of the language with the inconsequentiality of the reality to which it refers.

Although down-and-outs who sleep in ditches, they cling obsessively to a sense of order, and their conversation reflects this. 'We always find something, eh, Didi, to give us the impression that we exist?' And although down-and-outs, they speak in the language of men of reason.

The dialogue often has a knockabout humour:

Which of you two stinks?
He's got stinking breath and I've got stinking feet.

But although Al Alvarez says in his study, *Samuel Beckett*: 'It is as though a great fog of boredom enveloped every event and every word the instant it occurs,' it is not a boring play because, as in the earlier *Watt*, Beckett has slowed down the action to half the pace of normal life, so our expectation has been anaesthetised. And because the scenery is bleak, we are delighted to laugh at any absurdities that mitigate the boredom, as when Estragon's trousers fall around his ankles, or he explains:

ESTRAGON (*faintly*) My left lung is very weak! (*He coughs feebly. In ringing tones.*) But my right lung is as sound as a bell!

Completed in January 1949, *Godot,* as usual, was turned down. Since Beckett had once more collapsed into a state of total inanition, spending day after day in bed, it was his mistress Suzanne who tried to peddle his work. And after five rejections, it was her idea to approach Roger Blin, a director who had been a friend of Antonin Artaud. Blin liked it, and he and Beckett met in the early summer of 1950 to talk about it. Blin thought it ought to be performed as a circus, then reflected on the cost and decided it should be done as simply as possible.

Premièred finally in November 1953, it was, of course, the success that changed Beckett's life. But its original success was due to scandal rather than appreciation. Many people felt that it was an outrage that they should be asked to sit through a play 'in which nothing happens, twice'. It was like

Chekhov, only worse. Surely it was some kind of hoax? And the liveliness, and occasional bitterness, of the discussion, kept the Théâtre de Babylone full until Beckett became aware that at last, at the age of 47, he was famous.

Meanwhile, after writing *Malone Dies* in October 1948, then breaking off to write *Godot,* Beckett had returned to a final novel, *L'Innnomable*, that was the most uncompromisingly bleak so far. Here, a disembodied voice (although a mention of his crutches hints at Molloy) simply talks on into the darkness – after the first few pages, without paragraphs. There are not even anecdotes. The character sits in a shallow container, completely paralysed, and we gather through the gloom of the monologue that he will also lose his limbs, and end in a large pot full of sawdust outside a French restaurant specialising in turnips in gravy. The book ends: 'I don't know, I'll never know, in the silence you don't know, you must go on, I can't go on, I'll go on.' Few readers can have felt any desire to follow his example.

Without the success of *Godot*, Beckett would certainly have ceased to write; *The Unnameable* has the air of a farewell to life as well as writing. But fate decided to amuse itself at his expense; since he was convinced he had come to the end of what he had to say, how would he cope with fame? The answer was that Beckett declined to be coaxed out of his nihilism. If they thought *Godot* was a comedy, he would make it clear that he had no intention of being funny. He would show them that he was shaking his fist at these idiots and telling them that life was meaningless and they had better stop pretending otherwise. So for the rest of his life he went on writing plays and fragments of fiction in which the characters are forced to live in more and more undignified situations – confined to wheelchairs, to dustbins, buried up to the waist in sand, lying face downward in the mud. The more he cursed life, the more the critics applauded, until they awarded him the Nobel Prize.

It can be seen why, from the time I encountered Beckett's work in Paris, I had no doubt that he represented the lowest point on a curve that had begun its upward sweep with Rousseau and Goethe, and turned decisively downwards when Axel said: 'As for living, our servants can do that for us.'

This whole argument could be summarised in three words: Beckett *versus* Proust. Proust is saying: I may be feeling low and a bit sorry for myself, but there *is* something of tremendous importance out there, some revelation of immense meaning. And Beckett is saying: I can tell you, there's nothing important out there, just illusion. So let's all lie down and die . . .

It still seems to me amazing that critics can praise Beckett as a great writer. If Beckett had written plays in which he recommended the ideas of Hitler, we would have no hesitation in condemning him; he would probably have ended on trial. So why do we not recognise that a writer who poisons our cultural reservoirs by declaring that life is meaningless – and so probably been responsible for more suicides than *Werther* – is not equally guilty?

As noted earlier, one more member of the Beat Generation owed his emergence to Girodias. John de St Jorre records in *Venus Bound:* 'The publication of *The Naked Lunch* by the Olympia Press in 1959 lifted Burroughs out of obscurity.'

I was introduced to *The Naked Lunch* by its British publisher John Calder, who had invited Burroughs to the Edinburgh Festival in 1962 (together with Henry Miller and Alex Trocchi) and have to admit that I failed to share the admiration that Calder and Barney Rossett in America professed for the book, my taste for homoerotic sadism being relatively uncultivated.

Although the mood of *The Naked Lunch* is more savage and bitter than in *Cain's Book*, we can easily trace its source in Burroughs's first work *Junkie,* an account of his drug addiction. In other words, as in Beckett, we are dealing with the depletion of vitality that springs from boredom.

Ted Morgan summarises Burroughs's outlook in his biography *Literary Outlaw*: 'Nothing is true, everything is permitted. Every taboo that is broken, every act of outrage that is committed, is a justifiable act of insurrection against a bankrupt system of morality. Whatever his characters are doing, Burroughs seems to be saying, the actual conditions on the planet, created by the villains and morons in power, is worse.'

This is fundamentally the argument of de Sade: whatever outrage is committed by rebels against morality is justified because of the villainy of those in power. He goes on to deploy it in *Juliette* and *The 120 Days of Sodom*, to justify disembowelling women and torturing children.

The objection to this is clearly a logical one. I confronted it, for example, when a homicidal acquaintance, the Moors Murderer Ian Brady, used it in his book, *The Gates of Janus*, to which I wrote the Introduction, to justify the rape and murder of five children, on the grounds that those in authority are so corrupt that any gesture of protest is permissible. (He remained deaf to my objection that two wrongs do not make a right.)

To speak of murder is by no means irrelevant in the context of Burroughs. Sadistic sexual killers often lay out the victim's body in a display that is designed to create shock. *The Naked Lunch* is as close as it is possible to come on the page to displaying a mutilated corpse, or to screaming with rage and hitting people. Whole chapters are designed to arouse shock. In that sense the novel is as non-pornographic as a hospital report of a multiple car accident.

Anthony Burgess put the real objection in a review of a later Burroughs novel, *Cities of Red Night*, when he said: 'When we look at pederastic thrusts on every page we soon begin to yawn. Sexual strangulation is . . . soon boring.' And it seems to me that the practicable objection to the book as literature is that literature is intended to stimulate the imagination as food is intended to nourish the body, and that therefore a book full of descriptions that are intended to nauseate is like a restaurant that serves unappetising food.

Girodias sold American rights to Barney Rossett of Grove Press the same year, but Rossett was having problems publishing Henry Miller's *Tropic of Cancer* in the US. (Published in 1962, it became a bestseller, making Miller a substantial sum of money for the first time in his life.)

The Naked Lunch soon ran into trouble in Boston, and was adjudged obscene. But it won in the High Court in 1966, this decision virtually ending censorship in America.

By way of a footnote, it should be mentioned that one of my own books owes its inception to Girodias. Called in America *The Sex Diary of Gerard Sorme*, this sequel to *Ritual in the Dark* was suggested by Girodias. By contract it had to be offered to my British publisher first, and after reading it, Jim Reynolds of Arthur Barker Ltd decided that it could – in the post *Lady Chatterley* climate – safely be issued in England, where it came out as *The Man Without a Shadow*. This also ran into trouble in Boston in 1963, whereupon my royalties were seized by the publisher, Dial Press, to pay legal costs.

All of which explains why, when I returned from Paris to London in late 1953, I felt that I had left behind nothing I regretted. The surge of renewal that had come with the Liberation of France in 1945 was already fading. Sartre and Camus, who had told the postwar generation that they were free, had no advice about what to do with their freedom. Sartre drifted left, and defended Communism; Camus rejected this as an evasion of moral responsibility, and in *L'Homme Revolté,* outraged Sartre by saying that most leftists were not yet 'out of the pram'. But he had no better suggestions. And the driver and conductor of France's existentialist revolution left it parked in a kind of intellectual cul-de-sac.

I recognised my own reaction in George Orwell's response to his meeting with Henry Miller in 1937, when Orwell was on his way to fight in the Spanish Civil War. Orwell had written enthusiastically of *The Tropic of Cancer* and *Black Spring,* but when he called on Miller in Paris, he was shocked when Miller told him he was a fool to get mixed up in political and moral issues: 'Our civilisation was destined to be swept away and replaced by something so different that we should scarcely regard it as human – a prospect that did not bother him, he said. Everywhere there is a sense of approaching cataclysm, and . . . the implied belief that it doesn't matter.'

Orwell felt that bigger issues do matter and that Miller's nihilism was another name for irresponsibility. I felt much the same about Beckett, Girodias and the Tournon crowd. Alex Trocchi would write in 'Invisible Insurrection of a Million Minds': 'The individual has a profound sense of his own impotence as he realises the immensity of the forces involved. We, the creative ones, must discard this paralytic posture and seize control of the human process by assuming control of ourselves.' But this is precisely what Alex failed to do when he went to New York and became hooked on heroin.

My own attempt to 'seize control of the human process' had begun on Christmas Day 1954, when I sketched out *The Outsider* in my journal.

I certainly felt no confidence in my ability to change anything. It seemed obvious that the current of negativity was running too powerfully. I recollected the reception of Nietzsche's *Birth of Tragedy* and anticipated the worst.

What I had failed to recognise was the enormous number of people who felt I had described just how they felt. Slightly to my dismay, I found myself hailed as Britain's leading existentialist thinker. (In fact, its only existentialist thinker, if we exclude a young Cambridge graduate named Irish Murdoch who had also spent some time in Paris, and had just written her first novel, *Under the Net*.)

Apparently I was wrong, and it would not be as difficult as thought to set up a counter-movement to the Millers and the Burroughs and the Becketts.

But I wasn't wrong when I took my publisher's advice and fled to the countryside in 1957.

After London, I found Cornwall marvellously relaxing. We had originally thought of the Hebrides, about which I had romantic notions (although when I finally went there I found it wet and windy). Fortunately, a poet named Louis Adeane, who lived in the next room at Chepstow Villas, asked us if we would like to sub-rent his cottage near Mevagissey; he rented it from a local farmer, hoping to give up his office job in London and return there one day. He paid 25s. a week, and offered it to us for 30.

The cottage had thick walls made of a mud called cob, and was down a remote farm track, with a view of the sea. A stream ran below our front door, and made a sound like heavy rain. After the chaos of London it seemed almost eerily peaceful.

Ever since the publication of *The Outsider* I had been thinking about its sequel. One thing was clear: it could not be merely another collection of 'Outsiders'.

As far as I could see, the problem of modern nihilism had been brought about by the collapse of traditional religion. But unlike Chesterton, Eliot or Graham Greene, I had no hope that the answer lay in some kind of return to the Church of the past. Nor did I hope, like Aldous Huxley, that psychedelic drugs might give us back a kind of mystical awareness, since what was needed was fully conscious control of the process, and all drugs have the effect of reducing the mind to passivity. The transformation of consciousness, I felt reasonably sure, lay in the study of consciousness itself. And writing in my sunlit work shed, with the sound of the stream and the cry of gulls, the key to the transformation seemed much nearer than in central London.

Since the only people who had succeeded in bringing about a transformation of consciousness had been saints and mystics, then the next step had to be an attempt to distil the essence of their vision. That, I could see, would not be a popular step to take, but I was not in the business of being popular.

Before I could speak about Boehme and Pascal and William Law, I had to try and define what had gone wrong between the time of Pascal and the time of Sartre and Camus. It was a huge task, and I could see no simple way of organising the book. It would have to be in two parts: one about the history of religion, and one about individual religious 'Outsiders'.

And that, I can see in retrospect, was the reason that *Religion and the Rebel* was such an unmitigated disaster.

To begin with, I should have scrapped the use of the word 'Outsider', which had outworn its function and now caused only irritation.

Where history was concerned, it seemed clear that Spengler's conclusion – that the modern world is plunging into decadence and collapse – was overly pessimistic. Arnold Toynbee was closer to it in his *Study of History*, when he recognised that civilisations can be revitalised by their 'creative minorities' – that is, by Outsiders. But he also was unable to see any clear answers.

So I wrestled on with the book, which quickly became longer than *The Outsider*, feeling like an airman trying to fold up his parachute in a high wind. And at last I got it into some semblance of shape, although I was not sure that I would have trusted my life to it.

I was also fairly sure that it would be received with hostility. But *The Outsider* proved I might be wrong. So on the day of publication, in early October 1957, as I went up to the farm to collect the Sunday newspapers, I still hoped that things might not be as bad as I expected.

It was worse, ten times worse. In the *Observer*, Philip Toynbee called it a rubbish bin, while the *Sunday Times* reviewer said he never liked *The Outsider,* but still found this one disappointing. It did not get a single good review, and *Time* magazine summarised the disaster of its reception under the heading 'Scrambled Egghead'.

Oddly enough, when I had got over the initial shock at being publicly dismembered, I experienced a sense of relief. I was sick of being 'famous'. After the struggles of my teens I was used to swimming against the tide, and 'fame' was like being smothered to death in warm blankets. Now at least I could get back to working alone.

7 Joe for King

In March 1957, not long before Joy and I fled to Cornwall, Bill Hopkins asked me, 'Have you heard about this latest Angry Young Man?'

In fact, it was difficult not to have heard of John Braine, for all the serious journals had reviews of his first novel *Room at the Top*, and John Metcalfe's in the *Sunday Times* had begun: 'Remember the name: John Braine. You'll be hearing quite a lot about him.'

Bill and I agreed that it did not sound like the kind of novel we were eager to read. Its hero, the working-class northerner Joe Lampton, was apparently determined to rise in the world at all costs, and to that end seduces the boss's daughter.

Which is how he came to epitomise the adage, 'There's plenty of room at the top.'

About a year later I found a secondhand copy of it in our local market, in a Foyle's Book Club edition, and decided that it was at least worth the 4s. marked on the flyleaf. And when I started to read, I realised that this was a very impressive novel indeed.

I blamed the reviews for delaying my purchase, for they had made it sound as if the hero is a ruthless go-getter who cynically uses women to achieve his ends. Within ten pages I realised it was not like this at all. Joe Lampton is both sensitive and intelligent. But what was so refreshing was his sexual honesty. When I first read Hemingway's *A Farewell to Arms* in my teens I had been struck by the sentence: 'I was experiencing the usual masculine difficulty of making love standing up.' Braine had the same kind of honesty. He recognised frankly that when most young men look at a young woman, their first assessment is whether she is bedable. As Joe looks at his new landlady, Mrs Thompson, he tells us that although she possessed a good figure, he could still look at her 'without the least flicker of desire', then adds: 'though I wouldn't, to be perfectly frank, have thrown her out of my bed'. With those words –in the first five pages – I felt I could suddenly trust him.

Again, when he first meets the two girls with whom he will work at the library, and they flirt mildly, Joe observes: '[Beryl] had unformed babyish features and no perceptible breasts, but there was about her a disturbingly raw provocativeness as if, along with her School Certificate, she'd passed some examination on the subject of the opposite sex.' Joe obviously saw the world very much as Bill and I did.

So when he meets Susan Brown, the daughter of a wealthy manufacturer, at an amateur drama group, it is natural that the reader is deeply curious to know how long it will take Joe to persuade her to yield her virginity. I found it impossible to understand what Kenneth Allsop meant when he said die approvingly: 'Joe is a lout and a lecher, a money grabber ready to knock-up a virgin as a necessary detail of his master-plan.' This was the kind of crude, journalistic exaggeration that I had been encountering ever since I read the first articles about myself in 1956. Yet I knew Ken was a decent, sensitive man and a good critic. Clearly, there was something about the very nature of literary journalism that makes for oversimplification.

The truth is that Joe does not show the slightest interest in money. Neither is he a lecher, and when he allows himself to slide naturally into an affair with Alice Aysgill, a married woman in the drama group, she is as willing as he is. In due course, Susan becomes pregnant, and Joe is obliged to jilt Alice to marry her. Alice dies soon after in a car crash which leaves Joe with a deep sense of guilt. But in no sense can Joe be said that have engineered this result.

I was also impressed by the end of the book, in which Joe is attacked by two drunks, one of them the boyfriend of a woman he has been flirting with, and by remembering unarmed combat instructions from army days, leaves them groaning on the pavement.

What I found most invigorating about the whole book was that Braine had obviously thrown off the 'defeat premise' that had dominated the serious novel since Goethe's Young Werther, whose suicide triggered an epidemic of imitations across Europe.

This was a problem that had preoccupied me for a long time. Why is it that, for the past two hundred years, the heroes of 'serious fiction' have been defeated men? Of course, there are plenty of non-tragic heroes, from D'Artagnan to James Bond. But the novels in which they figure are essentially for uncritical adolescents. Among serious writers, it is as if the unstated premise is 'you can't win'.

Literary critics would reply: because an age like ours is too complex for the novelist to create an uncomplicated hero like Tom Jones or Roderick Random. Yet here was John Braine defying the trend and creating an intelligent hero whose outlook is cheerful and positive.

I must admit I also felt a twinge of anxiety. If Braine had really solved this problem of 'the age of defeat', then he was a major contender in the mid-twentieth-century literary stakes. Bill and I felt no threat from Osborne, Amis or Wain, but it looked rather as if Braine might be in the same heavyweight league as Hemingway.

I wrote to Braine care of his publisher, and received a handwritten reply from Bingley, in Yorkshire, in which he invited me, if I was ever in that area, to stay the night at his home.

Since Joy and I often drove from Cornwall to see my family in Leicester, and since Bingley was less than two hours further north, we took the next opportunity to take him up on the invitation. It was in October 1958, and I was due to speak at a *Yorkshire Post* literary lunch.

We pulled up outside a solid-looking semi-detached house near the bottom of a hill. The man who came to open the door was large, but not yet fat, had a Yorkshire accent, and wore horn-rimmed glasses.

He looked at our car – an ordinary Standard saloon – and said: 'That's posh.'

'It's about the cheapest model you can get, except a Baby Austin.'

John said defensively: 'Well I've got a Baby Austin.'

There was none of the male dominance I had expected from the author of *Room at the Top*; he struck me as mild and good-tempered, and rather like an overgrown schoolboy, swaying back and forth on the rug as he talked, his hands clasped in front of him. Nine years my senior – I was 27 – he gave the impression that he was already preparing for the onset of middle age.

John had been a librarian before the success of his novel. His wife Pat, a slim, pretty girl with a transparent complexion, had been a schoolteacher. They had a year-old son named Anthony, and seemed a typical middle-class couple.

While Pat prepared the dinner – with some help from Joy – John drove me to the local pub. He had only just passed his driving test, and was an appallingly bad driver. Although the pub was only ten minutes away, I had the feeling that I had developed a few white hairs by the time we got there.

John was the local celebrity, and obviously enjoyed his status. Joy and I had wondered what a bestselling novelist was doing living within a few miles of his birthplace instead of moving to London. Now I understood. Being a big fish in a small pond gave him a sense of security. There was a certain underlying lack of self-confidence, which he concealed by playing the bluff Yorkshireman, making wry jokes about his waistline, and referring to himself as 't'Master'.

How, I wondered, had such a person managed to write *Room at the Top*? The next day, as he was taking us on a short tour of the area, he explained.

John had decided from an early age that he wanted to be a writer, because his mother was a librarian, and his father, the foreman in a sewage works, had a literary knack that had enabled him to win several magazine competitions. At eighteen, in 1940, John became a librarian, then went into the navy. But they discovered he had a tubercular spot on one of his lungs, so he was invalided out three years later. He went back to librarianship in Bingley, and joined an amateur theatre group.

It was there that he met the girl who became Susan in *Room at the Top*.

She was beautiful and – as far as John was concerned – upper-class, for she was a colonel's daughter. To his astonishment, she obviously found him attractive. She also had a masochistic streak, and when she allowed him to take her virginity one evening after rehearsal, she obviously enjoyed the pain, and was excited by the blood on her thighs. John found it unbelievable that this embodiment of loveliness enjoyed being treated with a certain roughness and semi-raped.

He wanted to marry her, and was now gripped by the urge to become something more than a librarian. He had published a few articles in small Labour journals like *Tribune* and the *New Statesman*. These had caught the eye of the literary agent Paul Scott, himself a novelist, who noted the colloquial freshness of the style and thought Braine might have a novel in him. He asked John to call, and when they met in 1951, put to him the notion of writing a novel, and Braine went back to Yorkshire to think about it.

The affair with the colonel's daughter revived the notion, and he decided to chance his luck on a literary career. So he took his savings – £150 – out of the bank, and launched himself on the capital.

But it was discouraging work. Occasional articles, and a few broadcasts, were not enough to pay the rent of his bedsit. His outline of a novel called *Joe for King* was rejected. He was shattered when his mother was killed when she walked in front of a bus, and he went home for her funeral. But back in London, an attack of laryngitis turned into tuberculosis, and he was – as he put it – 'shipped back to Bradford on a train'.

He spent the next eighteen months in the sanatorium where he had spent his last months as a sailor. There he heard from the colonel's daughter, telling him she was going to marry someone in her own social set. And John decided to write her out of his system by putting it all into a novel.

Offered to various publishers in 1956, it was turned down by four of them before being accepted. And at about the time Joy and I were on our way to Ireland pursued by the press, John was tasting the first fruits of literary success.

As in the case of Osborne and his first marriage, I was struck by the parallels with the story of myself and Joy. There was an obvious basic difference though: that I wasn't in the least interested in Joy as a representative of another social class. I was glad she had been at university, and spoke without a local accent, but what attracted me was her gentle, sunny nature and delightful smile.

John, like myself, came to London fairly frequently, and it was when we were there together in early 1959 that he introduced me to his friend Robert Pitman, the journalist who would take me to meet Donleavy. On that visit to London, he stayed in the house where I kept a pied-à-terre, about a quarter of a mile from our old address at 24 Chepstow Villas. This was in a meaner part of Notting Hill, at 25 Chepstow Road; buses roared up and down, and the houses were narrower. In fact, the rundown tenement in which Bill Hopkins had found a room was owned by a notorious slum landlord named Peter Rachman. This was really a brothel, with prostitutes in the lower two storeys, and a few 'respectable' tenants living there to prevent the police from closing it down. The girl in the ground-floor room had a short clothes line outside the lavatory, on which she hung her knickers – bright colours like yellow, red, orange and purple.

Bill occupied a large room overlooking Chepstow Road, and above him, in an identical room, was one of our closest friends, a journalist named Tom Greenwell, who was one of the most delightful and good-tempered men I have ever known. Tom was tall and thin, in his mid-thirties; he freelanced for several newspapers, and had a regular evening job as a gossip columnist on the *Evening Standard*. He was tall and thin, with a beaky nose like Mr Punch. Because he worked evenings, we were able to use his room as a kind of social club, and he never seemed to mind how many people he found in there when he came in from work at one in the morning.

At the top of the building there were two small bedrooms, one of which I used whenever I came to London. John quickly agreed to share the rent with me. With his solid northern working-class background, I think he was delighted to find himself in this 'bohemian' set-up.

Another friend of John's, the writer Stan Barstow, also paid us a visit there. Son of a Yorkshire coalminer, Stan was a gaunt-looking man, who lacked John's self-assertiveness. And he made me laugh with a typical Braine story. The local Labour Party had asked John to write something for them. Typically, John replied: 'I'd gladly give you money. But the very thought of writing without being paid for it makes the pen fall from my nerveless grasp.'

In 1960, Stan made the move from writing short stories to his first novel, *A Kind of Loving*, the story of a draughtsman who gets a girl pregnant, then has to marry her and put up with her awful mother. It immediately established him as a master of northern realism, and in the following year, was filmed with Alan Bates, and led to him being included by journalists among the Angry Young Men. Unlike John, he had the good sense to remain true to his Yorkshire roots and stay there, with the result that he has continued to publish distinguished novels and stories for more than half a century.

Another one of the 'regulars' at Chepstow Road was Stuart Holroyd, the good-looking young man I had met at Alfred Reynolds's Bridge gatherings. It was Stuart's decision to break away from Alfred's vague humanism and write a book about poetry and religion that had made me decide to write

The Outsider. Being a faster writer than he was, I completed *The Outsider* and had it accepted long before Stuart's book, *Emergence from Chaos,* was even finished.

The success of *The Outsider* had led Gollancz to accept it, and it was published in June 1957. But Gollancz made a fatal and appalling mistake: on the dust-jacket of *Emergence from Chaos,* after speaking about *The Outsider*, he went on to add that Holroyd's book had not been influenced by it, since it had been started earlier (a pardonable untruth under the circumstances). And he ended by declaring that Stuart was only 23.

This attempt to repeat the *coup* of *The Outsider* invited derision, and it got it; critics talked sarcastically about 'cradle-snatching'. The unfortunate Stuart came in for a storm of contempt and invective that was really directed at me. *Religion and the Rebel* was not yet published, and the critics were waiting for a target. They had simply had enough of Angry Young Men and every other kind of young man. In due course, Bill's first novel, *The Divine and the Decay*, would walk into the same hail of missiles.

Stuart took it all good naturedly, as he had every reason to. After all, a book that would otherwise have received half a dozen reviews in *The Times Literary Supplement* and other small-circulation journals had at least made his name known to every literate person in England. So he picked himself up without too much despondency, and went on writing. Soon he began another book about the spiritual problems of modern man, with a strong autobiographical flavour.

Literary celebrity had placed a strain on Stuart's marriage to the delicious Anne. As a disciple of Alfred Reynolds and a writer for small poetry magazines, Stuart had led a quiet and sober life. Literary parties and invitations to speak at colleges and universities now poured in, and launched him on a more bohemian lifestyle. Anne went off with the eighteen-year-old playwright Michael Hastings, the youngest of the Angry Young Men, and the author of a play dedicated to the memory of the late James Dean. And Stuart embarked on an affair with a pretty cousin.

Which is why, in the early months of 1959, Stuart, who had moved to a cottage in Surrey, also began to spend a great deal of time at 25 Chepstow Road, and slept in whichever bed happened to be free.

He had already written a play about the breakdown of his own marriage which owed an obvious debt to *Look Back in Anger;* this had been turned down by George Devine, who nevertheless invited him to write another play, and guaranteed that it would have at least a Sunday evening performance – with a promise of a longer run if it succeeded.

We came upon a remaindered book called *Peter Moen's Diary,* published in 1951. Its author, a Norwegian resistance fighter, had been imprisoned by the Gestapo in Oslo in 1944, and had succeeded in keeping a diary on pieces of toilet paper, painfully forming each letter by pricking it with a tack; Moen drowned on a ship on his way to a German prison, but was able to tell a fellow prisoner that he had thrown the diary pages down a ventilator, and they were recovered after the war. It is basically the story of a man who tried to use the miseries of his confinement to 'find God', although the diary makes it clear he did not succeed. Stuart, perhaps inspired by Sartre's prison drama of the Resistance *Mort sans Sépulture*, decided to turn it into a play.

It received its single performance on Sunday 9 March 1958. Osborne's friend, Anthony Creighton, was the director. It was not a good performance, and the lack of scenery made it little more than a rehearsed reading. The subject of a man trying to 'find God' in solitary confinement is bound to put a strain on the audience's attention and when, in the third act, the author introduces music and a kind of Greek chorus to comment on the action, the dramatic tension began to drain away. Even I, as a friend of Stuart's, was wriggling with embarrassment.

Then, just as the play reached its noisy dramatic climax, there was a loud shout of 'Rubbish!' I think that most of us assumed this to be rather a clever dramatic device – perhaps the devil intervening – until Christopher Logue came clomping up the aisle, and went out with a crash of the door. A moment later, Tynan followed him. As he went past my seat, I grabbed him by the arm and said: 'Listen Tynan, why don't you keep your bloody friends quiet?' Tynan shouted: 'G-g-g-get out of my life, Wilson!' and left with a crash of the door. At that moment the curtain came down to polite applause.

Outside the theatre, I joined Stuart, who was with a beautiful American girl he had picked up in Oxford, Bill and his girlfriend Gret, the Leicester playwright David Campton and Victor Gollancz and his wife Ruth. I was cursing with rage – what Logue had done struck me as a thoroughly dirty trick. It had certainly completed the ruin of Stuart's 'first night'. Then, when someone mentioned that Logue and Tynan had adjourned to the pub next door, we decided they ought to be confronted.

Tynan was standing at the bar, and Logue sitting nearby, tilted back in his chair with his feet on another one. I marched up and asked why, if Logue wanted to express his views, he didn't write his own play? But before he could reply, Stuart's wife Anne – who was there with her new attachment Michael Hastings – pushed past me and went for his throat. His chair went over backwards with a crash.

Before a brawl could develop, the landlord was ordering us outside.

We all adjourned to the flat of David's agent, Jimmy Wax, in nearby Sloane Street. And on my way to the bathroom, I passed an open bedroom door, and heard Bill's voice saying: 'Is that the *Daily Mail*? Have you heard about this brawl outside the Royal Court? . . . Well, there was Stuart Holroyd, Colin Wilson, Bill Hopkins . . .'

Bill told me later that he had phoned his brother Ted, who worked on the *News Chronicle*, to tell him what had happened, and that it was Ted who advised him to ring the other newspapers.

The next day, the story was all over the front pages. And it did us, of course, no good whatsoever, simply giving the impression that we were seeking publicity. If it was possible for my reputation to sink lower, it did so after the 'Royal Court row'.

Bill, I think, was not entirely to blame. He had always been gripped by a kind of romanticism, the belief that literary quarrels ought to be as spectacular as in the nineteenth century, when Hugo and Balzac and Dumas often came to blows in the foyer with critics. So when, the next day, BBC television rang Stuart to ask him to appear with Christopher Logue, Bill persuaded him to accept. We all gathered round a television to watch, and were surprised to see the two antagonists arguing amicably. In fact, Logue and Stuart became friends.

And this turned out to our advantage. Bill, always more interested in politics than literature, was trying to form a political group called the Spartacans, the name taken from Spartacus, the gladiator who led the almost-successful revolt against the Romans in 71 BC. The name was used again in 1918 by a Communist group in Berlin. But Bill's own politics were strongly anti-Communist. Sometime that summer, Logue rang Stuart to warn him that one of the London dailies intended to send a reporter to interview us, then do a story denouncing us as fascists. (This would not have been difficult, since it was easy to trap Bill into admissions of admiration of Hitler's visionary idealism.) Forewarned, Bill and Stuart took care not to fall into the trap.

And, as it happened, it was Tynan who got out of my life rather than vice versa. In the autumn of 1958 he flew to New York, to become guest drama critic of the *New Yorker*, and the following spring, to Spain to write a book about bullfighting.

I have to admit that Braine and I envied the permanent residents of 25 Chepstow Road, since the ménage included a floating population of female groupies. But then, we were both married, with homes far from London, and could only look on in envy as Stuart retired upstairs with some pretty drama student whose breasts were bursting out of her corsage.

Braine, meanwhile, was having severe problems with his next novel after *Room at the Top*, having concluded that Joe's success and translation to the Bradford uppercrust was a kind of dead end, he might have tried to follow Joe into his new life, but he knew little about the inner workings of the wool trade. The idea he finally settled upon – to return to autobiography, and tell the story of his life in a TB ward – was a disaster. How could you give any forward movement to a story about a man lying in bed and wishing he had a girlfriend? John's solution, as he explained to me in a little Italian restaurant in a Notting Hill basement, was to revive a fantasy from his childhood, about little ratlike men called the Vodi, ruled over by a toothless old witch called Nelly, whose mission in life is to make sure the good fail and the wicked succeed.

My heart sank as he explained it. What I liked most about John was that he was contemptuous of what he called 'wet' writers, who write books in which the hero lets himself be trampled and kicked. A prime example had been published recently, a second novel by a writer called Thomas Hinde, whose first novel, *Mr Nicholas*, had been a controlled and savagely accurate study of a middle-class domestic tyrant. But *As Happy As Larry* had been about a neurotic unemployed schoolteacher who might have been created by Chekhov, and who ends – as he expects – as a depressive failure. It was the kind of novel that made us both want to groan, an English version of a Beckett play.

Hinde was, in fact, a baronet whose real name was Sir Thomas Chitty, and Stuart knew him because he and Chitty were neighbours in Sussex, and Chitty was also described by journalists as an Angry Young Man. I had often noted that people whose lives had been too easy were more prone to pessimism than those who had had harsher beginnings. But John's life had been hard enough, and I could not for the life of me see why he wanted to write a novel about a 'wet' hero. I could only hope that this part of his life had to be written out of his system.

At that time, in the summer of 1959, John certainly had every reason to be pleased with himself. The film of *Room at the Top*, for which he had written the script, had just been launched at the Cannes Film Festival, and had been an enormous success. Although the director, Jack Clayton, had chosen the smooth and handsome Laurence Harvey to play Joe Lampton, and the French star Simone Signoret to play Alice Aysgill, he had taken care to preserve that gritty, realistic quality, and the film launched what became known as the British 'New Wave'. At least one scene was faithful to the original novel – where Heather Sears, playing Susan, loses her virginity on a lawn, and says with mild reproach, 'You hurt me Joe.'

But the film rights had been sold soon after the book's publication for a mere £5,000. And although the Penguin paperback had gone on to sell nearly a million copies, this only brought the author about a penny a copy – the hardcover publisher took half the royalties – so this represented less than £5,000.

In due course, John sent me the typescript of *The Vodi*. Realising he needed the reassurance, I praised it fulsomely. In fact, I found it hard to finish. There was a kind of clumsiness about it that extended even to the

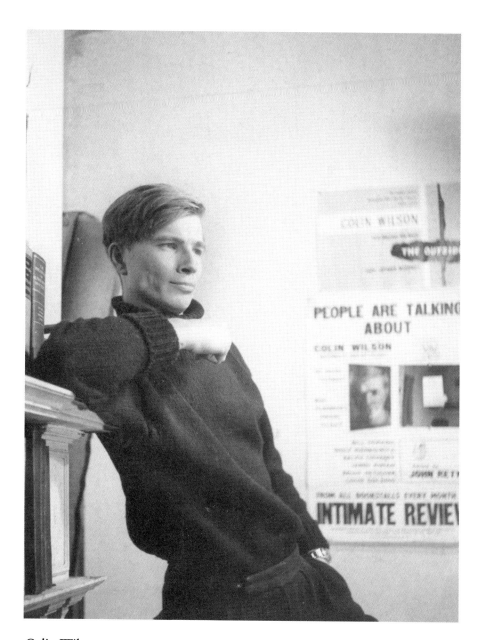

Colin Wilson
Me in my room in Notting Hill soon after publication of *The Outsider*.
(Author's private collection)

John Osborne
John Osborne, the first 'Angry Young Man' – whose explosions of rage and invective justified the label.
(Rex)

Kenneth Tynan
Probably the wittiest theatre critic since Shaw, Kenneth Tynan was finally destroyed by multiple addictions.
(Getty Images)

Alan Sillitoe (above)
The meditative pose gives a better notion of Sillitoe's achievement as a novelist than the more familiar Angry Young Man photographs.
(Corbis)

Arnold Wesker (left)
Here the jaunty stride gives some notion of the enormous energy that has sustained Wesker throughout some of the discouragements of his later career.
(Getty Images)

Iris Murdoch
When asked to write a piece for *Declaration*, Iris Murdoch, academic, philosopher and erotic novelist insisted she had nothing to declare. *(Rex)*

Alex Trocchi
Regarded as potentially the major writer of his generation, Alex Trocchi's writing career was sidetracked by his determination to try everything.
(Getty Images)

Kingley Amis (above)
Superficially cheerful and imperturbable, Kingsley Amis was a bubbling mixture of fears, guilts and uncertainties.
(Getty Images)

Maurice Girodias (left)
The piratical Maurice Girodias lit the powder-train of the swinging '60s in the early '50s.
(Corbis)

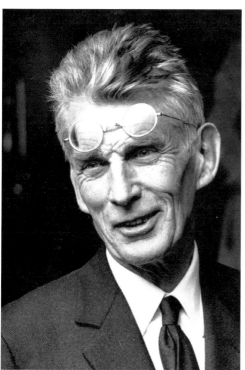

Philip Larkin (above)
The most popular British poet after John Betjeman, Philip Larkin would have preferred to be a novelist.
(Getty Images)

Samuel Beckett (left)
This uncharacteristic picture of Samuel Beckett, smiling and wearing a collar and tie, would undoubtedly have annoyed him.
(Getty Images)

Bill Hopkins (right)

Bill Hopkins suffered heavily from the backlash that hit the AYM movement before it had had time to get properly started.

(Bill Hopkins)

Doris Lessing

Although far from angry, Doris Lessing (pictured here in conversation with Aneurin Bevan) was one of the main driving forces behind the movement.

(Getty Images)

names: Noll Mainton, Jack Uplyme, Sister Lardress, while the factory where the hero, Dick Corvey, was employed is called Larton's, and the local pub the Tanbury Roynton. They may, for all I know, be genuine Yorkshire names, but seem to verge on the grotesque.

In the version I read, the action is also oddly contrived. Dick becomes attracted to one of the nurses when she slips on the polished floor, and he gets a glimpse of her underwear. In the published version, this is removed. But the plot remains as leaden. Dick takes her out for an evening, and it looks as if something might develop. Then, like the original Susan of *Room at the Top*, she decides to dump him for someone with more money and better prospects. And it is only in the last few words of the book that Dick rouses himself from his sense of defeat. 'I'm a fool – she's not married yet.' But this is the part of the story we would like continued. Does he make the effort and get the girl? His was a challenge John obviously felt himself unable to meet.

I found myself thinking of another north-country writer I admired, Arnold Bennett, whose novel *The Card* I read several times because its upstart young hero, Denry Machin, not only succeeds in becoming rich and successful, but in getting the girl by stealing her off the boat on which she is about to embark for America with her bankrupted parents. And when she asks pathetically, 'What are you going to do with me?' he replies, 'Do with you? – marry you, of course!', concluding one of the most delightful romantic endings in English literature.

And this, I realised, is the path Braine should have followed – the path of Arnold Bennett, who prepared himself to write a novel with a huge amount of preliminary spadework. When he decided to write a novel involving the drapery trade, he studied the drapery trade. When he decided to write a novel about a vast hotel, he studied the hotel trade. When he decided to write a novel about a wealthy newspaper magnate, he studied the life of a wealthy newspaper magnate.

In fact, the writer on whom Braine wanted to model himself was John O'Hara, the American novelist whose books display exhaustive social research.

When Joy and I first visited the Braines in Yorkshire, John told us that he was obsessed by the generation of young men from Bradford who were killed in the First World War, and intended to write a big novel about them, something spanning several generations. He undoubtedly possessed the literary gift to do it. What he did not possess was either O'Hara's passion for research, or Bennett's ability to painstakingly cover a large canvas.

The year John's novel reached the screen was also the year John Osborne and Tony Richardson, probably inspired by *Room at the Top*, decided to set up their own film company to make *Look Back in Anger*.

Understandably, none of the major film distributors was interested in financing a play that was all talk and no action, and it was not until Richard Burton agreed to play Jimmy Porter that Woodfall Films was finally launched.

It was also the year of Osborne's most spectacular disaster – a musical satire on London's gossip columnists called *The World of Paul Slickey*.

Its inauspicious origin was a play Osborne had written in 1955 while waiting for the production of *Look Back in Anger*. This was called *An Artificial Comedy, or Love in a Myth*, which Devine found atrocious and rejected. So did Tony Richardson. So did Devine's assistant William Gaskill.

The play was published on the day of the day of its first night, and its prefatory note would have given the critics a hint of what to expect. It begins:

> No one has ever dedicated a string quartet to a donkey although books have been dedicated to critics. I dedicate this play to the liars and self-deceivers; to those who daily deal out treachery; to those who handle their professional instruments of debasement; to those who, for a salary cheque and less, successfully betray my country; and those who will do it for no inducement at all . . .

In short, Osborne at his most combative and hysterical. A television interview he gave the evening of the opening, 14 April 1959, cannot have helped. Asked if he did not think it would arouse hostility, he replied 'I would say it's unlikely', and added patronisingly: 'Certain people may take umbrage – and let's face it, these boys can be pretty unscrupulous when they want – but I think that the majority of them – I hope – have the wit and the humour not to do this.'

This social satire had characters with names like Mrs Giltedge-Whyte, Father Evilgreene, and Terry Maroon (a crooner). It seems clear that the relative success of the musical interludes in *Look Back in Anger* and *The Entertainer* inspired Osborne with the notion of turning his satire into a full-length musical.

Since 1955 Osborne, like myself, had often fallen foul of the gossip columnists, of whom the best known were William Hickey of the *Daily Express* and Paul Tanfield of the *Mail*. Osborne decided to toss them into the mixture.

After that first night, I bought the play, out of curiosity, just to see if it was as bad as the critics had made out. The answer was that it was ten times worse.

It opens with the gossip columnist in bed with his wife's sister, the daughter of Lord Mortlake, who is on his deathbed. To avoid tax his property has been transferred to his children, but there are still two more days to go before the seven years is up. The jokes are embarrassingly feeble. When she asks, 'Oh darling, what are we going to do?', he looks at the tangled sheets and replies: 'Make the bed I suppose. We've lain on our bed – and now we must make it.'

The real problem with the satire is that it has too many targets: a Tory MP, a blackmailing priest, a pop singer, a trade-unionist butler, the monarchy (inevitably), drama critics, stage censorship, capital punishment, the taxman, and so many others that it is like a shotgun that scatters its pellets and misses everybody.

Boos were heard in the second act, and when someone complains that 'It's like a pantomime' there were cries of 'Hear hear !' The line 'What we want is a return to common sense' was received with enthusiastic applause. Finally, the curtain descended to a chorus of boos, with Noël Coward and John Gielgud joining in. As Osborne left the theatre, there were cries of 'Bloody rubbish', and angry members of the audience chased him down Charing Cross Road until he jumped into a taxi.

Slickey offers an interesting insight into Osborne's mentality. What infuriated that first-night audience so much was that the schoolboy humour was an underestimation of its intelligence that amounted to an insult. But then, *Look Back in Anger* and *The Entertainer* are expressions of the same juvenile emotionalism that assumes itself to be the centre of the universe, and *Look Back in Anger* would never have been taken seriously if it had not been for the praise of an emotionally retarded critic who saw his own personal frustrations reflected in it.

Osborne's response to this failure was to flee the country in his open-topped Jaguar with the play's designer, Jocelyn Rickards, leaving Mary Ure to explain his departure to the press. It was the end of their marriage.

This was hardly a surprise. In her autobiography *The Painted Banquet*, Jocelyn Rickards comments: 'I had learned from John that she was not altogether the forbearing, saint-like character she appeared. She was not above starting the day by hurling all the Copeland Spode breakfast china at him, leaving him in a sea of toast and tea-leaves.'

One evening in the autumn of 1958, John Braine and I were at Bob Pitman's flat in Kensington, when Bob showed us a novel he was just reviewing for the *Sunday Express*. It was called *Saturday Night and Sunday Morning*, by Alan Sillitoe, and Bob said he was one of the most typical Angry Young Men so far. Neither of us reacted with much interest – we both felt that the Angry Young Man mania had come to the end of its natural life, particularly when Bob outlined the plot – a young Nottingham factory worker who boozes himself insensible every Saturday night, and ends by marrying a girl he has got pregnant.

Apparently the novel was, to some extent, autobiographical. Bob had interviewed its author, who was then 30, and obviously felt he was a major discovery. Sillitoe had been born in Nottingham, a city only 25 miles north of my home town, Leicester. He was the son of an illiterate factory worker who had spent much of the 1930s out of work (the depression had hit Nottingham much harder than the more prosperous Leicester), so the family often went hungry. Sillitoe had worked in a bicycle factory, like the hero of his novel, and escaped to become an air-traffic controller at the local airport. At the age of 20 he was sent to do his National Service as a radio operator with the RAF in Malaya, but on his return was hospitalised with tuberculosis. It was while in hospital that he began writing short stories and a novel.

He was invalided out of the RAF with a small pension of 45s. a week, which was enough to live on at that time. In the following year he met the American poet Ruth Fainlight, and they went to live abroad together in France, Italy and Majorca. In 1959 he lived in Notting Hill Gate, my old stamping ground, where I was introduced to him by Laura Del Rivo.

Alan was slim and slightly built, and – like me – had taken the trouble to get rid of his Midlands accent. Unlike Braine, he struck me as an intellectual, clearly a person who had been reading obsessively since childhood. (His father had been furious with him for saving up his pocket money to buy *The Count of Monte Cristo*, when it might have been spent on food.) Yet his cast of mind was more down-to-earth than my own, and he did not strike me as a person who has a natural interest in ideas.

In Deya, Majorca, he had been to see Robert Graves, and with his encouragement began to write *Saturday Night and Sunday Morning*. Before that, he had spent most of a decade receiving rejections.

The novel's hero, Arthur Seaton, works at a lathe in the same bicycle factory where Sillitoe had once worked; the job is boring but well paid, and Arthur lives for Saturday night, when he can get drunk – when we meet him he is falling downstairs after he has consumed eighteen pints of beer and six gins – and occasionally gets into a brawl. He also likes sleeping with girls – even other people's wives – and spending a day fishing in the country. He tells the reader: 'I'm just too lucky for this world.'

This would also prove true for Sillitoe, whose first piece of luck was being invalided out of the forces with a pension, and whose second was publishing his novel just at the time when Tony Richardson was looking for material for films with a documentary flavour. Richardson's friend, Karel Reisz, suggested the Sillitoe novel and Richardson – who was seen as a kind of Diaghilev of the Free Cinema movement – found the cash.

It was as successful as *Room at the Top*, as a result of which the paperback went on to sell five million copies. Tony Richardson then directed Sillitoe's long story *The Loneliness of the Long Distance Runner*, about Colin Smith, a Borstal boy, imprisoned for thieving, whose hatred of authority is so great that he deliberately loses a race against public schoolboys to defy the governor. Beautifully filmed by Walter Lassally (who had previously shot Shelagh Delaney's *A Taste of Honey*), it made a star of its leading actor Tom Courteney as *Saturday Night and Sunday Morning* had of Albert Finney.

When I read *Saturday Night and Sunday Morning* I thought it the best novel I had read since *Room at the Top*. But I still felt that, compared to Braine's novel, it was lacking the dimension of Joe's strong moral sense. This novel, like many of Sillitoe's early stories (contained in his volume *The Loneliness of the Long Distance Runner*), seems to take for granted the assumption that people living on the bottom rung of the social ladder have the right to steal as a kind of protest against their condition and against those in authority – the people Arthur Seaton calls 'the bastards'. (His motto is 'Don't let the bastards grind you down.') I had always been interested in crime and the criminal mentality – which is why Bob Pitman's wife Pat and I were collaborating on *An Encyclopedia of Murder* – but mainly because I saw crime as a futile waste, not only for the victim but for the perpetrator.

This is why I felt there was a certain naïvety in Sillitoe's Rousseau-like dream of a just society in which man is no longer in chains. It failed to take into account the dark side of human nature, based as much upon boredom and lack of purpose as on evil and violence.

In Sillitoe's case, this generalised rebellion against authority led to a virtually Marxist social philosophy. My misgivings had been echoed by a scriptreader who had said of *The Loneliness of the Long Distance Runner*: '. . . this story is blatant and very trying Communist propaganda, and particularly worrying for us because the hero is a thief and yet is held up to the admiration of silly young thugs.'

The period Sillitoe was writing about was, of course, the fifties, when Harold Macmillan was telling us 'You've never had it so good' and would be succeeded in 1964 by Harold Wilson's Labour government. And Sillitoe, who had believed passionately that a Socialist government would bring about the millennium dreamed of by his long-distance runner, felt the first cold breath of disillusionment. The old Communist ideal is still there in his travel book *The Road to Vovograd* (1965), but can be seen fading steadily throughout his 1960s trilogy that begins with *The Death of William Posters* (1965), in which the Nottingham working-class hero Frank Dawley walks out on his wife and leaves England to go to fight with Algerian rebels against France. Bill Posters is not a real person, but the hero's ideal rebel, his name taken from proclamations on walls that 'bill posters will be prosecuted'. But Bill Posters actually dies in Algeria; Dawley grasps the reality of violence after ambushing and killing German mercenaries, recognises that we are all in the same boat, and that another dream has turned to ashes.

The irony of Sillitoe's anti-British sentiment can be savoured in the second novel of the trilogy, *A Tree on Fire* (1967), in which the brother of one of Dawley's closest friends, Albert Handley, a rebel painter, blows his brains out on a ship returning to England because he feels that this country has become degraded beyond hope of redemption. Nevertheless, Dawley returns to an England he now hates, planning to become part of a revolutionary commune, organised by Handley, that will withdraw from British society.

The third novel of the trilogy, *The Flame of Life,* is its most puzzling, since it is so inconclusive; the revolutionary commune simply drifts apart for no particular reason. At the climax of the book, the Spanish wife of one of Dawley's comrades, who died in Algeria, tries to kill him with a revolver because she blames him, but misses. Albert Handley's wife leaves him for a layabout named Posters who has introduced the commune to pot smoking. And the deceased John's final letter is read aloud to them all, advising them to forget violence and 'seek the more spiritual way'. Dawley's first wife divorces him and conveniently marries someone else, leaving him to settle down with his mistress and children and presumably live happily ever after. And as the reader closes the book, he is inclined to wonder what it was all about, and whether the author knows either. All that seems clear is that Sillitoe has renounced his hope of hanging the bourgeoisie on lampposts.

As I read the first two volumes of the Frank Dawley trilogy, I felt that they epitomised all that I rejected in the social philosophy of Angry Young Men like Osborne, Braine and Sillitoe. If you were to accept their vision of England as accurate – for example, the kind of England Osborne seems to evoke in *The Entertainer* – you would certainly feel like blowing your brains out.

In fact I rejected the whole attitude, for exactly the same reason that, in the second half of the fifties, I rejected this Angry milieu and the pessimism of Samuel Beckett. I felt that it failed to take into account the *inner lives* of individuals, and that ultimately, this was all that matters. What *can* happen to individuals who have wrestled hard enough with the problems of their own time, is that they finally begin to experience what Jung means by 'individuation', a peculiar inner 'solidification' that makes them far more resistant to the erosion caused by the sense of futility that haunts the Archie Rices and Joe Lamptons and Frank Dawleys.

There was another writer of this period who interested me because he seemed to embody these same social ideals: Arnold Wesker. 'Discovered' by Tony Richardson, he decided to become a playwright after seeing *Look Back in Anger.*

Joy had been to see *Roots,* and described it to me in such glowing terms that I lost no time in reading it, then went on to the rest of the 'trilogy', from which I quickly concluded that Wesker was a more substantial and interesting playwright than Osborne.

Wesker was born in East London on 24 May 1932, the son of first generation Jewish immigrants, both earning a slender living at tailoring, so that his background was almost as poverty-stricken as Sillitoe's. His mother was an enthusiastic and committed Communist, his father slightly less so.

In spite of my own temperamental dislike of Communism – and any other form of totalitarianism – I could actively sympathise with their convictions. In my teens I read Douglas Hyde's *I Believed*, a book describing his own journey from Communism to Catholicism, and was excited and moved by his description of the poverty in Bristol in the 1930s, and the rate of suicide among bankrupt businessmen. In similar circumstances, I would probably have joined the Communist Party. So I understood how a Hungarian immigrant in the East End would have dreamed of a Communist Britain as a Utopia. You do not have to agree with someone's ideas to sympathise with them – particularly if, as in Wesker's case, they are expressed with a vitality that is its own justification.

As a schoolboy, Wesker had been headstrong, and at one point was expelled from school. When he left school he was unsuccessful in his application to join the Royal Academy of Dramatic Art, and took jobs as a plumber's mate and kitchen porter. On family advice he decided he needed a trade, and became a pastry cook. At the hotel in Norwich where he worked he met his future wife Doreen, who was a waitress, known as Dusty because her hair was the colour of gold dust. They saved a hundred pounds and went to Paris together, where she became an au pair and he a pastry cook in a restaurant – an experience on which he would base his first play *The Kitchen.*

In 1957 he obtained a place at the London School of Film Technique. But, when he saw *Look Back in Anger*, in the following year he wrote *The Kitchen.* Seeing Tony Richardson outside the theatre he asked him if he would look at the play; Richardson agreed. But in the event, Wesker felt dissatisfied with it, and in six weeks wrote instead a play about his family background, *Chicken Soup with Barley,* which covers twenty years from 1936 until 1956 and was virtually as ambitious as Noël Coward's *Cavalcade.*

Richardson liked it. Devine, less enthusiastic, recommended it for the Belgrade Theatre in Coventry. It made a strong impression there, and subsequently at the Royal Court, whereupon Devine commissioned its sequel *Roots*.

The theme of *Chicken Soup with Barley* is fundamentally similar to that of Sillitoe's Posters trilogy: the way that the postwar Labour government led to a sense of disillusionment for Socialists who had expected it to bring the Golden Age. The mother, Sarah, is its driving force and central character. By comparison, the father, Harry, is weak and apathetic. He does not like demonstrating and marching with banners. After two strokes, he becomes senile. But Sarah remains as strong and idealistic as ever.

Chicken Soup with Barley was, as Tynan would point out, the first British political play. It starts with the daughter's fiancé going off to fight the fascists in Spain, and continues with Mosley's march in the East End. Stalin's trials later cause one of the family members to defect. In the last act, Ronnie – obviously Wesker himself – is disillusioned by the Soviet invasion of Hungary. But when he tells his mother angrily: 'You didn't tell me there were any doubts,' she replies: 'All my life I've worked for a Party that meant glory and freedom and brotherhood. You want me to give it up now?'

The second party of the trilogy, *Roots*, deals with a girl based on Wesker's wife Dusty, who came from a Norfolk background. Like Dusty, Beatie has been taught a great deal about music, art and politics by her lover. But Beatie has not fully absorbed it, and many of her opinions are regurgitated parrot fashion.

Her mother is a down-to-earth countrywoman who has no sympathy for her daughter's newly acquired culture. But Wesker does not fall into the obvious trap of making her into some kind of ideal archetypal female, as Lawrence might have done; she is narrow and stupid.

So *Roots* is not about the clash between illusion and reality, but about two semi-illusions, which gives it far more power and realism. Beatie becomes the symbol of every intelligent person trapped in an environment that offers no chance of development. The play is moving because the audience suffers her frustration and is made to think about it, as Beatie wants her family to think about it. The ending of the second act, in which Beatie persuades her mother to listen to the Bizet L'Arlesienne suite, then is so carried away she begins to dance to it, is a great moment of theatre. And so is the final scene, in which Beatie is shattered by a letter from Ronnie telling her that he feels they have to separate. She reacts to her mother's unsympathetic 'I told you so' with an explosion of her own impatience, in which she tells them that 'Ronnie's right – it's our own bloody fault' and then, suddenly aware of her own eloquence, turns to them with an ecstatic smile, and says: 'D'you hear that? D'you hear it? Did you listen to me? I'm talking. Jenny, Frankie, mother – I'm not quoting no more . . . God in heaven, Ronnie! It does work, it's happening to me, I can feel it's happened. I'm beginning, on my own two feet, I'm beginning . . .'

What has happened here is one of the most remarkable scenes since Ibsen's Norah decided to walk out on her husband and family at the end of *A Doll's House* and to go out into the world in search of her individual self-development. For me, it is one of the most moving moments in modern drama.

It also underlines why I rejected the anger of Osborne and Braine and Sillitoe. Like Rousseau, they dreamed of an ideal society, but it was no more than a romantic daydream, and the rebels of 1789 who tried to turn it into a reality only succeeded in creating a bloodbath, demonstrating, as Camus said, that 'innocence, as soon as it begins to act, commits murder'. Frank Dawley's dream leads him to Algeria to fight with the FLN, but this brings the ideal Socialist state no closer. John Handley's suicide is a demonstration of this failure. And the communal experiment of *The Flame of Life* once more underlines the failure. The real answer to the problem – as Wesker realises in *Roots* – lies in the self-development of the individual. Which explains why I feel that Wesker stands with Doris Lessing as one of the few Angry writers with something vital and important to express.

The final play in Wesker's trilogy, *I'm Talking About Jerusalem* (1960), might have been written to drive home the point that the answer lies in the evolution of the individual. Ronnie's sister Ada and her husband Dave move to the country to try to bring their Socialist dream to life in terms that would have appealed to Ruskin and Morris: he will set up a workshop for handmade furniture.

The great temptation for a playwright of ideas is to use the theatre as a pulpit, but Wesker avoids this by keeping his characters alive and active. When they are asked by the removal men why they have come to the country, Ronnie says: 'Come on, Dave. Give them an answer . . . The world has asked you why you've come here. There stands the world, and here stand you two. You're on trial, comrades.' But instead of the explanatory speech we expect, Ada says: 'Don't arse around, Ronnie, the men want their tea.'

Again, we would expect their Communist mother Sarah to enter into the spirit of this attempt to build a Socialist commune. But again, Wesker demonstrates his realism: Sarah is trapped in the personal, and thinks that Dave has decided to move to the country to separate her from her daughter, so they merely squabble.

Nevertheless, Wesker again shows his capacity to make the audience share his dream. Dave has worked in a factory making doors and window frames, and seen the frustration of workers who are a part of a machine. He dreams of setting up his own handmade furniture factory in the country, where his family can be around him as he works.

Things begin to go wrong when the local squire – for whom Dave is working until he can set up his own business – dismisses him for stealing linoleum and then lying about it. Then they are joined by Libby, a disillusioned ex-Socialist, who once used a legacy to set up a commune of garage mechanics, and lost his money because they treated him like a fool who was asking to be swindled. He tells Dave: 'I dirtied up. Listen to me, Dave, and go home before you're dirtied up.'

The real reason the experiment fails is that his handmade furniture simply cannot compete with the modern machine-made product. After an unsuccessful attempt to turn their home into a boarding house, they give up and return to London. One more dream of building Jerusalem in England's green and pleasant land has failed.

Wesker himself was far from disillusioned. The trilogy had made him famous (and has since gone on to sell half a million copies). He rewrote his first play *The Kitchen*, a typically ambitious project with 29 characters, which presents the life of a kitchen and its cooks, waiters and waitresses over one day. Its dynamics are impressive, and the superb lunch-serving scene achieves the sense of frenzied control of a complex ballet.

The idea behind *The Kitchen* seems to precede the trilogy; it aims to show the unsatisfactoriness of being cooped up in this crowded environment and living a life of repetition. That, and the frustration of a waitress changing her mind about leaving her husband, leads one cook, Peter, to go berserk and start smashing things. The final speech by the proprietor Marango underlines his innocence; this is no capitalist exploiter. 'I give work, I pay well . . . I don't know what more to give a man . . . What more do you want? What is there more, tell me.' And Peter shakes his head as if to say 'If you don't know I can't explain.' Wesker underlines the point by intervening in the stage directions to say: 'We have seen that there must be more.' And this 'more' is, of course, the subject of the trilogy, and of all Wesker's work.

The problem with such a working environment is that it reduces workers to robots. Yet when I was working in a similar environment in 1955, washing dishes in the kitchen of a restaurant in the Haymarket, I soon made the interesting observation that working at a frantic pace brings its own solution to the problem; when the evening was over, and we all took off our uniforms and relaxed before leaving, there was a marvellous sense of warmth, of human contact, of comradeship.

That Wesker is also aware of this becomes apparent in his next play *Chips with Everything* (1962), which is based on his period of National Service in the RAF. This strikes me as one of his best plays, with one scene in it that is as memorable and dramatic as Beatie's sudden flash of self-discovery in *Roots*. Its central character, Pip Thompson, an upper-class recruit, who is in rebellion against his own class, is determined not to become an officer. Yet by the end of the play, he has discovered that, whether he likes it or not, he *is* an officer, a natural leader, and there is no point in pretending otherwise.

The scene in which this happens is remarkable. One of the recruits, Smiler, has run away because he feels persecuted by the corporals. He goes back of his own accord, and the others put him to bed. Then the pilot officer – who has been trying hard to persuade Pip to give up his protest and become an officer – comes in to take Smiler to the guardhouse. But he encounters a passive revolt, and one by one, the airmen sit on their beds. The pilot officer says that the whole hut is under arrest and orders the corporal to take them all to the guardhouse. Then Pip says: 'I suggest, sir, that you don't touch any of them.' In the speech that follows, he summons his natural authority, and addresses his fellows, telling them they are all good men. And as he speaks, he changes his uniform, from that of an airman to an officer. And when he has finished, the pilot officer hands him the list of postings, and Pip reads it aloud, the men come to attention, and a band plays the RAF March Past. Then the play goes into its final scene, the passing-out parade. The scene switches to the parade ground, and as the men present arms and the band plays, the flag is raised up the flagpole. And the stage instructions read: 'Let it be a tall flagpole.'

All this brings back to me my own passing-out parade at RAF Bridgnorth, and the memory of how, in spite of my general irritation with the RAF and National Service, I suddenly experienced a rush of happiness, and felt entirely reconciled to the RAF. This, I feel, is what Wesker has caught with unerring dramatic instinct.

And in Pip's transformation he has caught something even more important: a concept that, nearly half a century ago (in a book called *New Pathways in Psychology*), I labelled 'Promotion'. William James remarked that a footballer might play the game *technically* perfectly for years, and then one day, in a moment of excitement, he is carried away, *and the game begins to play him*, so that everything he does is perfect. In such a moment, an officer who has never felt entirely at home in his uniform, is suddenly transformed and *becomes* an officer. This is what Wesker has caught in the final scenes of *Chips with Everything*.

So again, this play, like the trilogy, is about coming to terms with reality. It is about power, and manages to say far more important things than if it was a straightforward piece of left-wing propaganda.

But Wesker himself had not given up the search for a practical solution, as his next major project, Centre 42, reveals. This was an attempt, backed by the TUC, to bring art direct to the people, and he was appointed its director in 1961. Its venue was the Roundhouse in Chalk Farm, and the experiment survived for nine years until 1970. Unfortunately, Wesker's 1992 autobiography *As Much as I Dare* stops before this period. It would certainly be fascinating to know just why the project finally collapsed. But presumably it may be taken as another interesting lesson in how idealism wilts in the face of practical problems.

It was during the Roundhouse period that Wesker wrote one of his most ambitious political dramas, *Their Very Own and Golden City* (1965), about an architect who plans to design and build no less than six 'golden cities'. He is inspired by the idea of the medieval cathedral builders, but since he has no church to back him – only union leaders and some unexpectedly sympathetic Conservative politicians – it is bound to end in compromise. But in presenting his story of a visionary architect and the practical men he has to deal with, Wesker has written one of the best political plays since Shaw's *Apple Cart* and *On the Rocks*.

It is sad to record that this play in the mid sixties represented a turning point in Wesker's fortunes, and that in Britain (though not abroad) he has since experienced a series of disappointments, which brought increasing exasperation, so that interviews with Wesker often make him sound more of an Angry Young Man than he did in his revolutionary days.

8 Declaration

It was depressing for his friends to see the effect on John Braine of the reception of *The Vodi*. Reviews were not hostile or dismissive, but lukewarm. The *Spectator* called it 'drab', while the *TLS* said the ending was 'contrived and perfunctory'. John proceeded to drink heavily. Pat Pitman told me of an occasion when he was so drunk by the time a taxi arrived to take them to dinner that the cab driver refused to allow John inside in case he vomited.

When John drank too much, he became impossibly boring. Alcohol released in him a desire for self-assertion, which took the form of wanting to display how much he knew. An academic type might have tried to show off his learning. John, being non-academic, wanted to show off his Yorkshire common sense. Pat told me how, at two in the morning, when she and Bob were struggling to keep awake, John decided to deliver a discourse on the types and varieties of kitchen stoves, that became more impassioned as he saw their eyes glazing over.

I recognised the syndrome as indicating a deep lack of self-belief. When a man is unsure of himself, he often takes refuge in playing a part, building up a personality that convinces the world that he is at ease with himself. But eventually this personality can easily become a prison, and the real man, who has remained a nervous child, is trapped inside its thick walls, safe but hardly able to breathe. This is what Ibsen did to himself, so that in old age he was like some formidable crustacean, peering with fierce eyes from the depth of his armour. But in *The Master Builder* Ibsen reveals what he is really like. The famous architect Solness now feels dead inside, but allows himself to be awakened by a beautiful young girl, the daughter of his friend Dr Wangel, who has worshipped him since she was a child. At Hilda's request, he climbs to the top of a church tower; but since he is terrified of heights, falls and is killed.

The opposite of the Ibsen syndrome is a poet like Yeats, who scorns concealment and dares to leave himself wide open to experience. And slowly, very slowly, this honesty results in the creation of a self that has no pretences, and needs no armour.

Braine had been encouraged by his father to be a rather bookish little boy, and had in due course become a librarian. But this was not a particularly satisfying persona; he looked forward to being called up; fighting against Hitler would give his life a sense of purpose. But while he was still a naval cadet an X-ray revealed tuberculosis, and suddenly he was once more merely a librarian-in-waiting.

The affair with the colonel's daughter filled him with determination to achieve publication; when that collapsed, he wrote *Room at the Top*, in which his fantasy persona has been a prisoner of war, and now works as an accountant in the Town Hall. But the fame the book brought did not bring real self-confidence; at 35 it was too late to become another person. So when he wanted to impress someone he put on his act of the hard-headed Yorkshire businessman. And when drunk he simply overdid it and bored everybody silly.

Amis, I sensed, suffered from a related syndrome. Although more smooth and socially accomplished than John, he was also deeply unsure of himself. My letter calling the bluff of his anti-culture pose and threatening to knock him off his pedestal was enough to arouse deep latent neuroses and make him a lifelong enemy.

But compared to Braine, Amis had one major advantage – his charm and good looks. John, I am fairly sure, did not even contemplate being unfaithful to his wife, because his self-image was of the frog prince in the fairy tale. In fact, a love affair would undoubtedly have done his ego a world of good. Amis, on the other hand, after the early discovery that he was attractive to women, set out to bed as many as he could. In his biography, *Kingsley Amis*, Eric Jacobs says: 'Amis made little effort to avoid temptation. Quite the opposite: he seized every chance of sexual adventure he could. "Will alert you to my next visit," he wrote to [the poet Robert] Conquest . . . "May want to borrow your flat . . ."' Jacobs also records:

> Amis was not unhappy or unsatisfied with Hilly. But he could not and did not turn down any promising chance of going to bed with another woman that presented itself. His opportunism in these matters was prodigious throughout his married life. Once, much later, while staying with other couples for the weekend, he found himself having to give a warmly ingratiating smile to all the women at the breakfast table, being boozily unable to remember which one of them he had made love to the night before.

Amis was lucky in that his obsession with adultery gave him what Braine lacked – a perpetual subject for novels. So when faced with the problem of a sequel to *Lucky Jim*, his infidelities in Swansea provided what he needed, and the result was sufficiently unlike *Lucky Jim* to give the critics the impression of versatility.

The plot of the novel that followed was presented to him by chance when *Lucky Jim* won the Somerset Maugham Award, which involved travelling abroad for three months. A wealthy friend put him in touch with an acquaintance with a villa in Portugal. Amis, who had been contemplating an anti-travel book as a kind of counterblast against writers like D H Lawrence, Graham Greene and Laurie Lee, decided to turn it into a novel, which became *I Like It Here*. Amis's journalist protagonist Garret Bowen is sent to Portugal by his publisher to try to track down a writer named Strether, one of a group of 1930s writers Bowen considers 'prancing, posturing phonies'. (Even the name, Strether, is a sideswipe at Henry James and the Paris-besotted hero in *The Ambassadors*.) He succeeds, decides Strether is as phoney as he feared, and returns to London, having conveyed to the reader that his attitude to foreign countries is similar to Jim Dixon's to Mozart.

Generally speaking, *I Like It Here* was not a success. Critics recognised it for what it was – a travel book disguised as a novel – and Kenneth Allsop remarks of it: 'Throughout it seems to me to groan with desperation, as if Amis wishes he had never taken it on.'

Which left Amis, like Braine, with the problem is what to do next. One critic suggested unsympathetically that his second novel, *That Uncertain Feeling*, in 1955, could be retitled *Lucky Jim Married* and *I Like It Here Lucky Jim Abroad*. But again, Amis's obsession with seduction came to the rescue. In a notebook started in 1955, he speaks of being influenced by a novel published two centuries earlier – Samuel Richardson's *Clarissa*. Its subject is the abduction, drugging and rape of the heroine by a spoilt young man about town called Robert Lovelace, who declares that the only thing he cares about is his 'own imperial will'.

Lovelace has been introduced into the Harlowe household as a possible suitor for her elder sister, but is much more sexually attracted by Clarissa. To escape marriage to a rich, elderly suitor, Clarissa agrees to elope with Lovelace. But instead of, as he promised, taking her to the house of a noble kinsman, he takes her to a brothel, then presses her to become his mistress. She escapes, is caught, and returned to the brothel, where he drugs and rapes her. By the time Lovelace has decided that he wants to marry her after all, she has sunk into a 'decline', which kills her. She is avenged by her cousin, who drives a rapier through Lovelace's body in a duel.

Amis's equivalent of Clarissa, Jenny Bunn, in *Take a Girl Like You*, is a young schoolteacher from the north. His Lovelace, Patrick Standish, reflects that God has fashioned her 'primarily as a bedroom amenity'. Jenny wants a faithful husband, Patrick only wants to get her clothes off. He finally achieves his aim by getting her drunk at a party and taking her virginity while she is unconscious. And the book ends with her resignedly accepting that although they will remain lovers, he is unlikely to stay faithful for long.

When it appeared in 1960 it received some bad reviews. The *Times* called it 'a sad disappointment', while the *TLS* reviewer said it was 'a very nasty book . . . the worst novel ever written by a man who can write a novel as well as Mr Amis'.

It was obvious that what bothered the reviewers was the basic nastiness of Patrick Standish, his immorality and shamelessness. How was a reader supposed to react to a novel in which the hero was what one critic called a 'shit'?

What the critics were failing to grasp – or perhaps preferred not to believe – was that *Take a Girl Like You* is a celebration of promiscuity by one who was devoted to it, and did not give a damn how many people he hurt in satisfying the addiction. In a letter to Larkin on 26 November 1953, Amis admits: 'I have sex all weighed up now; the only reason I like girls is that I want to fuck them.' But he hastens to admit that 'it is adolescent, cheap, irresponsible, not worth doing, a waste of time, not much fun anyway really, a needless distraction from my real vocation . . . something I shouldn't be [doing] at my age and as a married man.' And his biographer Richard Bradford remarks in *Lucky Him* that the Patrick Standish chapters of *Take a Girl Like You* are littered with this kind of comment.

In other words Amis was aware that what he was doing in his endless seductions was not particularly creditable, but he still enjoyed it so much that it overrode all other considerations, including his wife and family.

Reprehensible though this may be, it must be balanced against the fact that promiscuity comes naturally to most talented people. Osborne had a string of casual affairs; so did Tynan and Wain. Arnold Wesker's wife Dusty told a journalist in 2002 that he had often brought their marriage to the brink of destruction: 'He did have a roving eye, right from the beginning,' and added by way of extenuation: 'This is the price if you marry someone like Arnold, who needs experience to write about.'

What had upset Yorick Smythies about Iris Murdoch's *A Severed Head* in 1961 was that it took for granted that promiscuity is enjoyable, an attitude its author certainly shared. On the other hand, she held fairly strong moral views on the matter, the most definite being that it is not permissible to hurt the vulnerable in pursuit of one's own pleasure.

Amis might have subscribed in theory but certainly not in practice. Moreover, it is clear that part of his pleasure came from the sense of behaving badly. In *Experience*, Martin Amis tells how his father took Hilly to dinner with his mistress and her husband; there was another couple present and, before the end of the evening, Amis had succeeded in dating the wife as well. This is not just the sheer delight in being allowed to remove the clothes of a woman who has not yet yielded; it is closer to the attitude of Lovelace in *Clarissa*.

This is also clear in Amis's 1965 novel *The Egyptologists* (written with

Conquest), about a group of well-off middle-class men who profess an enthusiasm for Egyptology because it provides them with an ongoing excuse to cheat on their wives. When the treasurer has an affair with an American research student and offers to leave his wife and marry her, she turns him down, on the grounds that the state of mind that led him to serial adultery is probably irreversible.

In Amis's case, it was reversed only by the break up of his first marriage, and the increasing alcoholism that led to sexual impotence at the age of 58.

This chain of events began in October 1962, when Amis was invited to appear on a panel at the Cheltenham Literary Festival by Elizabeth Jane Howard, the novelist who was then its director.

Jane – as she was known to friends – was exceptionally attractive; I had appeared with her on television a couple of times in the fifties and can vouch that she was incredibly beautiful. Hilly and Kingsley were staying at the same hotel and, at the end of the evening, returned there. Hilly went to bed, and Amis and Jane stayed up talking until the early hours. Amis, at this time, was planning to move to Soller, in Majorca, with his family, inspired by the example of Robert Graves; nevertheless, he and Jane exchanged phone numbers. Within a week he rang her in London and suggested a drink. And as they sat in the bar he opened the conversation by telling her that he had booked a double room in a nearby hotel, and that if she was against the idea, he ought to cancel it immediately. She decided to stay. And the next morning, both were convinced they were in love.

That winter he came to London several times and they were able to stay at the house of the publisher Tom Maschler, now running Jonathan Cape. Tom's fortunes had begun their steep climb with the publication of the book *Declaration* in 1957, a collection of essays by the Angry Young Men, and he had now signed Amis's next novel.

Hilly soon came to suspect what was going on, and sensed that this was more serious than his usual philandering. It was soon afterwards that she wrote on his back with lipstick: '1 FAT ENGLISHMAN I FUCK ANYTHING', preserved in a holiday snapshot

In July 1963, Amis returned to London 'on business', and then went to Sitges, in Spain, with Jane. When the *Daily Express* learned of their whereabouts – tipped off by Hilly, according to Amis – they sent a reporter. Amis and Jane hastily returned to England, but when Amis went to the house in Cambridge where he and Hilly were living (Amis having been appointed a fellow at Peterhouse in 1962), he found it empty – Hilly had not even left him a note. In the face of this fait accompli, Amis moved in with Jane in Maida Vale. Hilly divorced him and he and Jane married in 1965.

It seemed Amis was serious this time and (as far as is known) gave up adultery. But (as Jane describes in her autobiography *Slipstream*) he began to drink increasingly heavily, and to spend more time at his club, the Garrick. The marriage ended after fifteen years when Jane, sick of being treated as a kind of skivvy and maid-of-all-work, left him. (But asked by a reporter in later years if he ever regretted the break with Hilly, he replied 'Only all the time'.)

It was at Tom Maschler's house in Notting Hill that Joy and I had stayed overnight before our flight from London in 1957, at the time of the 'horsewhipping scandal'. We had been introduced to Tom by Bill Hopkins, whose novel *The Divine and the Decay* had been accepted by the publisher for whom Tom was working, McGibbon and Kee.

Like my own *Ritual in the Dark*, Bill's novel grew to some extent from the long discussions that Bill and I held as we walked around Paris at night in 1953. We were both admirers of the generation of writers who had been flourishing in 1900 – Shaw, Wells, Chesterton, Anatole France – and agreed that there had been a general decline since then. Bill admired Eliot and Joyce rather less than I did, and neither of us felt much enthusiasm for the generation of the 1930s, including Greene and Waugh.

The problem seemed to be the curious atmosphere of defeat that permeated the modern novel, and that seemed typified by the work of Beckett, to which the *Merlin* crowd had introduced us. And in philosophy – which interested me more than it did Bill – there was a dreary positivism typified by Ayer and Russell. I had bought the latter's *History of Western Philosophy* in my teens and detested what he had to say on Nietzsche. Russell seemed to find that the very word 'will' was tainted with Nazism, whereas for both Bill and myself it seemed to be the only valid starting point for philosophy. Central to it was Nietzsche's phrase 'how one becomes what one is' – that is, the question of how a person becomes aware of his true identity. It was for this, that Jung coined the word 'individuation'.

The central character of Bill's *The Divine and the Decay* Peter Plowart, is the co-founder of a right-wing political party, but although a powerful orator, is undermined by a sense of inner emptiness which expresses itself in appalling nightmares. Increasing disagreements with his co-founder have made him decide to have him assassinated. And to provide himself with an alibi, he has decided to take a holiday on the small channel island of Vachau (based on Sark). Bill had been to Sark to research the book.

There Plowart meets Claremont, the young Dame of the island, and as he becomes increasingly fascinated by her total self-possession, is convinced that she knows the secret that eludes him. She finds him attractive and interesting, but as he reveals to her his political philosophy, is increasingly horrified.

There is a typical episode in the power game that develops between them. Staying in her house, he goes to her bedroom with the intention of possessing her, if necessary by force. She opens her eyes and sees him standing at the side of the bed. Immediately, she throws off the bedclothes and allows him to see her naked. His lust instantly vanishes, and he knows she has defeated him again.

Later he takes her by force, but at the climactic moment she withdraws into herself, and once again he feels she has won.

When she learns why he is on the island, she decides that he has to die. Recognising her power over him, she tells him an interesting story: that she discovered the secret of inner power one day when she was swimming out to some rocks two miles offshore, and was caught by the currents at high tide. Suddenly, the rocks began to move towards her, and at that moment she experienced the revelation of her true identity. Since then she has done it several times, and each time the rocks have moved.

Immensely excited, Plowart wants to try it immediately. They both swim towards the rocks and are caught by the currents. But she is a far stronger swimmer than he is, and suddenly he realises that this was a ruse to drown him. Gripped by sudden rage, he begins swimming like a machine and, as he does so, it seems to him that the rocks are moving towards him. Claremont is pulled under by the current. But Plowart finally drags himself on to the rocks.

Fishermen come out to rescue them, but when they find he is alone, refuse to take him on board. As he struggles with them, one of the men falls overboard and is swept out to sea. The enraged fishermen throw Plowart after him. But one of them, a villainous outcast he has befriended, releases the lifebelt without being noticed. And as the book ends, Plowart struggles towards the lifebelt, shouting: 'I'm indestructible, you fools, indestructible!'

This, for Bill, was the essence of the book – that when the will is fully awake, almost anything is possible.

In 1956 Bill had outlined the plot of the book to Joy and myself in a café near the British Museum, the day before he went off to Sark; when he returned a few weeks later he outlined it to a young publisher named Tom Maschler.

Bill had known Tom as a budding photographer and would-be film director in Soho before he decided to go into publishing. The firm he worked for, McGibbon and Kee, was owned by the property tycoon – and Labour supporter – Howard Samuel. When Bill told Tom about the novel, Tom passed on this information to his boss. Since the newspapers were full of talk about Angry Young Men, Samuel decided to secure Bill by inviting him out for a lavish meal, and calling at his bank on the way to hand Bill a large wad of money – about £2,000. (Bill adds wryly that this was all the money he ever saw from McGibbon and Kee.) And it was Bill who suggested to Tom Maschler that he should gather together a group of Angry Young Men in a symposium. In due course, this was published as *Declaration*.

But by this time, *The Divine and the Decay* had already been published, and savaged by the critics. It was unfortunate for Bill, as it was for Stuart, that journalists associated his name with mine. *The Divine and the Decay*, published a few weeks after my *Religion and the Rebel,* received an unprecedented hostile reception. Kenneth Allsop remarked: 'Although there is an unwritten law of charity among critics to deal gently with a first novel, most of them waïved it in this case.'

Bill and I happened to be in Hamburg at that time – Bill had gone there to work on his second novel, and Joy and I were on our way back from a lecture trip to Oslo. We would meet up at about nine o'clock for breakfast, collect our mail, then walk down to a café in the Stephansplatz where the eggs and bacon were superb. Bill at the time had no idea of how his novel had been received, except for one lavish excerpt in *Books and Bookmen*, accompanied by a friendly review. I opened my post first, and howled with anguish at the reviews of *Religion and the Rebel* sent by Gollancz. Bill, busy smoking his first cigarette, commiserated, advising me not to take it too seriously, on the grounds that the critics would be forgotten long before I was. Then he opened his own envelope – from his girlfriend Gret – and a batch of reviews fell out. As Bill read on, his face darkened, and he suddenly cried in a voice of fury: 'The *bastards*!' Then he saw us smiling, and the three of us burst into roars of laughter.

With the wisdom of hindsight, I can see I should have kept silent about Bill and Stuart until their books were in print. But I can also see that, no matter what happened, the attacks on his novel were inevitable. A novel about a ruthless politician was bound to be labelled 'fascist' in the prevailing left-wing ambience of the fifties.

I viewed *The Divine and the Decay* as a philosophical rather than a political statement. In effect, contemporary psychologists like Watson, Skinner and Eysenck were preaching a mechanistic doctrine that was a restatement of the ideas that La Mettrie had advanced in 1748 in *Man the Machine* – that the human race will never be happy until we accept that we are machines pure and simple, and embrace materialism. Sixty years later, Maine de Biran tried to reverse the trend when he pointed out that doing something with *conscious effort* feels quite different from doing something mechanically. A sense of urgency somehow 'shakes the mind awake' and frees us from the mechanical self that does most of our living for us. When Plowart is making a speech, he feels fully alive. When he is alone, he soon feels becalmed, as if all his inner circuits have been disconnected. He wants to uncover the secret of the location of the master switch. And he thinks Claremont knows the answer.

If *The Divine and the Decay* had been published twenty years later, when Michel Foucault was writing books about power, it might have been understood. As it was, it sold minimally and vanished without a trace.

At least Bill's suggestion of a 'symposium' of the Angry Young Men bore fruit. I did not attend the launching party for *Declaration* in Chelsea, which may have been just as well, for I have an article about it that states that there was a plot to tar and feather me. This gives an accurate idea of how far the reaction had swung against the Angry Young Men, and in my case, how much the success of *The Outsider* and the endless publicity about it had created a groundswell of pure loathing.

Bill was able to attend the launch because he was just back from Hamburg. Since he had a phobia about flying, he returned to England by train before Christmas, and told us later that it had been an unprecedentedly cold and accident-filled journey.

For Tom Maschler, the book was probably the most important single move of his career. Since his name was on the title page as editor, it had the effect of making his reputation. *Declaration* sold incredibly well and went into many foreign translations. And as a result of its success, Tom was offered a job with a more prestigious publisher, Jonathan Cape. It was the beginning of his spectacular career in publishing, which ended with him owning the firm.

Bill's article in *Declaration*, 'Ways Without a Precedent', is his manifesto, his equivalent of Trocchi's 'Insurrection of a Million Minds'. It also throws a great deal of light on the aims of *The Divine and the Decay*.

It begins aggressively: 'The literature of the past ten years has been conspicuous for its total lack of direction, purpose and power. It has opened no new roads of imagination, created no monumental characters, and contributed nothing whatever to the vitality of the written word.'

Such assertiveness could only be justified by creating the kind of literature he is demanding – which, of course, is precisely what he intended to do, beginning with *The Divine and the Decay*.

After referring disparagingly to Samuel Beckett, Tennessee Williams and Arthur Miller, 'writers who have distinguished themselves by creating small men and women whose unlikely poetry is in their bewilderment', he goes on to state his own vision of what literature should attempt. 'It must begin to emphasise . . . that man need not be the victim of circumstances . . . It is the conquest of external conditions that determines the extent of Mankind's difference from all other forms of life.' He goes on: 'It is obvious that this concern with belief leads inevitably to the heroic. The two are joined as inevitably as flight to birds. The hero is the primary condition of all moral education . . .'

This emphasis on the hero suddenly clarifies his literary ancestry: Carlyle. This is something that often struck me in discussions with Bill –

that he is a twentieth-century version of Thomas Carlyle, fulminating against his own age and its lack of purpose. But, unlike Carlyle, he was disinclined to nostalgia about the past. His concern was wholly for the future.

Like myself, he recognised that the origin of the problem was the collapse of religion with the coming of rationalism. But – again like me – he saw that a religious revival was unlikely, and probably undesirable. But 'if we can trace belief to its origins and examine it in terms of plain, unadorned power, we have a potential weapon . . . I am convinced that it is an internal power comparable, when fully released, to the explosions of atomic energy.'

Such an assertion seems designed to arouse scepticism. But what he meant by it can be grasped in *The Divine and the Decay*. In spite of his fanatical drive, Plowart lacks the self-belief that would unite his inner forces. Knowing that Claremont has betrayed him and has planned his death acts on his inner being like the detonator of a bomb. And the rocks move . . . It is, in fact, a kind of 'magic realism', of the kind Iris Murdoch was aiming for in *The Sandcastle* (which, by coincidence, was being written at the same time as *The Divine and the Decay*).

For Bill, of course, the sheer venom unleashed by his novel and 'Ways Without a Precedent' was wholly unforeseen. He had expected – and looked forward to – controversy, but this was more like character assassination. Only someone who has been through it can know how bewildering and debilitating it feels to be violently attacked by strangers. Although Bill remained his self-confident self, I knew him well enough to know that this storm of detraction and disparagement had left him shaken. The second novel, *Time of Totality*, which he had started before travelling to Hamburg, progressed painfully slowly. And when the typescript was accidentally destroyed by a fire caused by a lighted cigarette, he made no attempt to rewrite it.

In the second volume of her autobiography, *Walking in the Shade*, Doris Lessing states that Bill Hopkins died young. (She was surprised and apologetic when I explained, forty years later, that he was still alive.) But the fact that he published nothing subsequently explains the misunderstanding.

Stuart Holroyd found himself in the same unenviable position after his essay in *Declaration*. Again, his name was linked with mine, which was enough to ensure that he would be attacked. Without that link he would certainly have been well received – he wrote well and clearly, and with a range of reference that suggested a university graduate.

In fact, he was from a working-class background, his father having been a milkman, a taxi driver and a commercial traveller. Stuart's school exam results had been so good that he had been accepted for a university place, but innate romanticism made him prefer the theatre, and he found himself a stage manager's job in the local theatre in Blackpool. We became friends after I met him at the Bridge group, and I had soon convinced him of the shortcomings of Alfred Reynold's doctrines. But to label him my disciple, as many critics did, was unfair, for he was an extremely able thinker. And recognising that part of the problem, as far as critics were concerned, was the fact that he did not have a university degree, he acquired Latin, and took a philosophy degree at London University under A J Ayer.

'A Sense of Crisis', which was Stuart's contribution to *Declaration*, is an excellent summary of what we both believed: that man's deepest desire is for freedom, and that this means far more than political freedom – it means the kind of freedom the Romantics dreamed about. And in fact, the appetite for freedom boils down to religion – it is what tormented Saint Augustine and made Bunyan's Christian cry 'What must I do to be saved?' Stuart writes: 'Man is not wholly determined from below, but also, and more essentially, from above. He is not only a social or political animal . . . He is also an eternal existing individual who stands absolutely responsible for his actions before God.'

I was not entirely happy about the use of the word 'God', since it tends to give a false impression of piety which provokes misunderstandings. Stuart himself understood the point, for he tells how, after sitting through a short religious film inserted unannounced in a cinema programme, he was told by the manager that the film mogul J Arthur Rank was a devout Methodist, and that he, Stuart, was the first person to complain.

He then goes on to cite William James, Karl Jaspers and Dr Alexis Carrel on the need for psychology to make an attempt to understand man's religious urges. (A decade later he would probably have mentioned Jung, but in the fifties, Jung had not yet achieved his position as universal guru.)

Where Stuart is in agreement with Bill is in his statement that what modern literature lacks is a sense of 'energy, vision and power', that modern man feels impotent and futile. Stuart seemed to see the answer in the idea of a new religion, Bill in the idea of a new kind of politics.

As to me, in my own contribution, 'Beyond the Outsider', I admit that I can see no obvious solution. 'I believe that our civilisation is in decline, and that Outsiders are a symptom of that decline . . . I believe that when a civilisation begins to produce Outsiders, it has received a challenge: a challenge to produce a higher type of man, and give itself a new unity of purpose, or to slip into the gulf after all the other civilisations that have failed.'

But although this sounds gloomy enough, I was beginning to catch a glimpse of an answer. I found it in H G Wells:

In the introduction to his *Experiment in Autobiography*, H G Wells has a passage that strikes me as being of peculiar importance; I cannot quote it in full, but here is its essence:

'Most individual creatures, since life began, have been "up against it" all the time, have been driven continually by fear and cravings, have had to respond to the unresting antagonisms of their surroundings, and they have found a sufficient and sustaining interest in the drama of immediate events provided for them by these demands. Essentially, their living was continual adjustment to happenings. [*Vide* Sartre in *La Nausée*: "When his café empties, his head empties too."] Good hap and ill hap filled it entirely. They hungered and ate, and they desired and loved . . . and they died.

'But with the dawn of human foresight, and with the appearance of a great surplus of energy in life such as the last century or so has revealed, there has been a progressive emancipation of the attention from everyday urgencies. What was once the whole of life, has become to an increasing extent, merely a background of life. People can ask now what would have been an extraordinary question five hundred years ago. They can say: "Yes, you earn a living, you support a family, you love and hate, but – what do you do?"

'Conceptions of living, divorced more and more from immediacy, distinguish the modern civilized man from all former life . . . We are like early amphibians, so to speak, struggling out of the waters that have hitherto covered our kind, into the air, seeking to breathe in a new fashion . . ."'

And this, it seemed to me, was clearly the answer. The distress of Outsiders is the distress of those early amphibians who dragged themselves out of prehistoric seas and wanted to become land animals. But they had flippers instead of legs.

Wells had also said once: 'The bird is a creature of the air, the fish is a creature of the water, and man is a creature of the mind.' But our problem is that we are not yet creatures of the mind. You only have to notice that feeling of suffocation that comes over you when you have spent too long reading a book to know that we are not yet creatures of the mind. We need to slip back into the sea to take a rest from the land.

But surely one thing is absolutely clear: that so long as we accept the nihilism of the Becketts and Henry Millers and William Burroughses, we are never going to evolve. Even Tynan, with all his laziness and preciousness, could see there was something all wrong with Beckett. *Yet he could not put his finger on it*, and when he had to review

Endgame, had to content himself with a parody instead of going in to the attack.

It would be another five years before I would begin to see the outline of a solution, and this was due to my acquaintance with the American psychologist Abraham Maslow, whose central insight was that all healthy people have what he labelled 'peak experiences', moments of a sudden upsurge of sheer delight. Moreover, the more these 'peakers' think and talk about peak experiences, the more frequently they have them, *and the more they can induce them in other people.* This last is the all-important discovery that could provide the answer to the future of civilisation.

The contributions of Bill, Stuart and myself separated us clearly from the other writers in *Declaration*: Osborne, Tynan, Doris Lessing, John Wain, and film director Lindsay Anderson. All, with the exception of Wain, were leftists, and Lindsay Anderson was a member of the Communist Party.

Amis had declined to contribute on the grounds that he hated this 'pharasaical twittering' about the state of civilisation. The real reason, fairly certainly, was that he knew he had nothing to say. His pose of cultural saboteur would hardly make for a serious contribution, and since Oxford, he had fallen oddly silent about his former leftist views.

Wain, who was essentially a writer of ideas, was glad to accept Tom's invitation. And in fact, his essay, 'Along the Tightrope', is one of the best in the book.

The writer's subject matter, Wain says, is 'what it is like to be human'. And his task is to humanise the environment. When the early Church was preaching that man's only job was to get to heaven, writers like Chaucer were there to remind people that living in the present can also be worthwhile. When Dickens or Mrs Gaskell wrote about the harshness of factory life, they were somehow reconciling us to industrial civilisation and making it more human.

After talking sensibly about his own work, he ends with a comment that sounds as if it is directed at Amis: 'I do know that the best hope for a significant and valuable literature is that those who have chosen writing as a profession should *do their best* – should think of their work as serious, and not be afraid to be earnest about it.'

As I reread this after more than forty years, it strikes me again that Wain was one of the best critical minds of his time. Then I see the quotation from Henry Miller that stands at the head of the article, and am reminded of what was wrong with Wain: 'The world is only the mirror of ourselves. If it's something to make one puke, why then, puke, me lads, it's only your own sick mugs you're looking at.' Yet Wain failed to see how far this applied to himself, and that the touch of bitterness and paranoia that spoiled his novels came from inside himself.

Osborne's essay, 'They Call it Cricket', begins by admitting that he is the last one to hand in his contribution, and the reason soon becomes clear: he has no constructive ideas. He explains: 'I want to make people feel, to give them lessons in feeling. They can think afterwards.' This was a reaction to a comment I had recently made – that what I wanted was to make people think. The objection to Osborne's aim is that all you have to do to make people feel is to excite their pity – as Dickens does in the death of Little Nell. But nothing in *Look Back in Anger* excited anything in me but irritation at Osborne's self-pity.

Osborne then goes on to attack the British press ('the liars of Britain'), the Tories ('genius for self-deception and arrogance') the Duke of Edinburgh (who had appeared on children's TV), the Haymarket Theatre (a 'permanent Old Ladies' Home'), the Queen ('a gold filling in a mouth of decay'), the BBC ('highly trained palace lackeys') and the Church of England ('the spiritual spiel of the wide boys of the Church'). There are also plenty of casual sideswipes at individuals, such as T S Eliot and a left-wing journalist called Marquand. Clearly, he is not really at home in an article that demands organisation, since all he seems to be able to supply is a ragbag of his favourite hates – a problem that would also be the downfall of his next play, *The World of Paul Slickey*.

Tynan's contribution, 'Theatre and Living', is a curiously muted performance, which makes no mention of his extreme leftism. About the kind of plays he likes he says: 'I want plays that affirm candour, valour, grace and sensuality, and plays that recoil from determinism, because determinism denies free choice, and without free choice there can be no drama. As Samuel Beckett's *Fin de Partie* showed, the play that is bound to a mechanistic universe is also bound to despair.'

As to positive convictions, he explains: 'I ask for a society where people care more for what you have learned than for where you learned it; where people who think and people who work can share common assumptions and discuss them in the same idiom; where art connects instead of separating people; where people feel, as in that new Salinger story [*Zooey*] that every fat woman on earth is Jesus Christ . . .'

The blandness of the passage suggests that Tynan, like Osborne, became embarrassed when asked to hammer out a piece of sustained thinking. Furthermore he pads out the remainder of the article with a long and dubiously relevant letter he wrote to the son of a friend about to go to Oxford, devoted mainly to advising him not to enter journalism – a letter he admits to not having sent.

Lindsay Anderson, who comes next, had been, like Tynan, a wunderkind, but his domain was not theatre but film.

His background was comfortable middle class, and when he went to the exclusive Cheltenham College, he became the friend of the brilliant Gavin

Lambert, a young homosexual who flaunted it (unlike Anderson, who was ashamed of it) and admitted openly that he was a 'tart'. They shared an enthusiasm for films and wrote two scripts together. At Magdalen College, Oxford, he shared room with Peter Brook, who would achieve eminence as a theatre and film director, and played a bit part in an experimental film. He left a year later without taking his degree – it is said because he clashed with his tutor, the intellectual bully C S Lewis, who disliked homosexuals – but three years later took over the Oxford Film Society's magazine *Sequence*. In this he set out to castigate the British postwar film industry, which he felt to be weary and out of ideas; within two years he and his fellow editors had made it so influential and exciting that they had became celebrities, and soon were being photographed for the fashion magazine *Vogue*.

As a director, his style was gritty and bleak. His first film *Thursday's Children* was a documentary on deaf-mute children, and won the Oscar for the best short film. His second, *Dreamland,* was a harshly realistic look at the Margate funfair. He would go on to become one of the major influences on the New Wave cinema movement of the 1960s.

Anderson's essay in *Declaration*, 'Get Out and Push', is very much in the same Tory-bashing vein as Osborne and Tynan, and it provoked two pages of cold fury in Kenneth Allsop's *The Angry Decade*, where it is described as a 'hectoring effusion' and 'this beating of the left breast'. In fact, Anderson attacks Amis as a coward and Wain as 'an empty-headed avuncular Tory'. Then he goes on to discuss me and my rise to fame, talks about my 'doctrine of the neo-Superman', then says: '. . . it is not the Wilsons who matter, but the thought that we live in a society where the expression of a philosophy so *jejeune* . . . can elevate a young writer to instant celebrity.'

Oddly enough I felt no resentment at this attack, for it was obvious that he was simply using *The Outsider* furore as a stick to beat the literary establishment. In fact, the blunt and down-to-earth tone of the essay made me feel that he was the sort of person I would like. Indeed, he lived up to his own admonition to get out and push with classics like *This Sporting Life, If . . .* and its sequel *Oh Lucky Man.*

In spite of the obvious brilliance of these films, Anderson was much underrated as a film director, and his final film, the autobiographical *Is That All There Is?* (1993) has a sequence in which he speaks of the immense difficulty he had in obtaining funding. It was such struggles that probably contributed to his death of a heart attack at the age of 71.

I have deliberately left speaking about Doris Lessing until last, for she strikes me as one of the most interesting of my contemporaries. Starting off as a leftist – in fact, as a Communist – she developed an evolutionary vision of humankind that places her far beyond such labels as 'angry' or even 'feminist'.

She was born in Persia in October 1919 – as Doris May Tayler – and her family moved to Southern Rhodesia – now Zimbabwe – when she was five. Her father had been hoping to make a fortune farming maize on a thousand or so acres of bush he had bought cheaply, but practical problems and his own depressive temperament defeated him, and the farm proved unproductive. Her mother was an ex-nurse, obsessed with discipline, and sent Doris to a convent school, which she hated. The two would never see eye to eye. Her formal education ceased at fourteen. She left home – partly to escape her mother – and took a job as a nursemaid. It was at this time she began to read books on politics and sociology, and to write stories.

Rhodesia was a frustrating place, a stagnant backwater where the lives of women were completely circumscribed, and once they were married and had children, were virtually over as far as further development was concerned. White men dominated the white women, but the women dominated the blacks, and Doris was instinctively revolted by this, since she saw the 'natives' as human beings.

Hearing there were jobs in the telephone exchange in Salisbury, she moved there and was taken on. She met the 'Left Bookclub crowd', who recommended her to read the *New Statesman,* but found them disappointing. She was reading D H Lawrence, Tolstoy and Dostoevsky. Then finally, at nineteen, she did what she was expected to do – got married. He was a civil servant named Frank Wisdom, who spent much of his time drinking with the boys (as most Rhodesian men did), and fathered two children by Doris. Feeling again that she was stagnating, she left her husband and children. She became a member of another left-book club, this time Communist, and ended by marrying its driving force and organiser, Gottfried Lessing. They had a son, Peter.

By now she was writing her first novel, *The Grass is Singing.*

This is a remarkably assured performance that draws in the reader from the first page with a newspaper report of the murder of a white farmer's wife, Mary Turner, by a black servant. The novel then tells the story of how this came about.

Approaching thirty, Mary has no particular desire to marry, but since an unmarried woman is regarded as 'odd', finally accepts a white farmer, Dick Turner, who scrapes an inefficient living from a farm as unsuccessful as Doris's father's. She finds the struggle spiritually deadening, but has an ambivalent attitude to the black houseboy whose natural grace and vitality at once attract and repel her.

If this were a Lawrence novel, they would become lovers. In Rhodesia this was unthinkable – one black who became his white mistress's lover was executed. And the tormented and ambivalent relationship between servant and mistress ends in her murder.

Now, having found herself as a writer, she decided to go to London with her son. *The Grass is Singing* was accepted by a British publisher in 1950, and established her name. She went on to publish the first two novels of a sequence she would call *Children of Violence*. The central character, Martha Quest, she acknowledged to be based on herself.

She became a contributor to *Declaration* almost by accident. Tom Maschler approached Iris Murdoch and she declined. He wanted at least one woman in the book, and asked Doris. She also declined, since she had no desire to write a 'think piece'. But his pleas finally won her over, the result being that she figures as the first contributor in the book, with an essay called 'The Small Personal Voice'. Doris was certainly a more suitable contributor than Iris would have been, for she was deeply committed, while Iris was still engaged in trying to back out of the existentialist cul-de-sac.

Her piece seems to me one of the best in the book for, although she had been a Communist – and was even now ceasing to be one – she was in transition, looking for a more satisfying belief. She writes: 'What is the choice before us? It is not merely a question of preventing an evil, but of strengthening a vision of good which may defeat the evil.' And it is because she is searching for a vision of good that she stands out among so many writers whose vision of the world is negative.

Unlike her fellow Communist Lindsay Anderson, she is dubious about 'Socialist' art. The optimism of novels about the five-year plan and collective farms strikes her as boring, and she is glad to go back to reading Tolstoy.

On the other hand, she is equally out of sympathy with Sartre, Camus, Genet and Beckett. She says: 'I believe that the pleasurable luxury of despair, the acceptance of disgust, is as much a betrayal of what a writer should be as the simple economic view of man; both are aspects of cowardice.'

Of her fellow 'angries', she is critical of Braine because, although Joe Lampton shares the values of Stendhal's Julien Sorel, 'he does not see himself in relation to any larger vision. Therefore he remains petty'. She criticises Amis for his lack of conviction, and for saying he envies writers who have a cause to inspire them.

Of Osborne she says little, although she might have quoted the actor Miles Malleson, who accompanied her to see *Look Back in Anger* and said unhappily 'But bad manners isn't social criticism.' And she says of Jimmy Porter: 'I thought [he] was infantile and as self-pitying as the youths who killed themselves because of *Werther*.'

She criticises me for saying: 'Like all my generation I am anti-humanist and anti-materialist' – quite justly, if I did say it, for I could hardly speak for my generation, and even if I could it would not be true, for it did not apply to most of the people in the book, let alone a whole generation.

She ends by defending the importance of the novelist. 'The novelist talks, as an individual to individuals, in a small personal voice.'

In 1958, after *Declaration*, came a third novel about Martha Quest, *A Ripple from the Storm*, which describes her membership of the Marxist group after the break up of her first marriage, and her marriage to its leader. But it was clear that writing this kind of semi-autobiographical novel was not the answer; she was trapped in it. As a result, she began work on something far more complex and demanding, her best-known novel, *The Golden Notebook*. This is an extraordinarily rich and intellectually versatile work, which would become a virtual Bible for the Women's Liberation movement.

The origin of *The Golden Notebook* seems to have been certain reflections on the idea of a novel about a writer or artist, in the tradition of Thomas Mann's *Tonio Kroger*. This developed into the idea of a writer, Anna Wulf, suffering a writer's block, and attempting to remove it by self-analysis in diaries or notebooks, and (after the trauma of the desertion of her lover Paul) by undergoing psychoanalysis. Anna actually descends into psychosis and insanity before struggling out of it, and writing a short novel called *Free Women*, about a person like herself.

In *The Golden Notebook*, the five sections of this novel are separated by extracts from four notebooks analysing various aspects of Anna's past. There is the black notebook, concerned with her life in Africa, the red notebook, covering her life as a Communist, the yellow notebook, in which she writes private stories of her own life, and the blue notebook, a diary. The fact that there are four notebooks indicates that she feels herself to be unable to unite the strands of her life, and they finally unite in the golden notebook of the title as she emerges from her mental torments.

The novel created a furore partly because Anna speaks so frankly of her sex life, which has involved many lovers. She has no desire to settle again into marriage – hence the title *Free Women* – yet the lack of a central male figure in her life is obviously one of the causes of her frustration.

What makes the book so remarkable is that it is obviously an attempt by Anna Wulf to unite many aspects of her complex life, and to achieve what Jung calls 'individuation', symbolised by the four notebooks coming together in and being superseded by, the golden notebook. The material sounds unpromising because so diverse, yet there is an underlying intensity that holds the reader fascinated. Anna finally overcomes her block to write *Free Women*, but feels that this can only be properly understood by revealing the complex mental life that cannot be contained in a novel. In the sense, one might say that Anna is able to have her cake and eat it.

The Golden Notebook clearly played a major role is Doris's own life. Anno's 'blockage' might be seen as the problem Doris was encountering as she wrote the *Children of Violence series, whose* autobiographical basis trapped her in an unsatisfactory form. In her personal life, this problem was symbolised by her mother's decision to come and join her in London; this is what caused her to seek out a psychotherapist ('because', she says in *Walking in the Shade*, 'if I didn't get some help, I would not survive'). And it was in part due to the stress of the situation that followed that she decided on what she describes as 'the most neurotic act of my life', and became a member of the Communist Party. In due course she would realise that this was another false direction.

Eventually, this 'blockage' was overcome, and the result can be seen in *The Golden Notebook,* and then in the fifth and last of the Martha Quest series, *The Four-Gated City* (1969), which seems to me not only the most important of the *Children of Violence* series, but in many ways the most important of all her novels.

In the previous volume, *Landlocked* (1965) the central event had been Martha's love affair with Thomas Stern, a Czech Jew who was a survivor of the war. He had finally died insane, but their close intimacy had made the two of them naturally telepathic, so that Martha was able to share his insanity without feeling repelled by it. This achievement of telepathic communication releases her into deeper awareness (and also enables its author to move beyond the purely realistic novel – there is an interesting parallel here with the break into 'magical realism' that Iris Murdoch made with *The Sandcastle*).

An unsympathetic reader might regard this as a step into an unreal mysticism – an attitude Doris herself would have taken during her Communist period. But anyone who has followed Martha Quest's development with sympathy – and recognised that the stressed and fragmented Anna Wulf of *The Golden Notebook* is another incarnation of Martha – will recognise that this is not an 'escape', but a logical and inevitable step.

At the beginning of *The Four-Gated City*, Martha is still a 'divided self' – the phrase is the title of the first book by the Scottish psychiatrist R D Laing, who argued that schizophrenia is the response of over-sensitive individuals to a society that imposes its crass and materialistic values like a straitjacket. (He admitted that it was inspired by *The Outsider*.) This was interpreted by his followers as the assertion that 'mad' people may actually be sane people reacting to a schizoid society (i.e., it is society that is mad, not they).The result is the kind of mental stress that drove Thomas Stern 'insane'. On the other hand Jack (Martha's lover in the first part of the book) is able to handle the vital current whose suppression causes schizophrenia, so their love-making is described in terms of the waves of the sea, in passages that cause us inevitably to think of Lawrence. The result is that as Martha begins to achieve internal unity, she also begins to develop psychic powers.

When Martha goes to live with the family of Mark and Lynda Coldridge, she again finds herself in a learning situation. Lynda is 'insane', and Mark and Martha become lovers, and she begins to take care of Lynda, and her emotionally disturbed children. *Children of Violence* is essentially a *Bindungsroman* (novel of education) in which Martha's inner development is charted. But it is when she ceases to care about her own evolution and to devote her energies to caring for the Coldridges that her true education begins, and she slowly develops powers of telepathy and intuition which are really the subject of the novel. In her youth Martha had experienced a kind of Wordsworthian response to nature, and now she finds it returning through this new self-forgetfulness. Oneness is found finally not in home or marriage or political involvement, but in the development of her ability to lose herself in others.

In the appendix to the novel, we learn that Britain has been subjected to some kind of nuclear catastrophe, and that a group of survivors, including Martha, have moved to an island off Scotland. The children of this group are already born 'psychic', and it is they and their kind who will take charge of the future of humanity.

When I first met Doris Lessing in the late fifties (it was at a revival of Ronald Duncan's *This Way to the Tomb* at the Arts Theatre) I found her sympathetic and likeable, but associated her with the political wing of the Angry Young Men, like Osborne, Tynan and Anderson, whose sympathies seemed to me too narrow. So no one was more surprised than I was to discover, through novels like *The Four-Gated City* in 1969, and the 'science fiction' series that begins with *Shikasta* (1979), that her preoccupation with human evolution had made her the contemporary with whom I felt the deepest sense of sympathy and kinship.

9　Downhill

Following their flight from London after the flop of *Paul Slickey*, Osborne and Jocelyn Rickards drove to Capri, and stayed for three weeks in a villa loaned to them by Graham Greene, who had been one of Jocelyn's former lovers. On their return to London, they lived together for the next two years. Osborne was shy and anti-social, and Jocelyn Rickards was a good cook and preferred quiet evenings at home with a book.

She would tell Osborne's biographer John Heilpern: 'He was the most complex man I've ever known. He was full of gaiety, but he could reveal little talent for enjoying himself. He had a talent for fucking up other people's lives, and his own.'

The marriage with Mary Ure was already coming to an end before Osborne met Jocelyn; she was a hard drinker, and when drinking, inclined to be quarrelsome. And she had started an affair with the handsome, blond actor Robert Shaw.

It was in September 1961 that Shaw came and introduced himself to me in the lobby of the Algonquin Hotel in New York. He was in Harold Pinter's play *The Caretaker*. When he mentioned the Royal Court, and I asked him if he knew John Osborne, he looked at me quizzically and said: 'Yes, I stole his wife. He's citing me as co-respondent.' He went on to tell me that the two often quarrelled violently in his presence, and that one evening he had said to her: 'If he ever throws you out, you can always come to my place.' 'And one night,' he said, 'there was a knock on my door and it was Mary.'

But this affair had still not developed when Osborne and Jocelyn Rickards fled to Italy. The British press not only chronicled their flight, but sent reporters after them. Fortunately they were safe in Greene's walled villa. But back in London a few weeks later, reporters were still surrounding the house in Woodfall Street, when Osborne returned. One evening, as Mary was falling asleep after too much to drink, she confided casually that she was pregnant. She did not say so, but Osborne inferred that the father was Robert Shaw. Not long after, the Woodfall Street house burnt down through an electrical fault, and Osborne moved in with Jocelyn in a house in Lower Belgrave Street.

Osborne wanted a child and, although she was less sure about the idea, the obliging Jocelyn agreed. But at three months she spontaneously aborted, and in retrospect knew this was for the best. It was just as well, for the inconstant Osborne was thinking of leaving her.

The rival attraction was a red-haired journalist and film critic named Penelope Gilliatt, whose husband Roger was a nerve specialist. She and Osborne had first met at the time of *Look Back in Anger*, when she interviewed him for *Vogue*. They renewed the acquaintance when Osborne moved in with Jocelyn in Lower Belgrave Street, and they met at a party. The Gilliatts moved in high social circles, and Roger Gilliatt had been the best man at Tony Armstrong-Jones's marriage to Princess Margaret.

Osborne liked redheads – his first wife Pamela had also been one – and Penelope Gilliatt was attracted to Osborne. In fact, according to Jocelyn, she went all out to get him.

Apart from the colour of her hair, they were not obviously well matched, for she was highly intellectual, and had just been appointed the *Observer*'s film critic, where she coruscated alongside Tynan. ('One of the characteristic sounds of the English Sunday is Harold Hobson barking up the wrong tree.') Osborne, while intelligent in his own intuitive way, was no reader. Even Jocelyn was slightly out of his class, with her taste for Henry James. However, he liked Gilliatt's energy and sheer enthusiasm.

Jocelyn was not the jealous type; she knew that, although they were living together, Osborne had one-night stands all the time. Gilliatt, herself given to bed-hopping (her lovers including Tynan and Ayer), was different, for her intentions were more serious. Clearly, she felt that Osborne was a more suitable mate than a doctor. According to Jocelyn, she was quite blatant about it. Besides, Jocelyn was five years Osborne's senior, while Gilliatt was two years his junior. His sexual ambitions may also have been stirred when, on his way to call on her, he met her on the stairs, arm in arm with a famous academic, who was wearing an unmistakeable 'post-coital smirk'.

One day in early 1961, Osborne received the proofs of his latest play, *Luther*, and hastened to Lowndes Square to read some of it to Gilliatt. When he left, they had become lovers. He says that on his way back to Jocelyn, he practised contorting his 'face into the most unsmirklike post-coital half-mask I could devise'.

Although Jocelyn was in love with him, she possessed something Osborne lacked: an ability to control her emotions. She merely watched with ironical detachment as Gilliatt 'lit up like a one-armed bandit' whenever Osborne came into the room.

When Tony Richardson suggested that the three of them should take a villa in the south of France for the summer, Jocelyn at first declined, until Osborne persuaded her by saying irritably that he was fed up with her mute attrition. No doubt the prospect of a Gilliatt-free summer also played its part in changing her mind.

La Baumette, in Valbonne, was an old stone farmhouse in a superb landscape of vines and woods. But Penelope Gilliatt declined to be exorcised, and sent Osborne special-delivery love letters every day, which Jocelyn had to sign (and tip the postman) for.

George Devine arrived in the process of having a nervous breakdown and was unable to stop weeping. The latest complication at the Court had been a painful clash with Nigel Dennis, whose follow-up to the unpopular *Making of Moo* was a satire on democracy called *August for the People*. Its hero Sir Augustus Thwaites, is finally driven to Swiftian madness by corruption. It had been violently attacked by the critics in Edinburgh, and Rex Harrison, who played Thwaites, then broke his promise to star in a five-and-a-half weeks' run at the Court in order to go to Hollywood to play Caesar in the Burton–Taylor movie. Blaming Devine for abandoning the promised Royal Court opening, Dennis brought to an end their five-year association, finally precipitating the breakdown. Devine had to remain heavily sedated for ten days.

Denied access to Devine by Tony Richardson, on the grounds that it would only make things worse, Osborne also seems to have experienced a kind of mild insanity, and thereupon penned a violent letter to *Tribune* attacking the politicians he felt were dragging England to destruction by condoning the Bomb, which began:

'This is a letter of hate. It is for you my countrymen. I mean those men of my country who have defiled it. The men with manic fingers leading the sightless body of my country to its death. You are murderers . . .'

When I read it – for it was quoted in every tabloid – I was reminded of Braine's remark that 'Truman's a bloody murderer', but with rather less justification since Truman had at least been responsible for the dropping of the A bomb, while Osborne's intemperate rant apparently achieved nothing but letting off steam, and revealing much the same chronic inability to exercise self-control that had irritated me in *Look Back in Anger*. The controversy rumbled on pointlessly for weeks.

A British major with a rifle turned up at the French farmhouse to remonstrate with Osborne, who ordered Jocelyn, 'Tell him to fuck off', which, surprisingly, she did.

When Mary Ure had her baby, they were suddenly inundated by pressmen, until Jocelyn told one of them, who happened to be a friend, the identity of the true father, and they all went away, to announce that Osborne was not the heartless parent he appeared to be.

When Osborne's secretary rang from London to say that the money he needed for Venice was in a local bank, Jocelyn noted that it was the time of the Venice film festival, which Gilliatt would undoubtedly be attending, and walked out to the swimming pool to say to Osborne, 'If you're going to Venice you must talk to me.' It was the wrong thing to say to Jimmy Porter, who snarled: 'I don't *have* to talk to anyone,' and dived into the pool.

Eventually he admitted that he was going to join Penelope, insisting that she had sent him the ticket. When he left, he made Jocelyn promise to await his return. Since Tony Richardson and some other guests also left, she then spent 'the bleakest week' of her life in the empty farmhouse.

When Osborne returned, he decided to go to London for an anti-Bomb rally organised by Bertrand Russell. They flew from Nice airport. In a taxi returning to Lower Belgrave Street, Osborne suddenly announced: 'I'm going to behave badly again, my darling,' and got out of the taxi close to the street where Penelope Gilliatt lived.

But Jocelyn's cheerful and unneurotic disposition served her well. She and Osborne remained friends for the rest of his life.

Gilliatt now moved into Osborne's country home, a mill at Hellingly, Sussex, which was soon surrounded by reporters. Osborne issued a statement saying that Mrs Gilliatt would be staying with him for some time. And the furore subsided. It was not until two years later, in 1963, that they were able to marry. It would last three years, until he left her for the actress Jill Bennett.

Yet to those who knew them it appeared a dazzlingly successful marriage. Everything seemed in their favour. Both were regarded as brilliant. Osborne had already written his next play, *Luther* which, to Devine's immense relief, had all the potential of a great success. And while they had been together in France, Osborne, Richardson and Devine had hatched a new project, a film of Henry Fielding's *Tom Jones,* which in due course would make all of them millionaires.

Osborne's next project, the two short *Plays for England*, were little more than amusing squibs, but kept alive his reputation as a critic of the establishment and opponent of the Lord Chamberlain. And the play that many considered his most substantial achievement, *Inadmissible Evidence* (of which more shortly), transferred to Shaftesbury Avenue and ran for months, then scored an equal triumph in New York.

Meanwhile, the Osbornes settled into the mill, an idyllic setting, where she worked in the granary and he – on *The Blood of the Bambergs*, the first of the two *Plays for England* – in the mill. The auguries could hardly have been better. Penelope obviously adored him, and after Mary Ure, he must have found her emotionally undemanding. The only cloud on their horizon lay in the fact that she was an immensely ambitious career woman, with a formidable academic record, and an obsessive and highly disciplined worker, while Osborne was emotionally self-indulgent and lazy, and often plunged into the depressions that accompany this makeup. He was also secretly irritated by her affectionate habit of calling him 'muddle-headed Johnny'.

This indicates what was basically wrong with the relationship – that she was naturally the more dominant of the two. And marriages work best if the dominance gap is the other way round, as the American psychologist Abraham Maslow discovered during the 1930s.

Gilliatt also took enormous pleasure in socialising; they also had a great house in Chester Square, and guests included the Oliviers, Lord Snowdon, Leonard Bernstein, Peter Sellers and the Tynans. But Osborne was a shy person, and this new lifestyle, while it made an interesting change from solitude and depression, must have struck him as basically rather futile. So while the marriage between the millionaire playwright and the successful journalist looked ideal to outsiders, strains were beginning to build under the surface.

Penelope even became pregnant to please him, but she was not a natural mother, and complained that the baby felt like a rat gnawing inside her. Her daughter was born on 25 February 1965, and was named Nolan, after a reference in a James Joyce pamphlet. If she had known that Joyce was referring to Giordano Bruno, burnt alive for heresy, she might have realised that the name was inauspicious.

Luther had received its try-out at the Theatre Royal in Nottingham on 25 June 1961, with Albert Finney, the star of *Saturday Night and Sunday Morning* in the lead. It was an enormous success, transferring both to the West End and New York, and helped to push the English Stage Company away from its usual state on the edge of bankruptcy.

It seems clear that after the *Slickey* fiasco, Osborne realised that he needed to find a completely new approach, and saw the answer in Brecht, particularly in *Galileo*, with its dramatisation of the clash between Galileo and the Pope.

I saw *Luther* for the first time on television in the sixties, and was impressed. Yet even then it struck me as a badly balanced play. The long first act is about Luther becoming a monk, and his arguments with his father. And when the play was televised again years later, I felt that this should have been shortened by a half. For there is a sense that the interesting part does not begin until the second act, when the Pope's 'salesman' Tetzel arrives in Jüterbog, selling indulgences – bits of paper forgiving sins – with all the techniques of an American advertising agent. When Luther hears about this from a peasant whose wife has just died (and has guaranteed her way into heaven by paying one gulden), he becomes indignant and preaches a sermon saying that God has already guaranteed salvation through faith, and that is all that is needed. From then on he and Pope Leo X are set on a collision course.

This is the point where the audience becomes truly gripped by the drama. They are on the edge of their seats as Luther nails his 39 theses to the church door, and is inevitably excommunicated. Then the play gallops forward a year to the Diet of Worms – in effect, Luther's trial – which ends with a defiant Luther declaring, 'Here I stand.' And then suddenly we have leapt forward four years, to the rebellion of the peasants, and to Luther's repudiation of their revolt.

It is all too fast, as if Osborne is making the actors gabble at twice the proper speed. We cannot understand how the heroic rebel has suddenly betrayed his people. And then, abruptly, the play is over, leaving everyone feeling cheated or baffled. We feel that Luther has been sold short.

Brecht would not have made this mistake. He would have kept the first act shorter, and allowed the drama time to expand and sink in. As it is, the play is like a huge torso with tiny legs.

Osborne's problem was that he wrote off the top of his head, and would not rewrite because it bored him. In the BBC television programme on the twentieth anniversary of *The Outsider* and *Look Back in Anger*, he explained: 'I always write very quickly – that's the easy, wonderful part . . . *Look Back* only took me twelve days, and *The Entertainer* something like eleven days.'

Still, in spite of its faults, *Luther* is undoubtedly his best play. Osborne had finally learned the trick of objectivity and discipline. Unfortunately, he soon forgot it.

The Brechtian techniques of *Luther* would again serve him well in the film *Tom Jones,* released two years later. As it opens, realism is abandoned in favour of a comic alienation technique with notices dropped into the middle of the screen like the old-fashioned dialogue in silent films, while narration is provided by the great Michael MacLiammoir.

The introduction of a jokey, tongue-in-cheek atmosphere into a film is always a gamble, since an audience wants to be convinced it is really happening. But in this case, high spirits and bawdy humour triumphantly carried the day. (Richardson's attempt to repeat the formula in *Joseph Andrews* in 1977 somehow lacked the vital spark, and merely produced a sense of *déjà vu*.) It would break box-office records in London and New York and make nearly a quarter of a million dollars for Woodfall.

The first play written during Osborne's marriage to Penelope Gilliatt was a satire on the royal family in which he wrong-footed the Lord Chamberlain by ostensibly basing it on *The Prisoner of Zenda*. It is about a royal wedding, quite clearly based on the 1960 marriage between Princess Margaret and the photographer Anthony Armstrong-Jones, who became Lord Snowdon.

In *The Blood of the Bambergs*, the male heir to the throne is killed in a car crash on the eve of his wedding, but the guardian of the King's Household decides the wedding has to go ahead anyway on the grounds that the prince's younger brother is homosexual and will not be able to provide an heir. An Australian press photographer, who is virtually the prince's double, and who happens to be asleep in Westminster Abbey, is persuaded to step into the breach. The bride, Princess Melanie, is quite clearly a harridan, as Princess Margaret was reputed to be, and her lines were spoken in an imitation of the Queen's voice. As her future bridegroom kisses her, at her invitation, she begins to struggle violently, shouting, 'I can't bear to be touched.'

As in *Slickey*, Osborne showed a lack of talent for satire, and the play goes on too long.

The evening was padded out with a second feature called *Under Plain Cover*, again clearly designed to provoke the Lord Chamberlain (who declined to rise to the bait). This time the inspiration was Genet's *Balcony*, in which customers in a brothel enact their fantasies; it is about a brother and sister, who are also husband and wife, and who spend their time acting out erotic fantasies involving knickers and 'correction'. It contains an amusing parody of the BBC discussion programme *The Critics*, in which the couple discuss lingerie in a stilted language that would be appropriate to an analysis of a novel by Virginia Woolf. But again the satire simply lacks the sharpness that might have been brought to bear if it had been written as well as directed by Jonathan Miller. When Osborne attempted satire, it usually turned into schoolboy smut.

Dramatically speaking, Osborne's chief problem was that when he thought in terms of serious work, he descended into the world of his own miseries and insecurities. The subject of Luther had been a godsend because the hero was able to rise above his personal problems – epilepsy and piles – and work out his salvation in terms of rebellion. But without historical inspiration, Osborne was at the mercy of his neuroses, and only financial success shielded him from the worries that might have otherwise kept him practically occupied.

There was to be one more impressive foray into history. *A Patriot for Me* is perhaps his most effective and integrated play so far. It is based on a homosexual spy who played a major part in destroying the Hapsburg empire.

Alfred Redl was a brilliant young officer from a poor background, who rose to head the Austrian counter-intelligence service, with such innovations as hidden cameras and recorders. Around the turn of the century, the Russian secret service 'turned' him with a combination of blackmail and bribery – at this time to be a known homosexual would have spelt social ruin – and in the days before the First World War he passed on to them Austria's defence and attack plans. He also betrayed fellow spies to their death. Caught by accident in 1913 in a routine investigation by an admiring young disciple, he was allowed to blow out his brains instead of being 'debriefed' to find out what he had given away and how the damage might be repaired.

Osborne saw the story of the scandal as another way of upsetting the Lord Chamberlain by openly presenting homosexuality on stage when it was still taboo. The major scene of *A Patriot for Me* was a 'drag' ball. The Lord Chamberlain opined that it was a 'pansies' charter of freedom' and banned it so, in order to bypass him, Devine had to turn the Court into a club theatre 'for members only', with a token sum paid at the box office to join. All this meant that its opening was delayed until after that of the play Osborne had written subsequently: *Inadmissible Evidence*.

The origin of the latter had been a letter Osborne saw in a newspaper agony column: a letter from a woman whose husband seemed to repel other people, although he struck her as decent, admirable and misunderstood. Worse still, she felt herself being dragged into this whirlpool of negativity he aroused.

Osborne found himself thinking in terms of a seedy lawyer involved in a middle-age crisis and sinking like a man in a quicksand. Working on *Inadmissible Evidence* left him, he admitted, feeling depressed and 'permanently despoiled'. It was perhaps the most downbeat play since Arthur Miller's *Death of a Salesman*. Strindbergian in its gloom, it unfortunately lacked Strindberg's sense of dramatic shape, and was virtually formless.

Presented at the Court in September 1964, with a remarkable young actor called Nicol Williamson playing the lead, it had remarkable success, and transferred to the West End, then to New York. Osborne's biographer John Heilpern regards it as a prophetic anticipation of his major nervous breakdown of 1966.

But its real significance is biographical. *Look Back in Anger* had been an outburst directed at all the things he disliked. The significance of *Inadmissible Evidence* is that it is an explosion directed *inward*. He is not shaking his fist at society but at himself. He was already on record as saying that he could not bear *Look Back in Anger*. Now it is as if he has conceded that the critics who called it a shriek of self-pity are right; the new Osborne alter-ego is admitting that the fault was his own weakness and self-indulgence. It raised the interesting question of where Osborne could go from there.

Sadly, the answer was provided by an external event: the death of George Devine.

A Patriot for Me finally opened on 30 June 1965. Devine was playing the baron and, on the hot evening of 9 August, he collapsed with a heart attack after the performance and, although he made a partial recovery, he died in the following January.

Osborne was inconsolable. He saw it as the end of an era in his own life. Drinking heavily, he took out his grief on Penelope, and announced that he was leaving her, struggling with her on the stairs to remove his suitcase. He spent the remainder of that night dozing in Kensington Gardens, then sitting alone in the downstairs room of the flat of the actress who had played the countess in *A Patriot for Me,* Jill Bennett, swigging brandy from the bottle. Then he changed his mind and went back to his wife and child.

This did not last, and in due course, Jill Bennett became the fourth Mrs Osborne. His decision to 'behave badly again' would prove to be his greatest marital disaster, and eventually led to his virtual destruction as a writer.

Osborne's first impression of Jill Bennett had been a poor one; he had seen her being rude to her husband, the playwright Willis Hall. Since then they had parted, and Osborne's opinion of her had risen when he saw how upset she was at the separation. As she sobbed on his wife's shoulder he began to feel protective about her. Before long he was sending her roses, and spending the afternoons at her Kensington mews flat.

The final break with Penelope came on an evening in June 1966 when they attended a memorial performance for Devine at the Old Vic, with scenes from various plays of the past ten years. After the curtain fell Osborne went backstage. Gilliatt went looking for him, and knocked on Jill Bennett's dressing-room door. It was opened by her husband, who told her briefly: 'I've left you. I'm going away with Jill.'

Gilliatt's reaction was a suicide attempt with an overdose. And Osborne's response to the summer of crisis was to have a nervous breakdown, and move into the Regent's Park Nursing Home.

June 1966 was also the occasion of Osborne's first total flop since *Slickey*. Tynan, who had been appointed literary manager of the National Theatre – working under Olivier – had asked Osborne to adapt a play by the classic Spanish dramatist Lope de Vega, *La Fianza satisfecha*, or *A Bond Honoured*. This was a religious play about a 'great sinner' who is suddenly converted by a vision of Christ. Tynan seems to have thought this should appeal to Osborne because the 'great sinner' commits a series of crimes, including blinding his father, trying to rape his mother and seducing his sister.

Tynan obviously hoped Osborne would take the opportunity to create an existentialist hero like Goetz in Sartre's *Le Diable et le Bon Dieu*, who seeks to prove his ultimate freedom by becoming first a great sinner then a saint. Instead, Osborne made no attempt to create a dialectic of immoralism, and left a confusing play as bewildering as he found it, although enlivened by more incest than Lope had dared to put in. The result was a fiasco.

The reason is obvious. *A Bond Honoured* should have been a play of ideas. But Osborne was incapable of creating a drama of ideas. He wanted to make people feel, not think, and Lope's play contained nothing to his purpose. It would have worked better if he had rethought the villain, turning him into a saturnine intellectual.

A Bond Honoured was to be the first of a string of theatrical disasters that continued for the remaining 28 years of his life.

Tynan, the man who had been indirectly responsible for the flop, was himself beginning to experience a similar decline in his own fortunes. And he himself would undoubtedly have traced the beginning of the downward curve to his wife's success as a novelist in 1959.

Before their marriage, his wife Elaine had been a neophyte actress. But lack of offers depressed her. At this point Tynan remarked that her letters revealed that she could write a good novel. So she began to write a semi-autobiographical tale about the sexual adventures of a young American girl in Paris. It flowed easily, and a casual remark by Sandy Wilson, the author of *The Boy Friend,* about dud avocados gave her the title. Since by now she had also given birth to a daughter, she found that writing, rather than acting, gave her more time to devote to their child.

Married life was still not entirely smooth. The main problem was still Tynan's devotion to whipping bottoms. On the first occasion she let him try it, she hated it so much that she seized the headmaster's cane and snapped it in two. Tynan, unaccustomed to being baulked, thereupon warned her that she could not blame him if he sought elsewhere for more obliging companions. She ignored the threat until he told her one day that he was about to be prosecuted for sending obscenities through the mail. It seemed that, through the personal column of a porn magazine purchased in Soho, he had begun exchanging fantasies with another sado-masochist. It proved to be a man, and not, as he thought, a woman, but this proved to be irrelevant when the Post Office opened the mail and talked of prosecution. His lawyer advised him to flee the country for a few weeks and he went to stay with friends in Spain until it blew over.

Elaine was shocked as she realised that S/M was not, as he had assured her in a casual admission before their marriage, a taste he had put behind him, but remained a powerful obsession. She accompanied him to Spain, and went on with *The Dud Avocado.* But the sexual disparity remained and finally soured their marriage. She wrote in her autobiography, *Life Itself,* 'Ken had . . . developed a deadening coldness.'

Tynan introduced her to Spencer Curtis-Brown, his own literary agent, who read her first three chapters and was enthusiastic. He asked her if she had any ideas about a publisher, and she said immediately 'Victor Gollancz', because he had published *Lucky Jim.*

Gollancz saw at once that she could write, and said that he would accept it on two conditions: if she called herself Elaine Tynan, and if she changed the title. Feeling secure with the backing of her husband, she said no to both, and Gollancz finally agreed.

To counterbalance this good news, Tynan announced his intention of going to Spain for two weeks with an actress called Carol Grace, who fascinated him. It was the only way, he said, to get her out of his system. Elaine was shocked, and told him that if he carried out his threat, she would divorce him. When he left for Spain on 20 July 1957 – two days after she had signed the contract with Gollancz – she went to a female divorce lawyer. When she and the lawyer returned to the flat after Tynan had left, she found no less than fifteen notes taped to the furniture, begging her not to leave him, and declaring that life without her would be absolute darkness.

She – and her lawyer – were baffled. If the prospect of losing her upset him so much, why was he deserting her for another woman?

If she had known anything about the psychology of the Right Man, as explored by Van Vogt, all would have been clear. By leaving him, she had attacked the foundation of his little sandcastle of illusion, in which he regards himself as the supreme master, like a sultan with his harem. He may sink into emotional collapse, or even commit suicide.

So Tynan's behaviour was typical. Mentally he had transformed the situation into one in which *he* is the one who is being deserted. It made no difference that this was outrageously untrue. The Right Man is a spoilt child who transforms reality to suit himself.

Sartre had once described this syndrome as 'magical thinking'. This is a strange and interesting exercise in self-deception, in which people convince themselves of a piece of wishful thinking which they know to be untrue; clearly it is a mild form of insanity, and Tynan suffered from it all his life. This explains, for example, his abandonment of his mother Rose after his father's death in 1948: this perfectly ordinary middle-class person was an embarrassment for this young disciple of Oscar Wilde, and he firmly turned his back on her. Finally, as his second wife, Kathleen Tynan, admits in *The Life of Kenneth Tynan*, 'extreme loneliness and self-effacing shyness began to take its toll', and she slowly went insane. Even Osborne's treatment of his mother was not as ruthless and heartless as this. But at least Tynan was open enough to write with bitter honesty: 'I could have postponed her death at the expense of my own absorption in self-advancement.'

Two days after Tynan had departed to Spain with his mistress, Elaine gave a party, to celebrate her book contract and her divorce. Among those present was the BBC political analyst Robert Kee, to whom she was deeply attracted, and he invited her out the next night. But early that morning the phone rang, and it was Tynan, who had just been caught in bed in flagrante by the detective Elaine had hired to get proof of adultery. He pleaded with her not to divorce him and she gave in. He said he would be on the next flight back. So her fling with Robert Kee had to be cancelled.

The Dud Avocado came out in January 1958 and became a bestseller. Typically, Tynan resented its success. Becoming a bestseller was competing with him.

Inadvertently, I added fuel to the flames. After the clash following Stuart Holroyd's play at the Royal Court I wrote to him suggesting a cessation of the hostilities that had been going on ever since *The Outsider* came out, since I certainly had nothing against him personally. I received a reply saying that he felt as astonished as Eisenhower would have done if Khrushchev had suddenly made peace overtures, and agreeing to give it a try. I can no longer recall what I replied, except that in a postscript I said how much I had enjoyed *The Dud Avocado*, and asking him to congratulate his wife on my behalf. I got no reply, and can now understand why. Elaine quotes him as saying: 'If you ever write another book I'll divorce you.'

In September 1958 Tynan was asked to become drama critic of the *New Yorker,* to replace the recently deceased Wolcott Gibbs. He and his family moved to America in November to find that *The Dud Avocado* had been on the bestseller list since July, and everyone they met at parties had read it.

As a theatre critic, Tynan made a good start by savaging Archibald Macleish's immensely popular *JB*, based on the Book of Job – his reaction was predictable since he detested religion – and being equally acerbic about Rodgers and Hammerstein's *Flower Drum Song* on the grounds that the sickeningly sweet native girls amounted to plagiarism from their own *South Pacific*. But finding enough biting things to say about other plays must have been harder than he expected, since this was an exceptionally dull season, with a high percentage of 'turkeys', such as a musical version of *Pride and Prejudice*. Broadway was as full of its own equivalent of Loamshire as London had been in 1955, and we may infer that he became tired of kicking the sawdust out of rag dolls from the fact that he included so few of his *New Yorker* reviews in his collection *Curtains*.

But America was an ideal place for what Elaine called his 'social game-hunting', the obsessive desire to meet – and if possible be photographed with – celebrities. New Yorkers did it all the time. 'Every morning, everyone in New York talked on the phone to everyone about the parties they'd been to the night before.'

A perfect opportunity for game-hunting came in March 1959 when Tynan was sent to Cuba to report on the Castro revolution, only three months old. He wrote to ask Hemingway, whom he had met in Madrid, if he could interview him, and received a positive reply. On the day before the interview he recognised Tennessee Williams drinking alone in the bar of his hotel in Havana, and approached him with some trepidation, since he had recently given a bad review to his *Sweet Bird of Youth,* but Williams proved forgiving – and was probably lonely – and they began to drink together. Tynan suggested that Williams should come with him to see Hemingway, and when Williams hesitated – since Hemingway had a reputation for disliking homosexuals – he went to the phone and verified that Hemingway had no objection.

At first the meeting went badly, as Hemingway snubbed Williams on the subject of honour among men. 'What kind of men did you have in mind?' asked Hemingway with what appeared to be a touch of homophobia. But when Tynan returned from the lavatory he found the writers engaged in a discussion on the relative merits of the liver and the kidneys. Williams subsequently accompanied Tynan to meet Castro, and was gratified to learn that the dictator admired his plays, particularly the one about the cat that was upon the burning roof.

Hemingway, it becomes very clear, was as self-obsessed as Tynan, and just as much of a magical thinker. In *Life Itself* Elaine Tynan describes how, at a lunch party in Malaga, Hemingway sat at the centre of a long table 'and held court', which meant he talked non-stop and expected silence from the sixteen other guests. When coffee came, George Plimpton (who was the host) rearranged the guests, and before placing Elaine next to Hemingway, whispered to her that if he called her 'daughter', she was 'in', and must then address him as 'Papa'. She felt momentarily rebellious, but 'when he called me daughter, I responded with a blissful, "Yes, Papa".'

Tynan, however, transgressed the rule that Hemingway had to be treated as a godlike authority. Sitting among a group of aficionados discussing a particular matador, whose kill Hemingway was praising, Tynan was heard to remark that on the evidence of *his* eyes, the kill was three inches off. 'I advise you Tynan,' said Hemingway sternly, 'to take your fucking eyes and stick them up your fucking ass.'

The next day, when Tynan and Elaine were seated in a bar after the bullfight, Hemingway approached them and asked her if she had appreciated the kill that afternoon. 'Yes, Papa,' she replied meekly. Then Hemingway turned to Tynan and said gruffly: 'Sorry about last night – too much vino.' 'Thank you, Papa,' said Tynan, taking the proffered hand. And when Hemingway had walked away, he said in tones of awe: 'I've been apologised to by a Nobel Prize winner.'

What had happened, of course, was that Tynan had also apologised by doing the required obeisance, and had therefore been forgiven. But it is typical of Tynan, the social big-game hunter, that what really impressed him was being apologised to by a Nobel Prize winner.

We can also see why Hemingway deteriorated as a writer in those last years. He was suffering from the same problem as Ibsen and John Braine: trapped inside a rigid alter-ego he had created to protect him from the world and from criticism, he was fighting for air. And because he had become too obsessed by how he appeared to other people, he turned into a caricature of himself.

Tynan himself was suffering from a version of this malady – the need to prop his self-esteem through social interaction. On a later occasion, Elaine caused her husband shock and distress by declining to go back to see Hemingway on the grounds that she was sick of social game-hunting and hanging around Big Personalities.

As usual, he responded by reverting to the spoilt child. 'My refusal devastated him, made him cry.' Tynan claimed that two of his articles had recently been turned down because the editors said they were half-hearted. That, he said accusingly, was because Elaine was no longer with him.

There may have been an element of truth in this. But was it because he was so deeply in love? Or was it simply the terror felt by the Right Man when his unassuming doormat rises off the floor like a magic carpet and threatens to sail out of the window, leaving him a prey to his inner world of self-doubt?

It was by now obvious that their marriage was no longer a happy one. Back in London, Tennessee Williams asked her why Ken was not with her, and she explained: 'It was a pattern . . . Ken would go off somewhere and after a while cables would plead with me to join him. Whenever I did so the fights would start at the airport.' Tynan was simply a person who did not know his own mind.

> . . . I had known for a long time that it was essential for Ken always to be at the apex of a love triangle consisting of a husband, his wife and a mistress. Since I, as his wife, was not fulfilling his requirements as a partner [i.e., unwilling to be flogged] he needed a mistress, went his thinking, but somehow the more he was with her, the more she became his wife – and I the desired mistress. What I also suspected was his growing need for me not only as part of a triangle but as a victim.

In other words, it was essential for Tynan's self-respect to see himself as the dominant one, beating the bare behind of a recumbent girl. Hemingway found his required sense of dominance by flinging his weight around and making women call him Papa. Since this was out of the question for Tynan, he had to achieve it by play-acting domination with a willing partner. This play-acting would become an increasingly important part of his life.

Persuaded to join her husband in Malaga by Tennessee Williams, she quickly recognised her mistake. He had already acquired himself another mistress.

Elaine's reaction was to go off with a Scottish laird named Peter, in whose bed she spent the night. When she returned to her own hotel that afternoon she found a thick envelope awaiting her at the desk, 'pages of professions of love followed by pages of accusations mixed with threats to kill himself . . .'

That night Tynan assaulted her and broke her nose, leaving her unconscious, with two black eyes, on the bathroom floor. Back in London, Tynan agreed to divorce in Mexico, where rules were slacker.

Tynan had returned to writing theatre criticism for the *Observer* in May 1960, and felt some disappointment that the world of the theatre had changed so little. He had enthused over Wesker's trilogy, and *The Kitchen*. Harold Pinter's *The Caretaker* announced the arrival of an important new talent (the earlier *Birthday Party* had failed to make an impact), although Tynan was uneasy at the threats of 'absurdism' in his work, and detected signs of paranoia in its mood of indefinable menace. *The Visit* by the Swiss dramatist Friedrich Dürrenmatt revealed that 'absurdism' could also have a disturbing moral dimension.

Bernard Miles's production of Brecht's *Galileo* probably inspired Osborne with the idea of *Luther*. Yet what was perfectly clear was that what Tynan's biographer Dominic Shellard calls 'the big bang theory', in *Kenneth Tynan, A Life*, that after *Look Back in Anger* everything had changed – was incorrect. Loamshire was as comfortably established as ever.

In the autumn of 1961, Tynan was suddenly plunged into another hysteria-inducing crisis, oddly reminiscent of the 1955 crisis that had led to his dismissal from the *Evening Standard*. A volume of his selected criticisms from 1950 to 1960, under the title *Curtains,* had appeared, and Terry Kilmartin, the literary editor of the *Observer*, asked the novelist Mary McCarthy to review it. This was asking for fireworks, since Tynan had attacked her own volume of theatrical reviews in 1959.

While acknowledging Tynan's wit, she nevertheless accused him of being a lightweight critic, who relied too much on parody rather than intellectual penetration – which had been my own feeling about his review of Beckett's *Endgame* – and lacked the ability of 'rational discourse'.

Kilmartin had thought twice and gone to the trouble of commissioning a rebuttal from Alan Pryce-Jones. Even so, Tynan very nearly repeated his mistake of 1955 and threatened legal action. Most of all, of course, he felt betrayed that a friend had commissioned the offensive criticism.

In the following month, his mother Rose died in a psychiatric ward. She had been mentally unbalanced for years; as long ago as 1955, one of her few friends, a Methodist minister named Frank Thewliss, had contacted Tynan and warned him that Rose was beginning to experience mental collapse. Before that, Tynan had brought her to London only when he needed someone to babysit his daughter while he and Elaine were abroad.

Now he tried belatedly to remedy his neglect, but it was too late. He admitted later that if she had been brought to London to live with them, her breakdown could have been avoided.

Her money – a considerable amount – came to Tynan who, as if feeling guilty, spent it all as quickly as possible.

Soon after this, Tynan himself experienced a curious mental breakdown. He had been producing a television programme called *Tempo*, and to cope with the pressure was drinking heavily and taking antidepressants. He and Elaine were already experiencing those stresses that would blow their marriage apart, one of them being that she had written a play called *My Place*, which was being produced at Stratford, then in London. One Thursday evening he sat down to write his Sunday column and sent it to the *Observer*. Terry Kilmartin rang him to say it made no sense. Tynan read it, and had to agree that it seemed full of odd irrelevances, such as comments on Lord Harewood, who was also on *Tempo*, and Orson Welles. Elaine asked him if he had felt anything strange as he was writing it; he replied that he had a feeling of complete arrogance, as if anything he wrote would serve. He had done three drafts, and they simply got madder and madder. It seems oddly typical of Tynan that, even when his brain began playing him false, it went naturally into the mode that his biographer Shellard calls 'celebrity bandwagoning'.

He went to see a psychiatrist, and told friends that his problems were due to the guilt he felt about wanting to divorce Elaine. (In fact, it was she who wanted to divorce him, but magical thinking made it impossible to face this.) Soon after this he moved out to live alone.

Tynan's reviews were losing their sparkle and betraying his depression. His days as a critic were clearly numbered. At this point, the National Theatre came to his aid.

The idea of a national theatre had been around since the nineteenth century, when Matthew Arnold had pleaded for a 'Comedie Anglaise'. Shaw had championed the idea in *The Dark Lady of the Sonnets*. In 1949, the National Theatre Bill went through parliament but no further. Tynan took up the campaign in his columns, and finally, in October 1962, Laurence Olivier was appointed its director. Tynan promptly wrote to him suggesting that he should be made its literary adviser.

Olivier detested Tynan, as most theatre people did, and asked his new wife Joan Plowright 'How shall we slaughter the little bastard?' But Joan, a sweet and kindly person (whom I had met many times in the mid fifties and liked enormously), pointed out that Tynan would be a good choice, since the younger generation would appreciate his association with it. So in February 1963, against all odds, Tynan became literary manager – or 'dramaturge' – whose job was to choose and recommend plays.

The first performance was *Hamlet* with Peter O'Toole, who had recently achieved fame in the film of *Lawrence of Arabia*. O'Toole was too lightweight to make a good Hamlet, and the critics were unenthusiastic; but his fame brought in the audience.

Some of Tynan's ideas were brilliant. He approached Robert Graves, who had just been appointed professor of poetry at Oxford, to ask him to improve Shakespeare's *Much Ado About Nothing,* and Graves rose to the occasion and made a good play of it. (As Shaw had pointed out, Shakespeare himself must have thought badly of it since he gave it such a dismissive title.) The result was impressive. So was *The Recruiting Officer* by the Restoration playwright George Farquhar, presented with a distinctly Brechtian approach. He persuaded Olivier to play Othello in black makeup, and Olivier chose to add a West Indian accent, which can hardly have been Shakespeare's intention, but apparently worked. Peter Shaffer's *Royal Hunt of the Sun* was such a triumphant panorama that Bernard Levin – one of the new critics influenced by Tynan's acerbic manner – called it 'the finest new play' he had ever seen. And a powerful performance of *Mother Courage* must have seemed to Tynan a proof that he was finally achieving in the theatre the kind of thing he had been aiming at since 1950.

On the other hand, for someone as politically committed as Tynan, the job was full of potential pitfalls. It was a natural part of his temperament to goad conservatives; but the ten-man board was full of conservatives, like Binkie Beaumont, Sir Kenneth Clark and the artist Henry Moore, so he had to tread carefully. The chairman of the board, Lord Chandos, had been a member of Churchill's wartime Cabinet, and would certainly have held Tynan's political opinions in abhorrence. This meant that Tynan had to disguise his revolutionary tendencies under a cloak of erudition.

A case in point was *Spring's Awakening*, written by the German expressionist writer Frank Wedekind in 1891. Regarded as one of the same school as Strindberg, it was about adolescent sexuality: the fourteen-year-old Wendla becomes pregnant by a classmate, Melchior, and dies during an abortion. In one of the scenes a schoolboy locks himself in the toilet with a picture of a naked Venus, and fairly obviously masturbates before he drops it down the pan. The play had been staged at the Court by Devine in 1963 in a club performance, but Tynan suggested presenting a toned-down version at the National. But although the Lord Chamberlain gave permission, the board said no, and declared that in future they would supervise all decisions. There was nothing for Tynan to do but to swallow his chagrin and accept.

During his period at the National, there had been another major change in his life: a new permanent relationship. She was an attractive secretary on the *Observer*, and her name was Kathleen Gates. She was married to a businessman, and was nine years Tynan's junior, the daughter of Matthew

Halton, a famous Canadian journalist and broadcaster. By the time Tynan moved to the National, they were living together, and they married in 1967. She adored and admired him, which was the main thing he needed from a wife. When she found photographs of 'chastisement' in their Mount Street home, she was deeply shocked; and when she confronted him with it, so was he, and said they must separate immediately.

Describing the episode in her biography of Tynan, she remarks: 'I never understood how deep-seated was his wish to think well of himself and how impossible for him it was to achieve this state of ease.' But the marriage endured, and it seems that, like Elaine, Kathleen learned to play a reluctant part in his spanking games, without ceasing to regard him with the admiration he required.

This was not always easy to sustain. Kathleen tells how, shortly after they had bolted together, her husband stormed in looking for her, and Tynan took refuge behind the settee. And one night, as he was taking her back to her mother's house in Hampstead, her husband emerged from the rhododendrons waving the gardener's hoe. As the men struggled, Tynan lost a few handfuls of hair. When they finally crept out of the house, Tynan declared they were being followed, and clambered into a dustbin. Kathleen reports that when he emerged, she was unable to find the right words of sympathy.

Yet Tynan could occasionally summon decisiveness. When he returned to Mount Street one night and found the semi-estranged Elaine in the kitchen with a man who was naked except for a tie, he sensed that the lover was a wet – in fact, he was a poet and BBC producer – and dived into the bedroom, seized his clothes and threw them down the lift shaft. The poet had to borrow a mac and his cab fare to get home.

In December of 1965, Tynan further alienated the directors of the National Theatre by what seemed to be a calculated act of exhibitionism. In a late-night television programme called BBC 3, asked if sexual intercourse could ever be presented on stage, he replied: 'Oh, I think so. I doubt whether there are very many rational people in the world to whom the word "fuck" is particularly diabolical . . .' The furore was tremendous; Mary Whitehouse said he needed spanking, and after that, Tynan found himself virtually banned from television.

The image of Tynan irredeemably obsessed by sex was reinforced by his next venture. In June 1966 he was approached by a producer who had been struck by Tynan's comment that sex and blasphemy should be explored on the stage, and asked him to think how this might be done. Inspired by a French painting of a naked odalisque lying on her side and exposing her rounded buttocks, Tynan had the inspiration for a 'classily erotic' show, which he decided to name after the painting as *Oh Calcutta!*, a pun on the words *Oh quel cul tu as* ('oh what a bum you have').

After many vicissitudes that brought him close to hysteria, it opened in New York on 19 June 1969, was a tremendous hit that ran for three years, and world productions grossed £360,000,000. But Tynan had signed a contract giving him only one per cent of the takings, he would receive only about a quarter of a million dollars which, spread over many years, was less of a fortune than it sounds. Paul Johnson, whose portrait of Tynan in *Intellectuals* is generally hostile, admits that at least Tynan was not greedy.

At the National, his next major clash with the board would cost him money as well as prestige. The German dramatist, Rolf Hochhuth, was writing a play called *Soldiers*, about Britain's saturation bombing of Germany towards the end of the Second World War. Tynan talked Olivier into doing it. But a secondary theme of the play was the death in 1943 of General Wladyslaw Sikorski, head of the Polish government in exile, in a plane crash, in which only the pilot survived. Hochhuth thought he had uncovered information suggesting that it was actually an assassination arranged by Churchill, the motive being that he wanted to break his agreement with Sikorski to keep Poland intact after the war, and instead to give half of it to Stalin.

Tynan lobbied hard to get the play presented at the National although he knew this would involve the resignation of Lord Chandos. As was inevitable, the board turned it down.

Tynan pressed on with his plan, and when the Lord Chamberlain's office was abolished in 1968 – partly as a result of the clash over Osborne's *A Patriot for Me* – Tynan, in association with the impresario Michael White, was able to go ahead with a production at the New Theatre.

This received immense publicity – as Tynan had hoped – but it backfired. The pilot of the plane, Edward Prchal, sued for libel, and Tynan found himself faced with a bill for £20,000. It was a crippling blow. He decided to return to the *Observer*, not as a theatre critic, but as a regular contributor. He was still the dramaturge at the NT, and remained so until it moved into its new location on the South Bank in 1976, but this was as much for financial reasons as for personal satisfaction; the latter had been reduced to a minimum by frustration and the knowledge that only the support of Olivier prevented the board from getting rid of him. (Typically, the paranoid Tynan became convinced that even Olivier was plotting to stab him in the back, which was untrue.) And he offered them the chance in April 1969 by asking for a six-month sabbatical. He told the board: 'Last year an X-ray revealed that I was suffering from an incurable but not incapacitating lung disease called emphysema . . .'

In this condition, air sacs in the lung have become damaged, usually by heavy smoking (and Tynan had been a chain smoker all his life). The muscles of his chest were, in effect, turning into armour plating. He had first suspected this condition in 1965 when, at a birthday party, he had been the only one present who could not blow out a candle. By the 1970s he was suffering from non-stop breathlessness, and even gave up smoking for a while.

Tynan was granted three months' leave by the NT board, but on condition that on his return he would be demoted to 'consultant'.

When he retired from the NT shortly after the Queen had opened the new theatre in October 1976, his marriage as well as his health had begun to run into problems. In a diary he began in 1971 he wrote:

> Since last November I have been seeing (and spanking) a fellow spanking addict, a girl called 'Nicole'. [Real name Allison] Her fantasy — dormant until I met her – is precisely to be bent over with knickers taken down to be spanked, caned or otherwise punished, preferably with the buttocks parted to disclose the anus.

She also, he explained, enjoyed exposing and spanking him. He added that they delighted each other because their fantasies exactly corresponded – unlike his sessions with Kathleen, who obviously found these fantasy games hard.

Finally, he admitted, he had confessed to Kathleen, who had been getting increasingly anxious about his loss of interest in her. He insisted – disingenuously – that there was no competition because Nicole was like curry as compared to Kathleen's French cuisine . . .

Threesomes, he confided to the diary, were particularly enjoyable for him because he liked an audience.

10 Iris Murdoch and the Gospel of Promiscuity

Of all the writers I met around the time *The Outsider* came out, the one I liked most spontaneously was Iris Murdoch. Intellectually speaking we had much in common, since we both saw ourselves as the heirs of existentialism.

Since this is a book about literature, not philosophy, I should offer the reader a brief explanation what that means.

'Existence-philosophy' originated around the mid nineteenth century with the Danish philosopher Kierkegaard, who was protesting about the abstractness of German idealistic philosophy, particularly Hegel's, who had undertaken to explain the whole purpose of life and history. To try to guide your life according to Hegel's philosophy, said Kierkegaard, was like trying to find your way around Copenhagen with a map of Europe on which Copenhagen is the size of a pinhead. Philosophy, he argued, should look at life 'close up', not from a mile in the air. Also, being deeply religious, he wanted to bring philosophers back to a question of how to find meaning in one's own life.

By the time it reached France in the mid 1930s, existentialism had shed the religious approach in favour of atheism, for it argued that you cannot see or touch God, but must take somebody else's word for his existence – usually a priest's who, you are pretty certain, knows no better than you do. We must live, as Camus put it, 'without appeal' to some higher authority. And to live 'without appeal' is also to accept that life is fundamentally meaningless – or at least, inscrutable.

This is the form in which Iris Murdoch encountered existentialism after the war, and which she accepted as the basis of her first two novels *Under the Net* and *Flight from the Enchanter*.

I had also encountered it via Camus and Sartre. But I had a fundamental objection to their notion of living 'without appeal'. It meant assuming the universe is meaningless, and my deepest instincts rejected the idea. I realised early on that the apparent meaninglessness of life is due to the fact that we are living with our faces pressed tight against everyday reality and its 'close-upness' deprives us of meaning; but our occasional 'bird's-eye views' and Proustian *moments bienheureux* make us realise it was there all the time. So I simply rejected the Sartre–Camus pessimism as a kind of schoolboy howler.

As I look back on the Angry Young Men period, I can see that the enormous and absurd success of *The Outsider* presented an obstacle to friendship with other writers, since most of those I met were aware of the non-stop publicity about Angry Young Men, and of the large advertisements that Gollancz took every week in the *Sunday Times* announcing that the book had gone into yet another printing. Any practising writer would have had to be a saint not to feel some degree of envy. Iris was an exception in that I had met her before publication, and we had been in correspondence since then.

A few days after publication she wrote to me: 'What a splendid send-off! I'm terribly glad and congratulate you very much. That is certainly the way to become famous – young and suddenly!' Clearly, she had no idea of how catastrophically wrong she would turn out to be. And she still had no suspicion two months later – although the tide was already on the turn – when she wrote, 'To know so much (not just to have read so much) so young gives you a marvellous start – and a start is everything since it just does take so long to achieve wisdom.' She goes on to add that she is getting married soon to John Bayley.

Her tone is affectionate and protective, and I suspect that, like Angus Wilson, she felt a kind of alarm as she watched me being snatched up like a leaf in the whirlwind of vapid publicity that ensued.

I am also inclined to believe that this is why she suggested, on at least two occasions, that she should try to get me into Oxford, where she herself taught. She probably felt that, in that still centre, away from literary parties and television studios, she could steer me towards a serious literary career.

I can now see she was right. Purely as a matter of literary politics, it would have been sensible to retire into the background and to focus on getting a degree in philosophy. But since I had spent the past ten years or so educating myself, the idea seemed pointless. Besides, I wanted to get on with finishing *Ritual in the Dark*.

After meeting Iris at the party for *Flight from the Enchanter*, I lost no time in finding a copy of her first novel *Under the Net*. (In fact, her second, *Flight from the Enchanter*, had been written first.) It had been published in 1954, and had immediately caused her to be classified with Amis and Wain (and later with the Angry Young Men). It was easy enough to find because it had been chosen for the Reprint Society book club, and could be picked up in any book shop in the Charing Cross Road.

Under the Net is a picaresque novel that, like *Hurry on Down*, gives the impression of hectic forward movement and comic invention. However, the first few pages make clear how much it differs from Wain and Amis. They write as if they are anxious not to be mistaken for intellectuals. Iris's hero enjoys writing and talking about ideas – in fact, he is writing in a French rather than an English tradition, and is obviously aware of the work of Sartre, Camus and Beckett.

The narrator, Jake Donaghue, is a likeable but lazy Irishman (Iris was born in Dublin), who makes a meagre living translating the works of a popular French novelist into English, but is too lazy to do more work than will keep him from starving. And since he is also too lazy to offer his girlfriend – who is also his landlady – any emotional security, he learns on returning from a trip to Paris that he has been superseded and has nowhere to lay his head. For the remainder of the novel he drifts amiably around London, apparently quite contented to be rootless.

The centre of gravity of the novel is a philosopher named Hugo Belfounder, based upon Iris's friend Yorick Smythies, who had been a pupil and friend of Ludwig Wittgenstein. The latter had died in 1951, and his enigmatic and obsessive personality had rubbed off on his disciples. Wittgenstein had been tormented into living like a monk by his guilt about his homosexuality, and the asceticism with which he punished himself led him to create a bleak, rationalistic philosophy that became the foundation of logical positivism.

Smythies, who was not homosexual, but still managed to live a fairly chaotic love live divided between two women, had taken over from Wittgenstein the view that language can only express falsehood. In *Iris Murdoch, A Life*, Peter J Conradi speaks of his 'absolute and exhilarating seriousness'. Iris, who had had many lovers, and describes herself as 'emotionally promiscuous', tended to look up to Smythies as a kind of guru and role model. On the other hand, her views were a thousand miles from Wittgenstein's reductionism and intellectual masochism, and she came to regard him as 'demonic'.

The novel's title, *Under the Net,* is also an image from Wittgenstein, envisaging a kind of transparent graph paper that we place over reality, in order to be able to impose some kind of order on it – what lies 'under the net' would otherwise be an unnavigable confusion. This view reflects her early existentialist preoccupation with living 'without appeal'.

Hugo Belfounder, a pacifist who has inherited an armaments factory, finds that he becomes increasingly wealthy against his will, so that even when he enters the film industry in a spirit of amateurism, he succeeds in becoming a film magnate. He and Jake Donaghue had met when subjecting themselves to experiments at a cold-cure establishment, and out of their non-stop conversation, Donaghue had constructed a kind of Platonic dialogue which, reluctantly, he allows someone to publish. Filled with guilt at what he considered his betrayal, he broke with Hugo – only to discover, years later, that when Hugo read it, he did not even recognise himself as its source, and envied his friend's brilliance.

Jake is also involved with two sisters, Anna and Sadie, one a singer, one an actress. Anna is in love with Hugo, who in turn is in love with Sadie, who is in love with Jake – the kind of emotional tangle Iris loved to spin, and came to specialise in.

The absurd and headlong plot involves a drunken pub crawl, kidnapping a canine film star, getting involved in a political brawl that wrecks a film set, and obeying a summons to Paris by his former girlfriend, who wants him to write film scripts at an enormous salary, an offer he rejects apparently out of a kind of Wittgensteinian masochism.

Back in London he takes a job as a hospital orderly, and is there when Hugo is brought in suffering from concussion after a political brawl. He breaks into the hospital by night to talk to Hugo, and there ensues a long dialogue which is obviously meant to be the heart of the novel, in which Hugo tells Jake that he intends to abandon his wealth to apprentice himself to a watchmaker in Nottingham.

In helping Hugo escape from the hospital, Jake is recognised by a fellow employee, thus burning his boats. And at the end of the novel, he pays out the few hundred pounds he has succeeded in accumulating during his wild adventures in exchange for the kidnapped dog – which he now knows to be too old to work – and so ends as broke as he began.

Even so, the book ends on a positive note. Jake calls on his friend Mrs Tinckham, who runs a newspaper shop in Soho, and her cat has just given birth to kittens. She asks him why two are tabby and two are Siamese, and Jake admits he doesn't know: 'It's just one of the wonders of the world.' Human existence may be meaningless, but while cats give birth to different types of kittens, the world must be regarded as absurd but delightful.

All is not as casual as it sounds. The book is dedicated to the novelist and poet Raymond Queneau, who preferred to write in the Parisian argot of working-class, unsophisticated characters, like the youthful drifter Pierrot of *Pierrot Mon Ami*, while an early reference to Beckett's down-and-out hero in *Murphy*, who protests against the meaninglessness of life by spending hours naked in a rocking chair, hints that Jake's refusal to take life seriously may rest upon existentialist foundations.

Pierrot is undoubtedly the more important of the two influences – in fact, it is hard not to believe that if Iris had realised the implications of *Murphy*, with its underlying world rejection, she would have questioned it on purely philosophical grounds. (But then, at that time the cheerful vitality of *Godot* had convinced most intellectuals that negation was a valid philosophical position.) The first thing that strikes the reader of *Pierrot* is its slapstick and sheer joy in being alive – the feeling that also pervades *Under the Net*.

It seems that Iris saw the latter as a philosophical statement about life and morality. On this level it fails, simply because the mad confusion of plot and incident leaves the reader too breathless to look for deeper meanings. Neither does it succeed in making clear what the author finds so impressive about Hugo Belfounder; here her novelist's instinct fails her, and we have to take her word for it that he is somehow the most important character in the book.

When I met Iris at the party at Gwenda David's in March 1956, I was also introduced to the writer Elias Canetti, who lived opposite – a bushy-haired middle-aged man with a walrus moustache, horn-rimmed glasses and a strong mid-European accent. As with Iris, there was instant mutual liking and sympathy. I loved German literature and music, and this cultured Viennese had known Musil, Thomas Mann, Hermann Broch and James Joyce, and I think he was pleasantly surprised to discover an English writer who was so familiar with European literature. I had no doubt that he and I were meant to become friends.

What I did not know, until many years later, was that Canetti was Iris's lover – like the slimly built Oxford professor John Bayley, who was also at the same party – and that there was considerable emotional tension since Canetti was of a jealous disposition and was meeting his rival for the first time. Neither, of course, was I aware that Canetti was a central character in her novel *Flight from the Enchanter* – in fact, was the enchanter himself. That evening – I later learned from Conradi's biography – Canetti more or less gave his blessing to the couple, telling Bayley, 'I like you' although, typically, he took offence when Iris left the party with Bayley, and thereafter refused to take her phone calls.

Iris had met Canetti through Franz Steiner, a Czech anthropologist and poet, to whom she had become engaged in 1952, when she was 31, he 41. He died later that year of heart disease, and Iris then turned for comfort to his charismatic friend Canetti, who lost no time in imposing his domination.

The key to Canetti was an obsessive, overwhelming egoism, which he concealed with his central European charm. A frustrated writer – his only novel *Auto da Fé* had aroused little attention in 1935 except for being burnt by the Nazis – he took out his frustrations in power games, especially with women. His wife Veza had only one arm – one female acquaintance suggested Canetti had bitten it off – and he expected her not only to put up with his mistresses but to bring tea after he had finished love-making.

He told me that the book he was now working on was – typically – about crowds and power.

Iris undoubtedly had a masochistic streak, and was inclined to admire strong-willed men. The gentle and intelligent John Bayley, who stammered, was an exception who must have appealed to her as a pleasant change. (He describes in his book *Iris* how they liked 'being children together'.) Canetti had ordered her not to sleep with Bayley, and she apparently obeyed.

Like *Under the Net*, *Flight from the Enchanter* centres around a guru figure, a film magnate, although, unlike Canetti, Misha Fox is wealthy. It also, like *Under the Net*, has an air of hectic improvisation. But this time the teenage girl Annette, who starts the action of running away from finishing school and swinging on a chandelier, is only one of many characters, and the book suffers from this lack of a central figure and an organised plot. Rosa Keepe, the nearest thing to a heroine, is an incorrigible fantasist, and the mistress of two Polish brothers – one of the first of Iris's characters to signal her central obsession with sex. Misha Fox, although he influences most of the characters, tends to remain in the background, for Iris was apparently anxious to dwell only on Canetti's pleasant side, and not on his ruthlessness and cruelty. The unpleasant side of Canetti is given to his henchman Calvin Blick, who serves as the villain.

Although entertaining and often funny, *Flight from the Enchanter* is even less of a unity than *Under the Net*, which is at least given a certain air of focus by the narrator hero.

About two months after Gwenda's party, *The Outsider* came out. Before this, I had told my publisher Victor Gollancz that I had met Canetti, and that we had liked one another, and Gollancz immediately asked me if I could persuade Canetti to review it somewhere. Dutifully, I wrote to Canetti, and received back a letter from Veza, telling me coldly that Mr Canetti *never* reviewed books. And although I replied apologetically, I somehow sensed that I would never again hear from Canetti. In retrospect I can see why. Canetti liked to see himself as the great European writer living in exile among fools who failed to appreciate him. The success of *The Outsider* must have galled him.

I failed to recognise this at the time, and felt slightly hurt by the way he had dropped me. But I subsequently came to know well another member of this circle, the novelist Rudolf Nassauer, whose first novel *The Hooligan* (1960) had been sent to me by its publisher, and whose dust-jacket contained glowing comments by Iris Murdoch, Canetti and Angus Wilson; Rudi told me that Canetti was totally dismissive about me. Nassauer, like Iris, was one of the group of disciples who regarded Canetti as a master.

Written in a classically precise style that owes something to Stendhal and Merimée, *The Hooligan* is a Dostoevskian study of the persecution of the Jews by the Nazis. His second novel *The Cuckoo* (1962) is just as well written, but I found it disappointing, since it struck me as too obviously personal, describing an affair between the narrator's wife and a brash American. It was impossible not to feel that it was written as an act of revenge.

Nassauer himself did not choose to enlighten me about the events that lay behind it, but I finally learned about them from Conradi's biography, when he tells how a young Bostonian, Allan Forbes, had arrived in

London after his mistress – and Canetti's ex – had died in his arms. To solace him, Canetti 'choreographed an affair' between Forbes and Nassauer's wife Bernice (who later became the novelist Bernice Rubens). This seemed typical of the 'Misha Fox' kind of behaviour Iris portrays in *Flight from the Enchanter*. Yet so great was Canetti's power over his disciples that Rudi's loyalty was unwavering, and remained so until, after Canetti was given the Nobel Prize in 1981, he found that the *maître* had become even more intolerably self-opinionated, and turned as bitter and critical as he had been formerly enslaved.

I borrowed Gwenda David's copy of *Auto da Fé,* which had been out of print for nine years. I found it both humorous (something I did not expect from Canetti) and impressive. Its hero, Professor Peter Kien, distinguished sinologist and obsessive book collector, even goes for walks with his briefcase full of books under his arm. I sympathised; I had been an obsessive book collector all my life. But as I read on, disappointment set in. The professor marries his scheming housekeeper Therese because she seems to treat books with such respect, and the chapter in which he holds a dialogue with Confucius and is persuaded by his aphorisms to offer Therese his hand is the most amusing in the book.

But pessimism and angst soon take over, and the novel becomes so claustrophobic that I had to force myself to go on. And the final chapter in which Kien piles up his books to the ceiling and then immolates himself is too melodramatic to convince. 'When the flames reached him at last, he laughed out loud, louder than he had ever laughed in his life.' That is absurd – a man with flames licking around his legs coughs, chokes and screams, and if he is still determined to kill himself, would go and jump in the river. Canetti is so determined to symbolise old Europe going up in flames that he abandons all realism, and in doing so, makes the reader aware that the whole novel is little more than the fantasy of a man who lives inside his own head.

As soon as his book, *Crowds and Power,* came out in 1962, I bought a copy, anxious to read this work that he regarded as his masterpiece. The result was again disappointment. This was not the well-formulated thesis I had expected – it read more like a series of notes on crowds and power accumulated over the years. It did not even have an index, and consisted of a series of short sections like separate essays. What seemed quite clear is that the reason it had taken Canetti so long is that he was simply unable to organise his ideas into a book. Like *Auto da Fé,* it failed to make a convincing unity.

Since Iris lived in Oxford (where she taught at St Anne's) and I in London, we were unlikely to bump into one another at literary parties. But a letter from her of 13 May – a fortnight before publication of *The Outsider* – refers to Chepstow Villas and mentions that 'I much enjoyed that evening with you and Bill', an occasion I have forgotten.

When I was invited to lecture at St Anne's, I accepted with pleasure. I took Bill with me, since he was eager to view a whole college full of girls. We had an interesting time, but saw rather less of Iris than I had hoped, since we spent most of the time with the professor who had invited me. But by then I had read enough of *Under the Net* to know that Iris had a taste for pub crawling, and so before I left, offered to take her to see some of the 'rough' Irish pubs at the bottom end of London's Edgware Road. An undated note from her family home in Chiswick tells me to expect her on Wednesday evening at five, and says she was 'looking forward to seeing you, Bill and cider'.

But Bill, I seem to recall, was working at the *New York Times* that evening, and in the event, it was Stuart Holroyd who came with us. Edgware Road was only a short bus ride from my flat in Notting Hill, and we went to a series of Irish pubs in succession, saving the roughest for the last. It was there that a gaunt old Irishwoman staggered past our table, stopped to peer at Stuart, whose good looks obviously impressed her, then raised her umbrella and poked him in the genital region, asking: 'Ish it a boy or a girl?'

I had been told that it was possible to buy 'red biddy' in this pub, which I understood to be a drink made from cheap red wine and methylated spirit which, like absinthe, was reputed to drive long-term drinkers insane. But when I asked about this, I was offered a bottle of a red-coloured ale which had a distinctly herbal taste, and which I was told was flavoured with bog myrtle. We were not tempted to try more than one.

I can no longer recall what we talked about, except that it was certainly not philosophy. And, unsurprisingly, I cannot recall how that evening ended.

When I moved to Cornwall in 1957 there were no more opportunities of seeing Iris. But we met once more by chance in the quadrangle of an Oxford College in about 1960.

I had gone, I think, on some journalistic assignment to interview philosophers for a Sunday supplement, and was on my way to see either Geoffrey Warnock or Stuart Hampshire. Once again I experienced the sense of enormous pleasure I always felt on seeing Iris, and regretted that we did not have a chance to see more of one another. My first novel *Ritual in the Dark* had been recently published, and I was able to tell her the film director Bryuan Forbes had inquired about taking an option. Unfortunately this came to nothing. (Iris had a similar experience when *Under the Net* was optioned in 1962.) And this was to be the last time I would see Iris.

But I continued to follow her literary career with interest, and bought her books whenever I saw them in book shops, until I had a dozen or so. I must admit that I finally began to find her sheer productivity disconcerting.

After her first two novels, it became clear that she felt the need to change direction. *Under the Net* and *Flight From the Enchanter* have an existentialist flavour because the writer seemed to accept the Sartrian premise that we are living in a world whose moral values are our own creation, in which the individual must rely on his own conscience and judgement. We are, says Sartre, 'contingent' – that, trapped in the present, in a continual flux of events, there is no way in which man can see himself as 'necessary'. Like the narrator of T S Eliot's 'Portrait of a Lady', we find ourselves repeatedly 'not knowing what to feel or if [we] understand'.

But it was clear that, as Iris approached the age of 40 (she was 37 when I met her), she was beginning to feel dissatisfied with the bleakness of the existentialist landscape. The word 'existentialism' suggests a philosophy that accepts everyday human existence as its foundation, and that refuses, in the name of honesty, to go beyond it. But as the last pages of *Under the Net* make clear, Iris had come to feel that everyday human existence, the world of other people – and even of dogs and cats – can show us the way out of the cul-de-sac. Little by little, she was becoming increasingly preoccupied with morality, and with the nature of goodness. Now the quest was on to find a way of expressing that sense of some 'other reality'.

In fact, she does not exchange the free-floating morality of existentialism for the ordinary realism of novelists like E M Forster or Angus Wilson, but for her own peculiar brand of 'magic realism', which makes its first appearance in *The Sandcastle* in 1957.

Magic realism has been defined as a literary genre in which magic elements appear in an otherwise realistic setting, and in *The Sandcastle*, these 'magical' elements take some time to emerge. But when they do, it becomes clear that the novelist is rejecting the quotidian reality that normal people take for granted, and setting out to create her own kind of reality.

Bill Mor, Latin master at a minor public school, finds himself in middle age trapped in a marriage to an irritatingly strong-minded wife, and in a life that has become increasingly stultifying. Then Rain Carter, a girl half his age comes to the school to paint a portrait of the retired headmaster, and as they are thrown together, he is slightly puzzled to find that he is falling in love.

The 'other reality' begins to obtrude in the person of Mor's teenage son and daughter. Felicity is psychic. When she goes on walks, the Mor's dog – which has been dead for two years – accompanies her. And she takes for granted occasional glimpses of a shape-shifting spirit she calls Angus, who is also visible to her brother.

Accidentally, the brother and sister discover a letter their father has written to Rain, admitting he has not told his wife the whole truth about their afternoon together, and they have soon sniffed out the love affair. To prevent her father abandoning the family, Felicity performs a witchcraft ceremony involving the tarot and a fetish figure of Rain Carter. The magic works, and the affair comes to an end with Rain's sudden departure. But at least the strong-minded wife has realised that giving way to Mor's desire to stand for parliament – which she has so far opposed – is the only way to save their marriage.

The Sandcastle is a pivotal work in that it enabled Iris to make a complete change of direction. The interwoven stories of *Flight from the Enchanter* revealed her gift as a storyteller, yet the reader feels that they have somehow failed to cohere. Now, by deliberately narrowing her canvas, she creates a unity, and by introducing the supernatural, she skilfully avoids being labelled a realist.

In her next novel, *The Bell* (1958), she builds upon the right she has established in *The Sandcastle* to assume 'another reality'. Michael Meade, its central male character, is a homosexual teacher who possesses a genuine religious vocation, and who is driven by a craving for a life of prayer and contemplation. But his desire to become a priest is frustrated after a sexual relation with a teenage pupil goes wrong and he is 'exposed'. Then he is presented with a second opportunity. He has inherited a fourteenth-century manor house called Imber, which is in the same grounds as a nunnery, and the abbess persuades him to turn it into a lay community. This is exactly the kind of life he has dreamed about.

The female protagonist, Dora, is married to an art historian who bullies and intimidates her. She has left him, but as the novel opens, has decided to return, and to join him at Imber, where he is researching manuscripts. Toby, a good-looking Oxford undergraduate, is strongly attracted to her. Unfortunately, Michael is also attracted to Toby, and it is when he gives Toby an innocent and spontaneous kiss that he inaugurates the chain of disasters that will bring the community to an end.

The story centres around the arrival of a new bell. According to legend, the old one is lying at the bottom of a lake, after it flew from its tower when a young man was killed trying to climb into a nun's bedroom. Toby, diving in the lake, comes upon the old bell, and tells Dora about it. She immediately conceives the idea of galvanising the community with a 'miracle'. When the nuns unveil the new bell, they will discover the old bell in its place. With the aid of Toby and a tractor, the old bell is recovered from the lake and concealed in a barn.

It all turns out disastrously. The villain is a drunken ne'er-do-well named Nick, who many years ago was the schoolboy who caused Michael's downfall. He is at Imber to see his neurotic twin sister Catherine take the veil. When Toby tells him about the kiss, the jealous Nick persuades him to confess to the administrator, who promptly resigns.

The inauguration of the bell turns into a comic disaster when, sabotaged by Nick, it again falls into the lake. Dora, who regards her scheme as the source of all these misfortunes, decides once more to abandon her husband and take a job far from London. Nick commits suicide, leaving Michael devastated and once again cast out upon a world in which he long ago ceased to feel at home.

The most powerful impression conveyed by the novel is of the author's insight into religion. Iris is on record as saying that she was an atheist, and no doubt she would have insisted that this remained true, in the sense of rejecting the God of the Bible. But in the sense that Jung meant when he said 'the soul possesses a religious function', she is obviously not an atheist. She has clearly undergone a major conversion since the days of *Under the Net*.

Even so, it is doubtful whether the bell itself is intended as a religious symbol; in fact, it is hard to decide just what it is supposed to symbolise, although it certainly seems to be associated with sex. It originally flew into the lake to signify its disapproval of the licentious nun. When the naked Toby drags it out of the lake, he flings himself exuberantly on Dora, and in the course of their embraces, they cause the clapper to strike the bell and wake everybody up. Earlier in the novel, Michael has a premonitory dream of being awakened by the sound of the bell – perhaps in anticipation of his own downfall through sex. Although sex had been a recurrent theme in the early novels, *The Bell* is the first in which it takes a central place. And it would continue to do so from now on.

Now according to her biographers, Iris had always been prone to love affairs, both heterosexual and homosexual, and after her marriage, to adultery. She was as preoccupied with sex as Amis.

Which explains why Yorick Smythies, the original of Hugo Belfounder, described her next novel as 'foul'. *A Severed Head* was published in 1961 – the three years that had elapsed since *The Bell* being the longest gap between novels so far. Conradi records that Iris was 'nauseated' by the praise received by *The Bell*, which left her feeling 'sunk in a sort of mush of insincerity and imprecise thinking and facile success'. She added: 'If only I could see how to get . . . out of the second class and into the first.' Ironically, this three-year effort produced her most 'facile success' so far.

The novel could as easily have been entitled *Change Partners*, for this seems to be the main activity of its six leading characters. Martin Lynch-Gibbon, a 41-year-old wine merchant, is having an affair with Georgie Hands, a young lecturer at LSE who adores him and would like to marry him, but knows he would never desert his wife, Antonia. The latter, a rather overpowering socialite, takes her husband for granted and treats him with casual selfishness, just as Martin does Georgie.

When Martin gets home from an afternoon in Georgie's bed, Antonia tells him that she is in love with her American psychiatrist, Palmer Anderson, and intends to leave him for Palmer. Oddly enough, her husband takes this very well, telling her that he is a little in love with Palmer himself, and is therefore quite prepared to tolerate a *ménage à trois*. Antonia, however, is not willing to accept this obviously convenient solution, which would relieve his guilt about his own infidelity (of which, of course, she is unaware).

Palmer's half-sister, Honor Klein, a 40-year-old anthropologist, arrives. She seems to regard Martin with a degree of contempt for his 'civilised' attitude to his wife's infidelity, and advises him that it would be quite easy to get Antonia back if he tried behaving normally. He declines, being quite content with the present situation. But when Honor finds out about his affair with Georgie, she loses no time in telling on him. The result is that Antonia and her lover feel aggrieved. Antonia now demands to be introduced to Georgie, and Martin does so reluctantly. Palmer obviously finds Georgie attractive, and we sense another exchange of beds is imminent.

In this tangle of infidelities, there is another odd twist. When Martin calls on Honor Klein, he walks into the bedroom to find Honor half naked in bed, and her brother pulling on his clothes. They, it seems, are also lovers.

Another character now enters this overcrowded scenario – Martin's brother Alexander, a sculptor, whom Georgie has always wanted to meet. When Martin goes to call on Georgie, he finds Alexander already there – he and Georgie have finally met socially (through Honor's machinations), and she has invited him back for coffee. Martin senses impending betrayal, which proves correct when Alexander later rings up to tell him that he and Georgie have decided to marry.

Antonia decides to return to her husband – but has only just done so when she learns about Alexander's engagement to Georgie. For reasons not immediately clear to the reader, she is shocked and angry – we discover why later, when it is revealed that she has long been having an affair with her husband's brother.

Just as there seems no room for further complications, Georgie attempts suicide – her engagement to Alexander seems to have been a ploy to get Martin back – cuts off all her hair, and goes to Palmer for psychoanalysis; naturally, they end by having an affair and going to America together. Antonia finally decides to leave Martin and go away with Alexander. And in the final scene, as if to tidy up the loose ends, Martin and Honor Klein look speculatively at one another and we can guess what they are thinking.

Soon after the novel's publication, Iris decided to turn it into a play, and showed the result to J B Priestley. Priestley, then 68, pointed out its imperfections and re wrote it. One year later, in June 1963, it opened at the Criterion Theatre, and ran for 1,111 performances.

It is not hard to see why Yorick Smythies described *A Severed Head* as 'foul'. This kind of bed-hopping hardly satisfies Wittgensteinian standards of seriousness. What Iris appears to be saying is that there is nothing wrong with adultery, and everybody ought to try it.

What puzzled me was that Murdoch novels had always contained symbols of some 'other reality', seen most clearly in the supernatural overtones of *The Sandcastle*, but I found this hard to detect in *A Severed Head*.

I stumbled on a solution in Malcolm Bradbury's 1973 essay on Iris Murdoch in *Possibilities: Essays on the State of the Novel* where he comments:

> . . . Miss Murdoch gives herself a very dialectical aesthetic, where the writerly task is to pass elegantly between the rocks of realism and symbolism . . . This one can see in *A Severed Head* . . . The novelist starts as a comic realist of social relationships . . . but we move . . . beyond this liberal theory of love as understanding, here to an account of it as morally imperative by virtue of its totemism, its violence, its irrationality.

And he goes on to speak of 'the dark gods of Honor Klein', leading us to recall that, at one point, she drives the highly civilised Martin to wrestle her to the floor and slap her. She also demonstrates her skill in symbolic violence with a Japanese ritual sword by beheading a statuette.

In other words, the answer to the question of the 'other reality' of *A Severed Head* lies in Iris's vision of sexuality itself. Whereas for Amis and Wain, sex was about male conquest, and the reader is expected to take freewheeling morality for granted, the sense of power it generates for Iris (as for Philip Larkin) is basically about 'forbiddenness'. This is why, in spite of having several mistresses, Larkin remained obsessed with pornography: reality could never compete with the intensity of that original fantasy of schoolgirls getting undressed in the dorm. So in Iris, the forbidden refuses to be translated into terms of normal sexual fulfilment. Martin is not anxious to marry Georgie because the essence of 'forbiddenness' would simply evaporate. Whereas the idea of Antonia being possessed by Palmer somehow underlines her desirability; he is even willing to serve them wine in bed. Neither is he shocked at learning that Palmer is his sister's lover. On the contrary, it makes Honor desirable, whereas before the discovery, he had regarded her with hostility. Sex is a kind of shimmering mirage that vanishes when you get close to it. Yet everyone is somehow obsessed by it.

In short, *A Severed Head* is about sexual underprivilege.

Now Bradbury's phrase about the dark gods evokes echoes of D H Lawrence and *The Plumed Serpent,* which at first seem inappropriate in view of Lawrence's known attitude to promiscuity. But this is to overlook the little-known fact that Lawrence himself went through a period when he preached promiscuity. This was in May 1912, when he and Frieda, the wife of a Nottingham professor, ran away together, and went to Germany, then Italy.

Six years earlier, soon after her marriage to Ernest Weekley, Frieda had had an affair with the brilliant Austrian psychiatrist, Otto Gross who, in reaction against a stern and rigid father, had become an advocate of total sexual freedom. Both Frieda and her sister Else became his disciples and mistresses. Frieda, who had married in 1877 at the age of seventeen, made the simultaneous discovery that she was naturally promiscuous, and that Otto Gross regarded her as a wonderful example of what a truly free woman ought to be. It permanently transformed her vision of herself.

Gross was a cocaine addict who died in his early forties; but Frieda worshipped his memory all her life. When she ran away with Lawrence, she put the gospel of promiscuity into practice on their 'honeymoon' by giving herself casually to a woodcutter in a shed in the Alps. Moreover, she told Lawrence about it, and persuaded him that she was right to do so, and that his male jealousy was merely a remnant of patriarchal dominance that belonged to the past. Lawrence permitted himself to be convinced, and in a novel called *Mr Noon,* which he began in 1920, appears as the advocate of sexual freedom and promiscuity – although the fact that he failed to finish it suggests that his attitude remained ambivalent.

Gross's doctrine of sexual promiscuity may sound immature, but this does him an injustice. In Martin Green's book *The Von Richthofen Sisters* (1974) it is presented as an outgrowth of Freud's doctrines, and obviously has much in common with the teaching of Wilhelm Reich, with whom Gross shared the belief that sexual freedom would bring about the millennium.

We can also sense a resonance between Lawrence's views and Iris's when Green quotes Frieda as saying that 'the religious approach to sex' had been her own small contribution to *Lady Chatterley's Lover.* For surely a kind of religious vision is what Bradbury is suggesting in his phrase about love as 'morally imperative by virtue of its totemism, its violence, its irrationality'. This is the notion that underlies *The Plumed Serpent,* a fantasy which describes how Mexico throws off Christianity and returns to the ancient blood religion of the Aztecs, complete with human sacrifice.

In *Psychoanalysis and the Unconscious*, Lawrence defines his own form of mysticism in curiously Blakeian terms when he says: 'Through the mode of dynamic objective apprehension, which in our day we have gradually come to call imagination, a man may in time add on to himself the whole of the universe, by increasing pristine realisation of the universal.'

This is certainly what William Blake meant by imagination – what the psychologist Pierre Janet labelled 'the reality function', the mode of 'dynamic objective apprehension' of the real, a Blakeian 'cleansing of the doors of perception'.

It might seem that the major difference between Lawrence and Blake is that Lawrence's concept of imagination is triggered by sex, and Blake's by his own visionary mysticism. But even this is untrue. New discoveries about Blake make it clear that sex played as central a part in his mysticism as in Lawrence's.

These discoveries are revealed in a book called *Why Mrs Blake Cried, William Blake and the Sexual Basis of Spiritual Vision,* by the American scholar, Martha Keith Schuchard, in 2006.

What she uncovered was an extraordinary religion of sexual mysticism practised in the 1750s in the Moravian Chapel in London's Fetter Lane by a congregation that included William Blake's parents. It aimed at religious ecstasy through sexual means, and another of its followers was the mystic Emanuel Swedenborg.

In due course, Swedenborg would become the greatest early influence on the career of the young artist and poet, William Blake, who was only seventeen when the Swedish visionary died in 1772.

The reason 'Mrs Blake cried' was because her husband wanted to go to bed with the maid. And at the age of 68, Blake shocked the lawyer Crabb Robinson by telling him that he believed that men should have access to 'a community of women', and not merely to one wife; when Robinson objected that surely marriage was a divine institution, Blake replied that this had not always been so, and that the Biblical patriarchs had many wives. He liked to cite the way that Abraham had slept with his wife's maid Hagar when his wife Sarah had been unable to bear a child.

So it seems that Blake held the same views on sexual freedom as Otto Gross, Wilhelm Reich, and Iris Murdoch.

The key may lie in that comment of Martha Schuchard's that the 'love feasts' (or *Agapes*) at Fetter Lane sometimes lasted all night, and that the congregation frequently experienced states of sexual/religious ecstasy that could be maintained for hours.

Could this have been the root of Catherine Blake's problem – that in his states of sexual/visionary ecstasy, Blake was capable of going on for hours, while his wife would have preferred getting to sleep? Which would have led Blake to feel that what he needed was a wider choice of sex partners.

It is natural for creative and dominant people to attach special importance to sex and, like Lawrence, to regard it as the key to insight into the meaning of life. It seems to promise some Dionysian explosion of power, the ability to rise above what Heidegger called 'the triviality of everydayness', the sense of mystical one-ness with nature that Lawrence describes in stories like 'Sun' and 'The Woman Who Rode Away'.

With *A Severed Head* we become aware of how far Iris Murdoch's quest had led her beyond the 'value-less' existentialism of Sartre and Camus to something closer to Lawrence.

It can be seen why I find her the most interesting of my contemporaries who emerged in the 1950s.

11 'Now That My Ladder's Gone...'

On 6 July 1960 Joy and I travelled to Tilbury to sail for Leningrad on a new Russian cruise ship called the *Bore II*; the other members of the party were John Braine, Bob and Pat Pitman and their son Jonathan. It was Bob who had discovered that we could travel to Russia at some preposterously low fare, and save hotel costs by sleeping on board the ship. The cheapness was an important factor, for Joy and I were, as usual, living off an overdraft. Joy was seven and a half months pregnant.

John's trip to Russia was to be a turning point in his life, although not in a sense he would have welcomed.

On board the boat, which smelt of fresh paint and pungent pink soap, John impressed me by announcing that he had given up alcohol. Pat told me later in confidence that this was on the orders of his doctor, who had warned him that if he kept drinking at his present rate, he would be dead within a year.

So in the bar, watching England recede, John drank lemonade, and talked about the virtues of teetotalism, while the rest of us drank a kind of very oily vodka. After two or three, you ceased to notice the odd taste, which was apparently due to fusel oil, and explained why the Russians drank it with a sprinkling of black pepper.

John stuck to his temperance vow until we went ashore in Stockholm at eleven o'clock one morning. We decided that the lure of an early glass of schnapps was irresistible, and went into a pavement café. John decided to join us in a glass, then demonstrated the behaviour of the true alcoholic by deciding to follow it with two or three more. Back on the boat for lunch, he went on drinking vodka, while we drank a sweet Russian white wine. After lunch he came back to our cabin, and went on to drink the whole of a bottle of cherry brandy I had bought that morning. From then on, he made no attempt to climb back on the wagon.

I could understand why this had happened. Sudden fame is a terrifying experience, because you know that all eyes are on you. And since John was essentially an autobiographical writer, and had used up most of the autobiography in *Room at the Top*, he must have felt like an actor standing on a floodlit stage and wondering what to do next. Alcohol restored his self-confidence, but only at the cost of turning him into a obsessive boozer.

From our 'floating hotel' in Leningrad it was about half an hour's walk to the Nevsky Prospect in the centre. The tall, gloomy tenements we passed, with their square drainpipes that stopped well short of the pavement (so when it rained you had to keep clear of the Niagara), reminded me of the cheap lodgings Raskolnikov describes at the beginning of *Crime and Punishment.*

When we inquired of our Intourist guide where Dostoevsky's house could be found, she was dismissively uninformative, and told us he was no longer read.

On our last evening in Leningrad, we were invited to a literary reception at the Astoria Hotel. John, of course, was the celebrity, since *Room at the Top* had been a bestseller in the USSR – even small Russian editions of foreign translations ran to fifty thousand – and they mistakenly assumed the book to be an attack on capitalism. I heard a stern-faced woman telling Pat Pitman, my collaborator on the encyclopedia of murder, that in the Soviet Union the murder rate was low, since most people were perfectly contented under Communism.

Few people spoke to me at the reception, but I assumed that this was because no one had ever heard of *The Outsider* and the Angry Young Men.

I discovered my mistake a year or two later when I received for review a book on Khrushchev's Russia by Alexander Werth. He mentions that an article in *Pravda*, by Alexei Surkov, head of the Russian Writers' Union, had attacked Camus and me as decadent Western writers. And it had appeared the day before our ship docked in Leningrad.

John, at any rate, was persona grata, and was invited to fly on to Moscow to give a talk; they would then fly him home, which meant he should arrive before we did. Oddly enough, we had another literary companion on the way home – John Wain and his new Welsh wife. It was then that Wain told me about the occasion he had stopped Amis pushing me off the roof.

We had only been back in Cornwall a day when I heard from Pat Pitman. It seemed that John had arrived at their house in a worse state than she had ever seen him, and she and her mother-in-law had taken refuge in the cellar, while from above them came the sound of John's ravings and of smashing glass. It seemed that he had quarrelled with Pat Braine and had been on a bender that had lasted for days; and was now drinking his way through their booze cupboard. When Pat's daughter, Katie, came home from school she found John in the midst of broken glasses, which he had hurled at the wall. The sight of her calmed him a little and he burst into tears. 'Eeh, Katie, when you're a bit older, will you come and look after me?' Katie replied without hesitation: 'No fear!'

At least this trauma seems to have helped restore John's creativity. His next novel, *Life at the Top*, the further adventures of Joe Lampton, has some of that warm glow of its predecessor. It is about Joe's life as a partner in his father-in-law's business, and his marriage to the desirable Susan Brown. All is not well; and she is already accusing him of selfishness. Drama is provided by a near-breakdown in the marriage, when Joe returns home unexpectedly from a journey to find Susan in bed with one of his friends. Divorce is avoided for the sake of the children, and he and Susan make up.

The new novel was soon made into another film starring Laurence Harvey. This was followed in 1970 by a television series called *Man at the Top*, with Kenneth Haigh – the original Jimmy Porter – as Joe, and then, in 1973, by another film of the same title. So John must have felt that the near-breakdown he had suffered in giving birth to the sequel had, after all, been fruitful.

I was in no position to find out, for by this time John was no longer on speaking terms with either Bill or me.

In 1964, Bill had met an American businessman named Bob Guccione, and together they devised a scheme for launching a *Playboy* imitation called *Penthouse*. They borrowed enough money to issue a glossy brochure full of half-naked girls, and promised the reader serious intellectual articles by authors like myself, Bertrand Russell and John Braine. To their delight and astonishment, letters, cheques and postal orders flooded in, and soon they had enough to print the first issue of a magazine that would make Guccione a multi-millionaire.

Playboy ran a regular feature called The Round Table, in which various guests discussed food (they were supposed to be at dinner), sex and censorship. Bill decided to run a similar feature. One day he rang me and asked me what I thought about sex. I replied, quoting Groucho Marx, that I thought it was here to stay. And so we continued talking for twenty minutes or so. At the end of that time he told me that he had been recording the conversation, and asked me if he could use it for the *Penthouse* symposium. I, of course, said yes.

Half an hour later Bill rang me again. It seemed he had repeated the procedure with John Braine, and when he told him that it had all been recorded, John's reaction had been indignant and explosive, and he called Bill several unkind names, of which the mildest was 'dirty little guttersnipe'. Bill wanted to know if I would ring John back and try to talk him round. But it was no use. John was furious. 'I've got a wife and children to support. I don't give interviews for nothing.'

I assured him – as Bill had told me to – that he would be well paid. But it made no difference.

Unphased, Bill rang Stuart and asked him what he thought about sex, ending by explaining that it had all been recorded and asking if he could use it in the first issue of *Penthouse*. Stuart, like me, said of course.

There was one more twist to the story. Because Stuart's interview had been less interesting then John's, Bill simply used what John had said and put Stuart's name on it. I had to chuckle at this typical example of Bill's Machiavellianism.

But John's behaviour struck me as rather discreditable. All this nonsense about having a wife and child to support amounted to moral evasiveness; what really worried him was having his name associated with a girly magazine. It was all bluster, another example of the Ibsen syndrome of hide-and-seek, pretending to be something you are not.

Penthouse went on to make as much money as *Playboy*, but Bill failed to benefit by it, since he had overlooked the importance of getting Guccione to sign a binding partnership agreement, and was soon forced out.

But although I ceased to see John, since we no longer shared a pied-à-terre, I continued to read his books. The next novel, *The Jealous God,* struck me as a reversion to the manner of *The Vodi*, with another 'wet' hero, a 30-year-old virgin who cannot work up the confidence to choose sex rather than Catholicism. For a novel of the sixties, this seemed almost anachronistic.

In 1966 John decided to flee from the cotton mills of the north and throw in his lot with the immoral southerners of the stockbroker belt. Now, novels like *The Crying Game* and *Stay With Me Till Morning* were about bed-swapping suburbanites in whom I found it difficult to take an interest.

Sometime in the seventies, John wrote me a letter saying that it seemed a pity for old friends to lose touch, and I agreed. Joy assures me that we went to look at John's new home in Woking – probably on a drive to London – and at the tiny office behind the fire station where he wrote, but all trace of that visit has vanished from my memory. Joy can only recall the huge kitchen. He was still, of course, living with Pat.

Pat fills in some of the details in an interview she gave to Roger Ratcliffe of the *Yorkshire Post* on the twentieth anniversary of John's death, on 16 November 2006. 'I never knew what he was going to be like from one day to the next. He made such a high drama out of everything. He'd either burst into tears or be verbally abusive. But in a strange way, after we split up, I sometimes began to find things were a bit boring. Sadly, though, my life with John had become too rich a mix in the end.'

The years of *Room at the Top*, *Life at the Top* and *Man at the Top* were a time of glamour and plenty, with friendship with writers like J B Priestley and John Betjeman. But this kind of success generated a certain dependence on the lifestyle. 'What he fed on was praise,' says Pat.

This began to diminish after his rejection of leftism in 1969, as did his ability to live in the style to which success had accustomed him. When they moved south, they had four children – three of them girls – but as his novels were less and less successful, they moved into smaller and smaller houses. For a worrier like John, this was the worst thing that could have happened, and the bottle became his refuge. Hypochondria and depression made him less and less stable. Finally, they were failing to bring in enough to run the household. It was after John had pushed her to the floor in a drunken rage that she decided they had to separate, and in the early eighties, she became a supply teacher, while John moved into a small room in Hampstead, which one interviewer described as 'gloom at the top'.

The last time I saw John was in London, at a meeting of the PEN Club, at which I had been invited to speak. John was now with another partner – not, as I expected, a glamorous younger woman, but a perfectly ordinary-looking middle-aged lady. After my talk, John rose to his feet, and I sensed a kind of resignation in the audience, as if this was something they were accustomed to. He spoke of 'my old friend Colin', and referred nostalgically to happy days in Chepstow Road.

He must have gone on for a quarter of an hour. He had already told me that he had given up drinking, so it was no longer a sign of alcoholic loquacity.

John sent me his three last novels: *One and Last Love* (1981), *The Two of Us* (1984) and *These Golden Days* (1985). Since he was essentially an autobiographical writer, the first and last were novels about himself, or rather, about a middle-aged writer who has separated from his wife with some bitterness, and met a woman of his own age, with whom he has found total emotional satisfaction. *The Two of Us* moves back to the north in a sequel to *Stay With Me Till Morning,* in which his hero and heroine survive mutual adultery and end up happily together.

As to the novels about the middle-aged writer and his new love, I found them hard to read, for nothing is more boring than being told about a happy love affair in which nothing much happens. I wrote to John saying I had enjoyed them, but it was not true.

He also wrote two spy novels, obviously in an attempt to widen his range. *The Pious Agent* (1975) is about a Catholic James Bond who says a Hail Mary and crosses himself before he kills someone. But John had not even attempted narrative; the story is told as a series of dates, and is in the rather slow manner of Len Deighton rather than the compulsive flow of Ian Fleming.

The same, I found, was true of its sequel *Finger of Fire,* which has lines like, 'Who else would be members of a terrorist organization except Communists?' Now John had abandoned his leftism and his political views had become drearily predictable.

It astonished me that, after those recent novels, John was still able to make a living as a writer. It seems I was right. In 1985, it was reported that John had put up his collected notes as a novelist for sale at Sotheby's. Apparently they failed to reach their reserve price, and were withdrawn. That Christmas he had eaten his Christmas lunch at a community centre with indigents.

In the following year, Caroline Coombes, a girl we both knew, rang me to tell me that John was in hospital with a burst ulcer. I rang the hospital to try to find how he was, but they refused to tell me, since I was not a relative. In November 1986, Joy and I were in Tokyo, where I was lecturing, having dinner with my agent, when he mentioned that John Braine had died that day, during the course of an operation. I suddenly felt an acute sense of sadness, feeling how ironical it was that I should hear of the death of an old friend thousands of miles from home.

John had dedicated his 1970 novel *Stay With Me Till Morning* to 'Jane and Kingsley Amis'. Amis and Jane Howard had been together since 1962 and married since 1965. But by 1970, the marriage had begun to sour. To begin with, Amis seems to have reconciled himself to fidelity by drinking heavily, and his 1969 novel *The Green Man*, which has heavy autobiographical overtones, is about an innkeeper who owns a fashionable country hotel, has affairs, and drinks far too much.

Amis himself, by that time, often drank a bottle of whisky a day. He also spent much time at his club, the Garrick, and every week had lunch at Bertorelli's, in Soho, where he was joined by friends like Conquest, Anthony Powell and Bernard Levin, and sometimes by John Braine. The latter was accepted on sufferance, since after a few drinks he slipped back into his old habit of laying down the law, often on the subject of the lack of freedom in the Soviet Union, and how much better off we are in England. Since most of the others present were in total agreement with him – Amis, like Braine, had become increasingly right wing – long assertive speeches on the subject were unnecessary and wearing on the nerves. It was difficult for John's friends not to feel occasionally that he had become downright stupid.

Amis had moved out of London in 1967 to a large country house called Lemmons, in Barnet. He portrays it in *Girl 20* in 1971 – the title refers to the fact that the hero cannot even see these words in an advertisement without getting an erection. But it is a strangely bleak novel about a conductor called Vandervane, who has a seventeen-year-old mistress and a six-year-old son who tells adults to fuck off and urinates on the bathroom floor. He permits the older children to do as they like because it allows him to ignore them – an attitude Amis shared. I reviewed the book at the time and was surprised that it was so oddly sad and unfunny. But then, I had not been following his progress as a novelist since *Take a Girl Like You*, which I had given up halfway through.

In fact, *Girl 20* is as close to a confession of his own inadequacies as husband and father that Amis ever came. His indifference to his children produced traumas in all three. The eldest, Philip, was angry and troubled for years, leading to divorce and remarriage. The same was true of the second son, Martin. Their sister, Sally, who adored her father, became an alcoholic and virtually a nymphomaniac, and drank herself to death in 2000 at the age of 47. Amis's self-preoccupation amounted to a kind of solipsism.

In 1976 came one of his more puzzling novels, a fantasy about alternative history called *The Alteration*. Its premise is that the Reformation never happened, and the Roman church continued to dominate life until it had achieved a kind of mind control like Stalin's Soviet Union. In this world A J Ayer is a professor of Dogmatic Theology and Sartre a Monseigneur. The hero, a boy soprano called Hubert, has been castrated to preserve his beautiful voice.

This strange fantasy seems to have sprung from Amis's recognition that he was becoming impotent. Sex with Jane was now increasingly infrequent. He refused to accept that this was due to alcoholism because the very thought of cutting down plunged him into depression.

Depressions, panic attacks and phobias had been a part of Amis's life since his early days at Oxford, and Richard Bradford suggests that they may have been his reason for being so addicted to change – the feeling that a new place, new circumstances, would somehow change his life. The truth seems to be that he was like a poor sleeper, who tosses and turns, but never gets comfortable. After two years he began to feel restless in Lemmons, and in 1975 he and Jane began looking for somewhere closer to town – or rather, Jane did, for Amis had come to rely entirely on her for the practical side of his life.

In May 1976 they moved to Hampstead, where Amis was now writing a grim novel about impotence called *Jake's Thing*. The central character, Jake Richardson, is intended as an updated version of Lucky Jim, for we are told that he was christened James, while 'Richardson' seems to be a version of Dickson (Dixon). Jake, we learn, has simply lost interest in women. And since, as Amis once told Larkin, he liked girls because he liked fucking them, this also meant that he was ceasing to even like women. He was increasingly unwilling for Jane's friends to visit, and had ceased to love her. Now she irritated him, and he found her upper-class accent affected.

Jake's solution – which was also Amis's – is to consult doctors.

His satirical attitude towards psychiatrists had already been revealed in *The Anti-Death League*, but in *Jake's Thing* it has become the core of the book. In the first of these, an impossible Irishman explains that his first name, Proinsias, is pronounced Francis, 'the correct Gaelic spelling'. In the second, Jake has to sit in an upright chair with no trousers on, in front of a group of medical students, with wires attached to his penis, and then made to read passages of philosophy, alternated with glimpses of porno-graphic photographs, to gauge his sexual response. Amis told his son Martin that this scene really happened.

However, the main effect of this loss of sex drive is to make Jake aware he never really *liked* women; he only liked the fact that they would let him undress them. Now he no longer wants to do this, he realises that he can hardly stand them. So when, at the end of the book, his doctor tells him that he can probably be cured by careful drug treatment, Jake replies, 'No thanks.'

Clearly, most of this depressing drama was psychological, due to self-pity, for after telling Larkin that he has 'not had a fuck for more than a year', Amis adds with stoical bravado, 'and a wank for over a month'.

In September 1980, following a lunch with friends at a castle near Edinburgh, when Amis had been gratuitously offensive to the conductor Abbado, Jane decided she had had enough. She went to a health farm – to try to lose weight – and wrote to him to say she was not returning. This was in November, after fifteen years of marriage. Amis told his biographer this was ten years too long.

But Amis hated living alone; he found being on his own profoundly disturbing. He now wrote to Jane saying that if she would return, he would drink less and try to be a better husband. She knew him well enough to know that no alcoholic can control it at will; he would soon drift back to drinking as much as before. She wrote saying that she would return only on condition that he gave up drinking completely. He naturally refused.

To soothe Amis's fear of the dark, his son Philip – whose own marriage had just broken up – used to come and stay at night, and Martin filled in when this was not possible.

Eventually the house had to be sold, in order to give Jane her share; she was living on very little money with a woman friend. She received half the £265,000.

At this point, his children suggested that it would make sense for Hilly and her third husband Alastair Boyd to move in with Amis so she could look after him. Boyd was Lord Kilmarnock, a penniless Scottish peer, who had moved back to London from Majorca to take his seat in the House of Lords. Oddly enough, the arrangement worked perfectly, and the *ménage à trois* moved into a house in Kentish Town. So after 20 years, Hilly and Amis were back together again.

Now his chief preoccupation was to get his own back on Jane. In spite of the fact that she had been an excellent wife and a caring stepmother – it had been she who had been largely responsible for getting Martin an education and turning him away from drugs and into writing – he had slipped into the paranoia that was always hovering just around the corner – and decided she was detestable. He took his revenge in the most bizarre of his novels, *Stanley and the Women*, which is not only an attack on Jane, but on womankind in general. It is Amis's own version of *Look Back in Anger*. But whereas Jimmy Porter is convinced from the beginning that Alison is a part of a middle-class conspiracy against non-U people like himself, Stanley Duke is, at the beginning of the novel, wholly sympathetic to his wife Susan, with whom he is in love. It is only after he has been drinking in a pub with Bert, the ex-husband of his previous wife Nowell, an actress, that his views begin to change. By the end of the novel he has become a convert to the Strindbergian view that women are by nature evil, mean, predatory, grasping and totally selfish.

The second step in his 'conversion' is his suspicion that Susan was responsible for the mental breakdown of the son of his first marriage, Steve, who had come to see them in a state of obvious mental stress, and later stabbed her in the arm. Her reaction is admirable – tolerant and charitable. But Stanley comes to believe that she actually stabbed herself in order to get Steve committed, and out of their lives. And at the end of the novel, his suspicion is confirmed by the doctor who had examined the wound.

Because Amis had taken so much care to present Stanley as a decent and harmless person, who is converted to misogyny by sheer weight of evidence, he succeeded in concealing the mental unbalance that lay behind it, and although female reviewers reacted with indignation, most of the males were remarkably sympathetic. Financially, *Stanley and the Women* was one of his greatest successes.

Richard Bradford, after mentioning that Eric Jacobs, Amis's official biographer, deals with the last twelve years of his subject's life in 28 pages, asks if this indicates negligence, or perhaps discretion. He concludes: 'In truth it was neither. There was very little to write about.'

This is not to dismiss his last six novels as negligible. At least two of them, *The Old Devils* (1986) and *The Russian Girl* (1992) are as good as anything he ever wrote. But all arouse a strong sense of *déjà vu*, and two of them, *The Folks That Live on the Hill* (1990) and *You Can't Do Both* (1994) are frankly autobiographical. *Difficulties with Girls* (1988), a sequel to *Take a Girl Like You,* deals with the married life of Patrick and Jenny, with Patrick as unfaithful as ever, but with Jenny now far stronger, and capable of gaining the upper hand. There are times when it reads almost like another apology to Hilly. This seems to be even more so in *You Can't Do Both,* which is fictionalised autobiography which includes the story of Hilly's accidental pregnancy.

Hilly's presence is strong in most of them, since they were living together again, and he makes it clear that he still loved her. In retrospect, Amis looked back on his years with Jane as the worst mistake of his life, although Jane's autobiography, *Slipstream*, makes it clear that he only succeeded in achieving this view by some careful editing of the past.

But there can be no doubt about his pleasure in being reunited with Hilly, even if she was somebody's else's wife. The main plot of *The Old Devils* concerns the return to Swansea of a television celebrity and his wife, based on Amis and Hilly. This character, although in his sixties, is as randy as ever, and greatly enlivens the daily routines of a group of old friends who had succumbed to habit and boredom by seducing their wives.

Although sexually impotent, Amis obviously enjoyed writing about sex as much as ever, and it continues to play a central role. In *The Russian Girl*, a beautiful Russian poetess, who writes atrocious poetry, comes to London and has a love affair with a middle-aged professor whose own wealthy and eccentric wife no longer excites him. Even in the curious last novel, *The Biographer's Moustache* – probably written as a kind of joke to coincide with the publication of the Jacobs biography – the great novelist's wife is seduced by his faithful Boswell.

During these last years, Amis's routine remained unchanging. He wrote all morning, then devoted the rest of the day to eating and drinking, mostly at his club, the Garrick. The photograph on the dust-jacket of the biography – showing a man with bulging eyes and lobster-red complexion, staring unhappily at the camera – leaves little doubt that he was hovering on the verge of apoplexy. Something of the sort finally felled him when he was in Swansea in August 1995, but fortunately his biographer was on hand to drive him back to London and hospital, where he died on 22 October 1995.

Amis and John Wain had not been on speaking terms since the 1960s. In what Amis admits is a 'rancorous little digression' in his *Memoirs*, he gives his reason: that he had been told by a third party that Wain had mentioned that his reason for declining Amis's invitations to go and stay in Swansea was his fear that Hilly would 'break down the door to get her hands on him'. Amis had finally confronted him with the story: 'Instead of denying it, he remarked that it showed a grave deficiency in my informant's sense of humour. From this moment I considered myself released from any duty to keep to myself what I thought of his books, a specially handy dispensation when his *Life of Johnson* came out in 1974.'

Here we note the Amis paranoia. Wain said, quite fairly, that it was meant as a joke, which amounts to an apology. Instead of accepting it, Amis decided it justified him attacking the friend who had been responsible for getting *Lucky Jim* accepted.

In fact, the *Life of Johnson* is one of Wain's best books, displaying the kind of solid erudition that Amis's criticism never achieved.

A year earlier, Wain had been elected professor of poetry at Oxford, a position he held for five years.

I continued to buy his novels in paperback, simply out of a desire to keep abreast, but continued to find an oddly disagreeable flavour about them, which seemed to stem from Wain's self-assertive egotism, and his predatory attitude towards women. When I heard that he was writing a 'big' novel, set in Wales, I hastened to read *A Winter in the Hills* (1970), hoping that this would show what Wain could do when he chose to be serious. In fact, I was quickly put off by the central character, Roger Furnivall, who goes to Wales to learn Welsh, with the aim of teaching it at the University of Uppsala, where he is hoping to seduce long-legged Swedish blondes. And although Furnivall shows himself capable of standing up for the underdog in a dispute with a ruthless businessman who is determined to develop a monopoly on the local buses, I still found him a typical self-centred Wain hero, and never finished the book.

But I found his final novel, a trilogy called *Where the Rivers Meet* an exception. Set in Oxford between the 1930s and the mid fifties, it charts the life of Peter Leonard, son of an innkeeper, whose intelligence leads to him becoming a history don. He marries a farmer's daughter called Heather because he is overwhelmingly attracted physically – the treatment of sex is unusually uninhibited for Wain. When the war comes, he is transferred to the Ministry of Supply in London, and has an affair with an Irish girl named Mairead. At the end of the war, they agree to go their separate ways, although both are in love. Then Leonard discovers that Heather chose him as a second best, after a long and determined attempt to get pregnant by another man, to force him to marry her. He decides to leave her, and ends by going back to Mairead.

This is a huge novel, and Wain undoubtedly sets out to make it his masterpiece. One might say that Oxford is the real hero of the book, along with the great changes that came about when the Morris car-making plant opened in the late 1920s, and – Wain feels – destroyed the old rural Oxford and made it an industrial wasteland. So there is a sense in which *Where the Rivers Meet* is a nostalgic portrait of a vanished Oxford. On this level it is remarkably successful.

I was also glad to note that it is free of that bitter taste that is present in the earlier novels. This may have been because Wain had mellowed and ceased to be so competitive. Carpenter reports in *The Angry Young Men* that in his final years Wain was often short of money, and had to rely on handouts from the Society of Authors.

A passage in the second volume, *Comedies* seems to reveal a new level of self-knowledge. The hero is reflecting on the fact that Heather 'used' him to escape a family background she detested. 'It wasn't as if I was too good for such treatment. I wasn't a high spiritual type. I was a pretty selfish sod who had always, on the whole, behaved as a selfish sod behaves. Looking after Number One . . .'

Wain's health was poor towards the end, and he died in May 1995, at the age of 69, just before the publication of *Hungry Generations*, the third volume of his trilogy.

Philip Larkin had preceded him by ten years. He and Wain had remained friends to the end. On the other hand, Amis and Larkin had seen little of one another since Larkin had become the head librarian in Hull in 1955.

For a year after that Larkin lived in various bleak and uncomfortable lodgings, summarised in his poem 'Mr Bleaney'. In October 1956 he moved into a top-floor flat in a block owned by the university, and Monica was able to visit regularly. But she remained in Leicester, and his sex life was otherwise confined to masturbation.

This was not entirely a matter of choice. He kept a pair of binoculars on the windowsill of his office, so he could survey passing female students, but his occasional attempts to initiate relationships remained unsatisfactory. He envied Amis the ease of his conquests, but recognised that, with his thick spectacles, his skinny body and increasingly bald head, he was not qualified to imitate him. Although the majority of his staff were female, a group photograph in Andrew Motion's biography reminds us that librarians are seldom noted for glamour.

It was not until spring 1960 that he began to see possibilities in one of them, 31-year-old Maeve Brennan. He had offered tutorials to members of his staff who were interested in taking the Library Association exam, and she was among half a dozen who signed up. As others dropped out they were sometimes alone, and she occasionally made up a foursome with a married couple from the ground floor of his block of flats.

Maeve had been engaged but had broken it off. She was conventional, religious and ordinary, and he was apparently excited by her hairy legs and forearms. When she passed her exam they went out for a celebration meal, and in the taxi on the way home he embraced her. She was at first unwilling to have sex, but he eventually prevailed.

Monica, a regular visitor to Hull, soon found out – although he insisted they were 'just good friends'; but this also suited Larkin's purposes. Monica's mother and father had died in 1959, and he began to feel she might be thinking in terms of marriage; so Maeve was interposed as a barrier.

Fourteen years later, Larkin initiated a relationship with his secretary, Betty Mackereth, a woman of about his own age who lived with her parents. They seem to have entered this relationship not out of strong feelings, but simply to provide mutual sexual satisfaction.

Maeve regarded Larkin with immense admiration, which gave her a certain advantage over Monica, who saw him more realistically. In fact, Larkin was becoming quite a famous poet by the mid sixties, his third volume, *The Whitsun Weddings*, placing him immediately beside Betjeman as one of Britain's most widely read poets. Its opening poem, 'Here', is a lovely evocation of Hull and the surrounding countryside, of which Motion remarks: 'Sweeping like a camera on a helicopter over the "widening river's slow presence" towards the "surprise of a large town", he lingers over the civic details before veering on again to the country between Hull and the coast . . .' This is followed immediately by the deservedly celebrated 'Mr Bleaney', whose sketch of a bleak hired room evokes an atmosphere like Sickert's 'Ennui'. The lovely 'Whitsun Weddings' may be his finest poem, with the same 'helicopter' feeling as 'Here'.

Not long after publishing this volume, Larkin made a BBC Monitor programme in which he appeared with John Betjeman. Two years earlier the poet Al Alvarez had attacked him as 'parochial' in the Introduction to the Penguin *New Poetry*, and followed it up with an attack on his poetry's drabness in the *Observer*. In front of the camera, Betjeman asks him what he thinks of such critics, and Larkin replies reasonably:

> I read that I'm a miserable sort of fellow writing a sort of welfare-state sort of poetry, doing it well perhaps, but it isn't really what poetry is. But I wonder if it ever occurs to the writers of criticisms like that that really one agrees with them, but the kind of poetry one writes is based on the kind of person one is and the kind of environment one's had . . . and one doesn't really choose the kind of poetry one writes. One writes the kind of poetry one has to write or can write.

Here the innocent word 'environment' deserves attention. All Larkin's later poetry shows a man who feels trapped in his environment, in 'the triviality of everydayness'. All poets have their symbols of 'otherness', from Yeats's Celtic daydreams to Betjeman's nostalgia for the past. But Larkin's 'otherness' seems to be constricted by boredom and a kind of claustrophobia that was due to a lack of interest in literature or ideas.

The point is underlined later in the same programme when he reads aloud his 'A Study of Reading Habits', describing his childhood passion for escapist reading:

> When getting my nose in a book
> Cured most things short of school,
> It was worth ruining my eyes

To know I could still keep cool,
And deal out the old right hook
To dirty dogs twice my size.

Later, with inch-thick specs,
Evil was just my lark:
Me and my cloak and fangs
Had ripping times in the dark.
The women I clubbed with sex!
I broke them up like meringues.

Don't read much now: the dude
Who lets the girl down before
The hero arrives, the chap
Who's yellow and keeps the store,
Seem far too familiar. Get stewed:
Books are a load of crap.

On first reading you suspect he is being ironic about some yobbish illiterate, as 'Naturally the Foundation will Bear Your Expenses' is of the globe-trotting self-satisfied academic. Then you realise that the reference to thick lenses must refer to Larkin, and that he is admitting to the loss of the romanticism of his teens, and to his acceptance of the bleaker, gloomier world he now feels trapped in. In that sense it resembles Yeats's 'The Circus Animals' Desertion', in which Yeats speaks of the heroic legends that sustained his youth as a kind of ladder to escape reality, and ends:

> . . . Now that my ladder's gone,
> I must lie down where all the ladders start,
> In the foul rag-and-bone shop of the heart.

But Yeats at least was still sustained by the idea of human evolution and 'profane perfection of mankind'. Larkin seems to be describing total emotional bankruptcy.

In this there are clear parallels with Amis, whose 'project' also collapsed in mid-career. Amis's project was basically sexual conquest – to have as many mistresses as a sultan has wives. It is clearly stated in *Take a Girl Like You*, where Patrick is determined to exercise his 'own imperial will' and possess Jenny, even if it means raping her when she is unconscious. But it all collapsed: first with Hilly's desertion, then with his disillusionment with Jane and her final desertion – by which time he was impotent anyway. But that 'project' *was* what Amis had 'to say', and when it evaporated he had nothing to say, even though he half-disguised this in novels like *Difficulties with Girls*, in which Patrick continues to plod on his rather weary treadmill of adultery.

Larkin's own indication of the collapse of motive occurs in 'Ambulances', the poem he wrote immediately after 'books are a load of crap', in which ambulances become a symbol of

> . . . the solving emptiness
> That lies just under all we do.

And it was at this point, when he was still only 38, that death began to dominate his thoughts. In 'Aubade', written in 1977, he describes 'waking at four to soundless dark', then, as he watches it grow light

> . . . I see what's really always there:
> Unresting death, a whole day nearer now
> Making all thought impossible but how
> And where and when I shall myself die.

Which is why, as Bradford puts it, 'the years between late 1974 and mid-1979 saw the decline and death of Larkin as a poet'. When John Betjeman, the poet laureate, died in May 1984, Larkin, who was widely expected to succeed him, turned down the job with the comment: 'I didn't give up poetry; it gave me up.'

In 1974, when the block of flats in which he lived was put up for sale by the university, he bought himself a grim, box-like house of the type that might have contained Mr Bleaney's room. Why he chose this is a mystery, for he was sufficiently rich to have bought any he liked. There seems to have been a kind of masochism involved that comports with his deepening sense of meaninglessness. He admitted that he hated it from the moment he moved in.

In 1983, Monica began to experience severe headaches, blurred vision and shingles, and it became apparent that she would need regular care. She moved in with Larkin. But his health was also poor; his eyesight was growing steadily worse, he was becoming deaf, and an enormous gain in weight to seventeen and a half stone caused him to develop high blood pressure. His drinking remained excessive. Hospital tests to investigate a pain in his lower abdomen revealed a cancer of the oesophagus. An operation revealed it had spread to the rest of his body.

He spent his final three months back at home, tended by Monica and regularly visited by his other two mistresses. On 28 November 1985, he died after a sudden collapse.

Amis and Hilly attended his funeral. It was the first time Amis had been to Hull; Larkin had carefully kept him at arm's length.

12 Watch It Come Down

It usually gives me a certain pleasure to begin the final chapter of a book, particularly one that, like this, has been more than two years in the writing. But in the event, the relief has been tempered by a feeling of sadness as I contemplate the wreckage of so many of my contemporaries scattered over the literary battlefield. For example, although I disliked Osborne's work, I get small satisfaction from recording that his decline as a dramatist is one of the most spectacular in the history of British theatre.

Osborne is also in many ways the most puzzling of the casualties. For the first ten years of his career, from *Epitaph for George Dillon* in 1958 to *A Patriot for Me*, in 1965, he seemed to know roughly where he was going and what he was trying to achieve, even if the structure of the plays was occasionally chaotic. But from *Time Present* in 1968 to *Déjàvu* in 1992 it is frequently difficult to make out what he thought he was trying to achieve. In a play like *A Sense of Detachment* in 1972, an anarchic conversation piece in which the main event is an old lady reading aloud from a pornographic catalogue ('Then we finish with a girl masturbating herself in both her holes at one time'), the purpose seems to be simply to shock the audience, the equivalent of giving them all the V sign.

The journalist Frank Marcus, who joined Osborne in the balcony several times during the run, said they took bets on when the first person would storm out, and the more there were, the more Osborne loved it. This sounds like masochism. But that was as early as 1972, a mere four years into his hectic decline.

This is often blamed on the marriage to Jill Bennett – and certainly, the pages Osborne devotes to her in *Almost a Gentleman* are among the most bitter and splenetic that ever poured out of him. Osborne's biographer John Heilpern makes her sound positively demonic, quoting Osborne's agent Robin Dalton: 'Psychologically, she broke his balls. [She] killed him.'

But writers are not killed by their wives. They are killed by something in themselves.

Here I need to add a personal note. Some time in the late 1980s – she separated from Osborne in 1977 – Jill Bennett came to our house in Cornwall with her current boyfriend, an *Observer* journalist who was there to interview me. Having read about Osborne's divorce case, I observed her with interest, expecting a typical self-centred actress – when people think the world revolves around them they find this hard to conceal.

But Joy and I both found her so charming and amusing that she would have been welcome to stay much longer. Joy went out with Jill and her beau to visit the artist Graham Ovenden on Bodmin Moor and had the opportunity of talking to her at length. When Joy later read the pages about her in Osborne's autobiography she found in them a person she did not recognise.

In happier times Osborne himself had described her in a play (*The Hotel in Amsterdam*) as 'playful, loving, impetuous and larky'. This was the Jill Bennett we met, not the avaricious, hysterical virago of *Almost a Gentleman.*

From this I infer that it was their chemistry that was incompatible. She was extraverted and socially inclined; Osborne was introverted and prone to depressions. Basically it was the same kind of mixture as with Penelope Gilliatt. But Jill was more temperamental and impulsive. Doris Lessing told Heilpern: 'She was madly in love with him. But as far as I can make out, he objected to the fact that she was an actress and behaved like one. Lying in bed until lunch time, drinking too much'. This probably aroused disagreeable echoes of Mary Ure.

Osborne's problem was that when he felt negative, he allowed it to darken his mind like a giant storm cloud over a landscape, and when that happened he exploded with appalling bitterness. The success of *Look Back in Anger,* with its negative tirades, had obviously reinforced his belief that vituperation was an acceptable mode of self-expression.

On occasion this could push him to alarming limits. One Sunday in 1972 Jill and Osborne were driving to Dulwich for lunch and bickering as usual. Osborne said: 'If you say that one more time I'm going to smash the car into the roundabout ahead.' Defiantly she repeated it. He accelerated, and they hurtled on to the Wandsworth roundabout and stopped in the middle of the flower bed. Unfortunately Osborne hadn't noticed the police car behind them. They breathalysed him, and he lost his licence for a year. Jill Bennett fractured her ankle, and so had to abandon a role in a play in which she was about to take the lead.

The Hotel in Amsterdam was originally written to be presented in tandem with *Time Present,* but for various reasons was delayed. Neither made any great impact, although *Time Present* transferred to the West End and won her the award as Best Actress of the Year.

Hotel in Amsterdam seems to be an oddly trivial and pointless little drama in which a group of people connected with a film escape from its domineering producer – based on Tony Richardson – and flee to Amsterdam for a weekend. Laurie, the writer, is obviously Osborne, and as usual the play centres around him. (Osborne, I note in passing, seemed incapable of writing plays that were not about himself.)

I saw the television production when it was revived after Osborne's death, and found it incomprehensible. For the first of two acts, the six characters talk about nothing in particular and the play seems merely a conversation piece. In the second act, Laurie's wife's sister arrives in the process of some kind of emotional crisis, then Laurie tells his script editor's wife that he loves her and she admits to loving him, and then a phone call informs them that the egomaniac producer has committed suicide. The play seemed all loose ends, and if it had a point – apart from wishful thinking – it simply failed to come across. Yet this was written while he was in love with Jill Bennett and still happy. Like *Time Present* it makes us aware that Osborne had simply lost direction as a dramatist.

As a footnote, it should be added that Osborne had just written the film script for Tony Richardson's latest venture, *The Charge of the Light Brigade*, but had become increasingly unhappy as it became clear that Richardson wanted to turn it into an anti-war film. In the event it was a total flop, and caused a bitter estrangement between the two men.

Osborne's loss of direction is confirmed in the next play *West of Suez* (1971), in which a distinguished writer named Wyatt goes to visit his four daughters who live on a subtropical island that was once a British colony. They seem to be living in the past, in an atmosphere that is almost Chekhovian, and are all suffering from boredom. When Wyatt – who was played by Sir Ralph Richardson – finally appears late in the play, (as usual Osborne's construction seems slapdash), he is interviewed at length by a lady reporter, and conveys his feeling that everything is going to pot. This island, like the England of *The Entertainer,* seems stuck in decay, in the face of which, Wyatt informs us, he still clings to the old bardic belief that 'words alone are certain good'.

A young American drifter finally explodes and tells them that they strike him as 'pigs barbecued in their own shit'. Doom is on the way. They will be swept away by his rebel friends. 'We think, we fuck and we shit and that's what we do and you're on the great gasping end of it.' All this seems as tedious in its way as these dull British colonials stuck in the past. And then, when apparently out of sheer boredom Wyatt says he must go to bed, a group of armed islanders burst in and shoot him dead. His son-in-law, apparently unfazed, says mildly that there is an old English saying: 'My God, they've shot the fox.'

Like the suicide of the producer in *The Hotel in Amsterdam*, it seems like an artificial crisis that has been introduced arbitrarily to give the play a conclusion.

In the following year, 1972, as if driven by some illogical compulsion to see how much boredom audiences could be persuaded to endure, he wrote the disorganised and bewildering *A Sense of Detachment*, which opened at the Court to baffled and outraged reviews. Heilpern describes it as 'an accident waiting to happen'. 'Osborne wrote it on amphetamines – his uppers of choice – and it speeds and swirls plotlessly like a racing state of mind. Dunlop [the director] shrewdly believed the freewheeling piece was like living inside Osborne's head.'

Interruptions from the audience are written into the script – 'Load of rubbish', 'Get it off' – while Michael Redgrave's wife Rachel Kempson, playing a dignified old lady, had to deliver lines like 'Did you ever fancy getting hold of a pretty young girl scout and fucking her up the arsehole?'

It looks as if the play was Osborne's theatrical equivalent of driving his car into a roundabout, a kind of suicidal gesture. And, as he seemed to expect, the reviewers were outraged, the *Daily Telegraph* critic commenting: 'This must surely be an end to his career in the theatre.'

This was not quite true, but it might have been better for Osborne if it had been.

Penelope Gilliatt, who had moved to America and become a successful film critic for the *New Yorker,* returned to London for a visit, and when Osborne called on her to see their daughter Nolan, remarked as they were saying goodbye: 'You've really fucked up your life, haven't you?' And in gloomily recording this in his journal, Osborne admitted: 'It was hard not to agree with Penelope.'

In fact, three of his plays were rejected in 1973. He adapted Shakespeare's *Coriolanus,* obviously identifying with the rebellious patrician who is dragged down by the mob, but it was turned down by 30 producers. His adaptation of *The Picture of Dorian Gray* fared no better. The rejection of an anti-women's lib play called *The End of Me Old Cigar*, Heilpern records, 'sent him spiralling into the worst depression he had known'.

It deserved to, being one of the most feeble things he had written since *Paul Slickey.* It is about a female brothel keeper who aims to bring about a kind of feminist French Revolution by filming the perversions of her upper-class clients through one-way mirrors, but is foiled by the treachery of her chauvinist pig of a boyfriend, who sells the films to a newspaper magnate who will destroy them. Osborne went out of his way to upset Tynan by taking a casual sideswipe at him as 'a lilac-trousered Oxford trendy with a passion for inflicting dangerously painful spankings'.

When Heilpern finally saw *The End of Me Old Cigar*, he records 'thinking in shock that Osborne, the hero of my school days, had lost his way'.

What was worse, Osborne was allowing these private torments to dominate his work. *Watch It Come Down*, his last play for a decade and a half, dramatised the state of virulent detestation between himself and Jill Bennett – or rather presented it on stage in all its gruesome, tasteless reality. It has lines like: '. . . will you for one minute, just stop that fucking pile of shit spewing out of your fucking mouth . . . or you'll get my fist right in the fucking middle of it.' This is not even Strindbergian; it is merely offputting.

What is worse, Jill Bennett, the true target of all this loathing, was playing the wife.

The play is set in a disused railway station, in which an old writer, based on Lytton Strachey, is dying. Ben, Osborne's alter-ego, has bought it because it was cheap, and his mother lives in the attic with her cats and television. Sally, his bisexual wife, is enamoured of Jo, a girl based on Dora Carrington, the artist who committed suicide when Strachey died. Strachey himself is intended as a symbol of the decent old Edwardian world for which Osborne pines nostalgically. In short, we are in the standard Osborne set-up; the modern world and its nastiness, which he hates, contrasted with the dignified old world, which he sentimentally pines for.

The play, as usual, is lopsidedly constructed, with a long first act devoted mainly to the warring couple, and a short second act in which Strachey dies, Jo kills herself by flinging herself in front of a train, then some unspecified 'yobbos' begin to shoot up the station with automatic rifles, and Ben walks into a bullet. This ending is as abrupt and unprepared for as the marauding natives in *West of Suez*, and leaves the audience just as sceptical.

Osborne was delighted when Peter Hall, who in 1976 had just taken over the National from Olivier, decided to present it there. But the first performance in February 1977 was greeted with boos and cries of 'Money back!' As Heilpern sums it up: 'It's as if he tossed a hand grenade into his own play and his rotten marriage with it.' Osborne noted in his journal: 'I'm finished. My days in the theatre are numbered.'

On 21 June 1977, just as Jill Bennett was waiting to go onstage in *Watch It Come Down*, Osborne telephoned her to tell her he was leaving her – carefully selecting the moment when it would do most damage. She told him she would be driving down to Edenbridge right after the performance. 'I shouldn't,' said Osborne, and told her that her successor, Helen Dawson, another *Observer* journalist, was already installed in her place.

Watch It Come Down ran for only a few months. Osborne was furious when he returned from a short trip to America in June 1977 to find a note from Hall telling him it was being taken off, since it was playing to half-empty houses. In 1983 he got his own back in a review of Hall's diaries in the *Sunday Times,* which he dismissed as a 'numbing record of banal ambition, official evasiveness and individual cupidity'.

That Osborne was possessed by a kind of suicide urge is demonstrated by the curious affair of *The Entertainer* revival. In 1985, eight years after the failure of *Watch It Come Down*, Peter Hall, having forgiven Osborne's attack, suggested doing *The Entertainer*, with Joan Plowright in the part of the mother. Osborne went to Hall's office and agreed. Then he went back on his word and told Hall that she would be quite wrong for the part of Phoebe (based on his own mother). Hall, placed in the embarrassing position of informing Lady Olivier that she was being dropped, decided instead to cancel the production. Yet this was at a time Osborne badly needed a revival, since his finances had become disastrous.

In November 1986, Osborne and Helen moved from Edenbridge in Kent to Clun, in Shropshire. The sale of the Edenbridge house was intended to pay off his debts, which included a £100,000 overdraft and a similar amount in tax arrears.

The real problem was that ever since *Tom Jones* had made him a millionaire, Osborne had continued to live like a millionaire. And as the annual income from his plays diminished from £50,000 a year to £25,000, he continued to live as if it was four times that amount. And although the difference between the price of the Edenbridge house and the Clun house reduced his debts, the huge repair bill on their rundown new property sent them skyrocketing again.

When Jill Bennett committed suicide on 6 October 1990, Osborne hastened to add a particularly vindictive chapter about her to *Almost a Gentleman*, which was about to go to press. It was also in 1990 that Albert Finney broke it to Osborne that Woodfall Films still owed him £70,000 from *Tom Jones*. When asked by a mutual friend to cancel the debt, the wealthy Finney refused.

At this point, Osborne had a brilliant idea that should have restored his fortunes: a sequel to *Look Back in Anger*. He decided to call it *Déjàvu*, a deliberate misspelling of the French words meaning 'already seen'.

This time it was not 'pulled from the air', like most of his previous plays, but carefully planned, then written between December 1988 and April 1989, from notebooks he had filled with fragments of dialogue.

He sent the play to Richard Eyre, artistic director of the National Theatre, who had presented a revival of *Inadmissible Evidence,* and commissioned an Osborne adaptation of Strindberg's *The Father* (1989), which had been well received. But within a fortnight, Eyre replied:

> Dear John,
>   I am sorry not to have responded sooner to your play. I can't remember ever looking forward to receiving any play more, and my disappointment is perhaps partly due to my exaggerated high expectations.

He went on to suggest that it might be more effective as a monologue performed before *Look Back in Anger*.

But Osborne had already sent it to an independent producer, Robert Fox, who liked it and accepted it. He suggested that its publicity value as a sequel to *Look Back in Anger* would be enhanced if Tony Richardson would agree to direct it.

Richardson and Osborne had ceased to communicate years ago, after the *Charge of the Light Brigade* fiasco. But since Fox was soon to marry Richardson's daughter Natasha, he was hopeful. And Osborne was delighted when Richardson rang him from Los Angeles to say he thought *Déjàvu* was his best play since *Look Back in Anger*. He flew to London and there was a reconciliation.

The artistic director of the Court, Max Stafford-Clark, did not agree. He said it was 'dated'. Stephen Daldry, the incoming director, was of the same opinion.

Fox and Richardson were still willing to go ahead. Alan Bates – the original Cliff – agreed to play Jimmy Porter. But to their chagrin, Osborne said he was wrong for the part. Finally, Richardson returned to Los Angeles and Fox dropped out.

To increase Osborne's depression, he had been found to be a diabetic, and told to cut down drinking. Since he had been virtually an alcoholic for years, this was a severe blow.

Osborne's old Court friend Helen Montagu, now at H M Tennent, took up the challenge, and suggested Peter O'Toole as Jimmy Porter. This finally fell through because O'Toole felt the play needed cuts, and Osborne was unwilling.

Three years of frustration followed. And in 1992, *Déjàvu* was doomed by one final piece of appalling luck. The opening corresponded with one of the worst heatwaves in years, when London's theatres were half-empty anyway.

True, this was not the only reason *Déjàvu* was a failure. O'Toole had been right: it was simply far too long, nearly twice as long as *Look Back in Anger*. Worse still, it was almost actionless. In *Look Back in Anger*, Alison walks out on Jimmy, and her friend Helena steps into her shoes. Then Alison comes back and they are reconciled, so there is a happy-ever-after ending. *Déjàvu* ends with the middle-aged Jimmy Porter still spouting rancour at his Teddy bear, and the weary Cliff understandably asleep under his newspaper. Osborne had been simply carried away by all the notes he had made for the play, and tried to stuff them all into it, making it top heavy.

Osborne had added a stage instruction at the end: that in the event of 'audience dissent', loud martial music might drown them out. In fact, by the end of this marathon of talk, the audience felt too tired and dispirited to boo.

By 1993, Osborne's finances were dangerously low. His overdraft was now £150,000. He wrote to Robert McCrum, his editor at Faber, telling him that the problem was now 'literally to be able to eat'. McCrum went to Osborne's home with the Faber accountant to find out just how much his author owed. The answer was: far too much for Faber to be justified in bailing him out.

Osborne asked his agent if he could get him lecture tours in America, adding: '. . . it would kill me . . . but I think it would be as good a way to go as any.'

Wallowing in depression, he was now signing his name 'John Osborne, ex-playwright', or 'Yesterday's Man'.

He was persuaded to go to the Dorchester in September 1992 to receive a Lifetime Achievement award from the Writers' Guild, but was so incoherent when he made his speech that the audience began to boo. But it was not, as it appeared, drunkenness; Osborne was having a hyper-glycaemic attack because he had failed to take his insulin. The television writer Alan Bleasdale recognised what was really wrong. 'He's dying,' he told Guild President Alan Plater.

As a result of his diabetes Osborne was going blind, and was also losing his teeth. The dentist's bill came to £18,000. A grant of £6,700 from the Royal Literary Fund did not even begin to cover it.

The original manuscript of *Look Back in Anger* was put up for sale at Sotheby's, but failed to reach its reserve price of £40,000. It finally sold for half that sum to the University of Texas. The tax man took it all.

Suffering from pernicious anaemia and a failing liver, Osborne went into the Nuffield Hospital two weeks before Christmas 1994, with problems with his right foot. But when these healed a few days later, he was too weak to go home. He died in Helen's arms on Christmas Eve, a few days after his sixty-fifth birthday. His last word to her was 'Sorry'.

Kenneth Tynan, no longer an employee of the National Theatre after October 1976, had to think of how to make money. He had been forced to settle the *Soldiers* libel suit out of court, but was optimistic that a projected film about S/M in a *ménage à trois* might prove as profitable as *Deep Throat*, about a girl whose clitoris is where her tonsils should be. He was also mulling over ideas for a pornographic novel. Some of his diary entries read like notes for it. 'The full rectal presentation with the dear Scot's bum bursting as the pink piston of prick slides up and down is something I shall never forget.'

Soon after leaving the National, Tynan and Kathleen, with their two children, flew to California, where he spent the remainder of his life. Kathleen had found a Spanish-style house in Santa Monica Canyon. It cost $2,200 a month, and since their income was only £10,200 a year, this was more than they could afford, but since they would be hobnobbing with film stars, directors and editors, it was important to give an impression of wealth and success.

Fortunately, Kathleen was now contributing. For some time now, she had been a successful writer of film scripts, and was working on one about the 1926 disappearance of Agatha Christie. .

In the dry climate of California Tynan's emphysema improved, and the *New Yorker*, which had hired him to write six profiles for $44,000, was also paying his medical expenses. But relaxation had tempted him to take up smoking again.

In December 1977, when Kathleen was briefly absent, he went to an 'enema clinic' which advertised spankable girls. His assigned spankee was black and built like a Watusi warrior. He complained that smacking her black marble buttocks was like spanking King Kong. Besides, he said, spanking black girls conflicted with his ideas on civil liberties.

His sexual adventures in these last years seemed doomed to absurdity and bathos. When Kathleen was away, he continued to go to a clinic in North Hollywood. After paying $60, he was sitting with a girl across his knees and about to begin when another girl rushed in and told her to come at once. Two minutes later his girl returned to say: 'The cops are at the door. Hide in the closet.' There he recalled that his wallet was on the bed with his money and credit cards. As he stood in the dark, shaking so hard the coathangers rattled, she whispered that the cops were going to search the place, and he had better jump from the balcony. It was a fifteen-foot drop and he protested 'I can't make it.' 'It's that or jail.' He managed to drop without damage. Then it struck him that this had been simply a swindle to get $60 out of him. But later in the day when he rang the house, he learned that the girls were appearing in court, and heaved a sigh of relief at having avoided disastrous publicity that might have jeopardised his *New Yorker* job.

Sexual abstinence continued. He had not made love to Kathleen – to her distress – since 1973. The affair with Nicole was on hold, since she was in London, but he looked forward to mutual flogging sessions when they could get away on holiday.

On 29 May 1977 he wrote in his diary:

> Get up from nude sunbathing on lawn to discover viscous yellow fluid oozing from tip of prick. This, considering that I have not had sexual connection with anyone or anything (except my own right hand) since I was in London is really too much. Bankruptcy, emphysema, paralysis of the will – and now this! Feel that God is making his point with rather vulgar overstatement.

He goes on to mention a new magazine called *National Bottom,* which deals exclusively with events in and around the anus, and says he has taken out a lifetime subscription.

'Paralysis of the will' refers to a now-recurrent problem. His difficulty, he admits, is that he needs an audience, like an actor, and without this feedback, his creativity tends to dry up. A book about Wilhelm Reich, the prophet of sexual freedom (which should have been Tynan's ideal subject) had had to be abandoned in 1974. A piece on Tom Stoppard commissioned by the *New Yorker* took him six months

In November, he succeeded in escaping to Spain – on a *New Yorker* assignment – to meet Nicole. This girl in her late twenties, an out-of-work actress, had met Tynan in 1973, and proved to share his fascination for anuses and smacking. They had soon progressed to more complex scenarios. Through an advertisement, Tynan located a young married woman called Sally who had discovered her masochism as a result of reading *The Story of O*, and arranged for a threesome with Nicole. They played make-believe games, in the first of which Tynan and Nicole were a count and countess punishing a maid for theft and drunkenness. The girl, wearing Victorian knickers with a flap, lay over Tynan's knee, with the 'exquisite hairless little pink anus' exposed, and was given 25 smacks, then twelve blows with a hairbrush by Nicole. Then the countess had to be spanked for overspending on a dress – Sally was obviously fascinated by her bottom, and timidly expressed the wish that she might be allowed one day to spank it. Then both women retired to the bedroom to be whipped by the count, to whom they showed their gratitude by holding his penis. Sally then had to return to her husband and children. But next time, said Tynan, 'Nicole will surely end up on top of me, being whipped by Sally, while I fuck her and at the same time stroke Sally's already glowing bottom. A milestone!' concluded Tynan, 'if I were now to die!'

He admitted to feeling ashamed of these charades, in some of which he dressed as a woman. 'It is fairly comic and slightly nasty. But it is shaking me like an infection and I cannot do anything but be shaken until it has passed.'

There were even times when he suspected that he was possessed by something demonic. In St Tropez, he records 'a literally diabolical dream' of a masochistic girl in a cellar, naked and covered with excrement, her hair shaved off, and dozens of drawing pins driven into her head. 'At this point I wake up filled with horror. And at once, dogs in the hotel grounds began to bark pointlessly, as they are said to when the King of Evil; invisible to men, passes by. I really felt as if my mind had been the temporary harbour of an evil spirit, sent to deliver an obscure and obscene warning.'

In Madrid with Nicole in 1977 Tynan discovered that the great theatrical hit of the season was *Oh Calcutta!*, and that the journalists who interviewed him assumed it had made him a millionaire. The truth was that he had less than $600 in his American bank and an overdraft of £5,100 in London. As Paul Johnson says, whatever his faults, he was not greedy.

By January of the following year, cheques had started to bounce. By February he was sunk in depression, quoting Dr Johnson, in a sentiment that echoed Schopenhauer: 'That man is never happy for the present is so true that all his relief from unhappiness is only forgetting himself for a little while. Life is a progress from want to want, not from enjoyment to enjoyment.'

In spite of his feeling that God was determined to drive home a tiresome lesson, he prepared in 1977 to embark on a summer of sexual indulgence with Nicole in Spain. What followed was an incredible odyssey of disasters:

The plan was to take a villa in Mojacar with Nicole, breaking off to drive Kathleen and the children on a tour to Compostela. The first sign that fate disapproved was when his plane from Rochester to New York was grounded by engine failure, and his luggage was transferred to a second plane, which also developed engine trouble. A third plane was re-routed to Paris via Buffalo, Toronto and Amsterdam on four different airlines. 'Arrive to find all my baggage (eight pieces) has been lost. It turned up in Warsaw two days later.' He and Nicole picked up his Jaguar, which had come from London, only to discover that its power-steering had broken down so it was undrivable 'except by Superman'. It took three days to get it repaired, and they finally set out on their holiday. Two days later, across the Spanish border, the tyre exploded when they were driving at a hundred miles an hour on the motorway. Nicole demonstrated her skill as a mechanic by changing it, but the tyre was so damaged that they made the mistake of throwing away the wheel – Tynan eventually had to have another flown in from London.

Having endured sexual abstinence since the previous November, Tynan was making up for it with such vigorous abandon that he bent his penis so it swelled and became painful to the touch, even when half-erect. It seemed the problem was a broken blood vessel, which reduced it to the shape of an egg-timer. This, reports Tynan gloomily, makes sex a 'long and exhausting business'.

Suffering from extreme lassitude, he accepted Nicole's suggestion that he spend three days in bed. He sleeps while Nicole is at the beach and awakens to discover he has been robbed of his camera, gold pen and a thousand dollars, as well as his passport, air ticket, and $14,000 in travellers' cheques. His neighbours assure him he is lucky he was asleep; one woman who awoke and interrupted burglars had both kneecaps shot off.

An exhausting round of visits to police stations, embassies and banks ends in a two-hundred-mile trip to an American Express in Granada, during which a lorry passing too close on a mountain road badly damages the side of the Jaguar. A paroxysm of coughing caused by something that went down the wrong way causes a hernia. This forces him to wear a truss which finally ends all sexual activity.

As the date of Kathleen's arrival approached, he tried to book Nicole a plane ticket, but all seats were taken, so she had to move in with friends when the family arrived. 'Atmosphere is electric. My reaction is a simple desire to go to sleep for ever.'

His run of bad luck seemed to end with Kathleen's arrival and Nicolo's departure, and there followed a pleasant sight-seeing tour. But emphysema catches up with him in Leon, and he is forced to remain in bed for two days. A kind of nervous breakdown makes him talk gibberish and wipes the whole episode from his memory.

After Kathleen's departure, more disasters. Two friends from Mojacar take him to dinner. As they leave a young man snatches his new handbag and disappears at a sprint. Tynan runs after him but falls badly and cuts both knees. So he once more loses his passport, air tickets and traveller's cheques.

This time the authorities are deeply suspicious, and getting it all replaced involves days of standing in queues in temperatures of 102° at police stations and embassies, knowing that if there is any delay his visa will expire and he will be unable to re-enter America.

Finally back in Los Angeles, 'destiny gave me a final tap in the balls to remind me who was boss. Of my eight pieces of luggage, seven appeared on the carousel at LA Airport. The eighth, containing all my *New Yorker* research and the manuscript of the Mel Brooks profile (32,000 words) which I'd finished in Spain, was lost. It turned up next day in Rio de Janeiro.'

By 1979, he was on oxygen all the time, with a portable machine for daytime use. For that year there are only two pages of diary entries.

In July 1979, Tynan flew down to Puerto Vallarta in Mexico, where he would spend the morning in bed, sometimes dictating letters to the wife of an American friend, who served as his secretary, and after a lunch of Tequila and a fiery chilean soup at a local restaurant by the sea, another siesta, then the evening in a restaurant surrounded by noisy tourists.

In August he was joined by Kathleen and the children. When they played a word game and Kathleen forgot the rules he snorted: 'It's my fucking passion and you can't fucking well remember how to play.' She countered: 'I'm not good at games.' 'Life's a game,' he told her.

But one morning, as he struggled to sit up, he said: 'Life itself is my enemy.'

Later that year he signed a contract to write his autobiography, with advances amounting to a quarter of a million pounds. When a book of his *New Yorker* profiles, *Show People*, was published in the spring, he went through the gruelling round of publicity, and Norman Mailer, with whom he had dinner, found him as brilliant as ever. But on his return to Los Angeles he collapsed and had to go into intensive care. By April he weighed only 117 pounds, or just over eight stone.

Incredibly, he survived more than a year, until 26 July 1980, when he died in Santa Monica, at the age of 53.

His friend Tony Richardson, of whom he had seen a great deal in Hollywood, would die of aids in 1991. Tynan's wife Kathleen would die in January 1995 at the age of 57.

Alex Trocchi, while not a close friend of Tynan, had attended a wedding reception in his Mayfair house for his friends John and Sue Marquand. His biographer Andrew Murray Scott records that Alex 'was rather sceptical of Tynan', remarking that 'I don't like people who are more far out than I am'. What he undoubtedly sensed was that Tynan was not genuinely 'far out', because his desire for social acceptance was too strong.

In New York he had become a celebrity around Greenwich Village, since the Beat Generation had just arrived on the literary scene. As his biographer puts it: 'he wanted to leave no convention unflouted'. When his job as a scow caretaker bored him, he gave it up and lived in the rooms of various friends in the Village.

At a party there he met a slim, beautiful girl called Lyn Hicks, eleven years his junior, and an executive secretary for an advertising firm. Her well-off bourgeois parents lived in Hicksville, New Jersey, so he referred to her as Miss Hicks from Hicksville. They got married in Tijuana, Mexico, in August 1957. Soon she was pregnant – and also on heroin. They rented an amazingly cheap – cockroach infested – apartment in the Village, which soon became a centre for the Beats. He did some reviewing, wrote a long poem *The Sacred Grove* (which has since vanished) and a spoof novel about the lesbian poetess Sappho supposedly translated from a medieval Latin manuscript.

Cain's Book came out in April 1960. The New York police were already aware of him as a drug addict, and during this period he was arrested and thrown into the Tombs – the New York police cells – again and again.

But it was when he obtained a drug prescription from his doctor at the request of a sixteen-year-old girl, unaware that she was under age, that he landed himself in the deepest trouble of his life. When she was caught with it on her in 1961, Trocchi's name on it meant that, under a new law of New York State, he had become eligible for the maximum sentence – death.

He had no chance of paying the enormous bail – $5,000 – but George Plimpton (whose father was a rich lawyer on Wall Street) stepped in and paid it.

He then made a gesture that was the equivalent of Tynan saying 'Fuck' on air: on a live television programme being broadcast nationwide he gave himself a fix on camera. As far as the New York cops were concerned, that made him Public Enemy Number One. If he landed back in jail now, they would throw away the key.

On a trip to Hicksville to see Lyn's parents, he gave them their chance. On their way home by rail, both were longing for a fix. They began to do it on a station platform. As their train was arriving, the agents bore down on them. Alex saw them in time and jumped aboard the train, leaving his wife and child behind. At his destination, the vast rabbit warren of Grand Central, he managed to slip out without being seen. From there he made his way to the Phoenix Bookstore on Cornelia Street, where the owner, Larry Wallrich, risked his own freedom by sheltering him. For several days he hid out in a back room furnished with a bed. The assistant, Diane Di Prima, spent days on the telephone to various friends, and finally raised the money for his return trip to Scotland. Jane Lougee was now married to Baird Bryant, once co-editor of *Merlin*, and he gave Alex his passport. George Plimpton involuntarily contributed no less than two Brooks Brothers suits when Alex called on him, found him out, but succeeded in gaining access and putting on both suits, one over the other. So attired like a wealthy businessman, he caught a bus from the Port Authority terminal on West Fortieth, and made his way to Montreal. With the help of a young poet, Leonard Cohen, he spent four days there before taking ship for Europe.

In Glasgow, now suffering agonies from withdrawal symptoms, he rushed into the first chemist shop he saw and got himself a fix – in 1961 there was little drug addiction in the UK, and heroin could be obtained on prescription. As a registered addict, Alex soon had a regular supply.

To his enormous relief, Lyn had been given a two-year probation instead of the prison sentence he feared. But it took most of a year before she and their son Mark were able to join Trocchi in Scotland. At the first opportunity, they moved to London, and found a cheap room in Kilburn.

Money was scarce, and Alex's need for twelve grains of heroin a day meant that it remained scarce. The royalties he had coming from America – for *Young Adam* and *Cain's Book* – were blocked by a court order because he was a fugitive. He was forced to live on pittances from selling his manuscripts to a bookseller, and occasional royalties sent to him by Girodias, who was continually trying to persuade Alex to sell all his copyrights, and waiting like some patient vulture for the day when urgent need for cash would force him to do it. Drugs seemed to have destroyed Alex's ability to do what he did best – write fiction. Instead he wrote essays like 'Invisible Insurrection of a Million Minds' and 'Sigma, A Tactical Blueprint', in which he foretold a cultural revolution brought about by men who recognised the need for an evolutionary change in consciousness. Both were frequently and widely reprinted.

Guy Debord, founder of Situation Internationale, disapproved of them as aiming at too large an audience, and told Alex: 'Your name stinks in the minds of decent men', and excommunicated him on the grounds that he associated with 'mystical cretins' like Allen Ginsberg, Colin Wilson, Timothy Leary and R D Laing. In fact, of course, I had not seen him in years.

As a footnote to Debord's career, it may be noted that he would achieve maximum notoriety in the Paris students' revolt against de Gaulle in 1968, in which he and Daniel Cohn-Bendit ('Danny the Red') were the two main leaders. After de Gaulle defused it by announcing elections, Situation Internationale became famous and its members' works bestsellers. But in post-1968 France they were irrelevant and were slowly forgotten. Debord, after expelling most close associates from the movement, soothed his frustration by eating and drinking in gargantuan quantities. (He had always been a heavy drinker of red wine.) As he became immensely fat he began to suffer from gout and insomnia. His health destroyed, he committed suicide on 30 November 1994 by putting a bullet through his heart. Alex had then been dead for ten years.

Alex needed to articulate this kind of Situationist wishful thinking as a counterbalance to his pessimism about society. He wrote in an unpublished notebook:

> I have needed drugs to abolish within myself the painful reflection of the schizophrenia of my times, to quench the impulse to get at once on to my feet and go out into the world, and live out some convenient, traditional identity of cunning contriving; acting, doing, asserting myself in the world of others, desperately as men do, and competitively, against short[ness of] time.

He failed to see that 'abolish within myself' was merely a synonym for 'escape', and that the best way to do this would have been to write, not take drugs. Publishers like John Calder would have been delighted to take his work (in fact, Calder would soon publish *Cain's Book*). This tendency to blame society for what is your own fault is a constant theme that, as we have seen, runs through the story of the Angry Young Men.

Yet his reputation was steadily increasing. In February 1962 he was asked to represent Scotland at the week-long International Writers' Conference in Edinburgh, whose other guests would include Aldous Huxley, Angus Wilson, Truman Capote, James Baldwin, Henry Miller, William Burroughs, Alain Robbe-Grillet and the Scottish poet Hugh M'Diarmid.

The latter, Scotland's best-known living poet, soon made clear his basic objection to Trocchi's comprehensive anti-authoritarianism and defence of drugs and free sex. M'Diarmid was a member of the Communist Party, and committed to the notion of a Communist utopia. Trocchi counterattacked by condemning most modern Scottish literature as parochial. The Scottish newspapers made much of their disagreement.

By now, Lyn was having health problems, due to her drug addiction, in spite of which she had a second child, Nicholas, in 1966. Trocchi had to go on National Assistance. In hospital in the Isle of Man, Lyn tried to kick the habit, and Trocchi was warned that unless he did the same, the only foreseeable future would be increasing illness and death.

Financial ruin was always hovering over them. At one point he was so broke he copied out by hand the whole of *Young Adam* and *Cain's Book* to sell to an agent for an American university, for a mere £35 each. In spite of which, he played a central part as compère in the poetry festival at the Royal Albert Hall in June 1965, and did it with his usual aplomb. Other poets there included Christopher Logue, Lawrence Ferlinghetti, Allen Ginsberg and Gregory Corso, and the occasion made Trocchi as well known in London as he was in Edinburgh.

In October, aware drugs were wrecking him – by the predicted increasing frequency of illness – he decided to kick the habit once and for all. He hired a room in Herne Bay, in Kent, for the experiment. He took with him enough heroin and cocaine for 24 hours, and other less powerful drugs, like methadone and psychedelics. The aim was to use these to help him break his dependence on heroin and move on to something less deadly.

As the day wore on, and his drug supply diminished, he tried to make it spin out, but was soon enduring agonising withdrawal symptoms. Finally he gave in. He took the last grain of heroin, then went out to search for a chemist, from whom he bought more. The effort to establish control had been a total failure.

Lyn was off heroin – for a short time – but her health was now poor. Alex sent her with Mark to Mallorca. After three days she rang him frantically to say that Mark had fallen out of a second-storey window and broken both arms. The hospital bill for five days was £125, far more than he could afford. He must have felt that fate had selected him for a special series of disasters.

In 1968, Lyn had to go into a mental hospital for a year. Then, in 1972, she contracted hepatitis, probably from a dirty needle, and in June 1972 she died in Guy's Hospital at the age of 35. Meeting Alex had obviously been the worst thing that ever happened to her. What made it worse was that he knew it.

Soon after, their fifteen-year-old son Mark contracted cancer of the throat, and it took him three years to die. This came about on 21 May 1977. Alex was shattered with grief and confesses to sobbing whenever he was alone.

Murray Scott observes, in his biography of Trocchi that, by 1970, he was virtually a forgotten man. His occasional windfalls came from gullible publishers who offered him advances on books that were never written – Tom Maschler at Cape gave him £750, the largest he ever received, on a novel called *American Nights* that never progressed beyond the title. Neither did a volume of reminiscences of his Paris days.

To make a little money, Alex opened a book stall in a local market, and in later years this was often his only source of income.

To look after his other son Nicholas, a pretty New Zealand girl, Sally Child, moved in. She was 24, roughly half his age. Alex's way with women was still hypnotic, and they became lovers. He wrote to her parents to promise that she would not be using heroin.

In 1979 he went to France to meet Jane Lougee, to take a trip to Majorca. Arriving four days late, he insisted on driving the car, and soon hit a mailbox. He decided to return to London.

His first wife Betty made the trip to see him and Scott says: 'She found him greatly changed, reminding her of the rabbit in *Alice in Wonderland* – "I'm late, I'm late . . ." She was surprised to see how like his father he had become, almost pompous, grandiose . . .' This recalls a comment Lyn had made years earlier: 'Alex, who is a great man, but no bargain, said: "I will not tolerate a world that rejects me." He thinks he is God, he really does.'

The end was clearly in sight when, in the autumn of 1983, he went to see his doctor with chest problems, and learned that he had a malignant tumour in his left lung. When he went into hospital, he was told there was a 90 per cent chance of a successful operation, and in fact the tumour was successfully removed. But after six months of recuperation, a bad cold turned into lobal pneumonia. He died on 15 April 1984, a year before his sixtieth birthday.

At his funeral at Mortlake ten days later, Christopher Logue read Marvell's 'Definition of Love', and a Miles Davis record was played.

Sally placed his ashes on the mantelpiece next to those of Lyn, Mark and two beloved cats. But one day, an unknown thief stole them, and they have never been recovered.

Epilogue

In this book I have not had time to talk about my own ideas because I have been too busy talking about other people's. Now I shall permit myself this indulgence.

From the perspective of my 75 years, I can see that the 'fame' that arrived with the publication of *The Outsider* 50 years ago, with all its publicity about Angry Young Men was, as far as my work was concerned, a total waste of time.

My work began from a simple insight that came to me in my teens: that a vast change came over the world in the late eighteenth century, a change that at first brought a wonderful surge of optimistic idealism, a promise of a new kind of future for the human race.

The herald of this sense of change was Jean-Jacques Rousseau, and his novel *Julie, or the New Héloïse*. This was about an aristocratic girl who is seduced by – or rather, who seduces, for it is she who takes the lead – her tutor St Preux.

But this was not the only reason the novel created a sensation. It was also due to Rousseau's ecstatic response to nature. For, as odd as this sounds, no one in the eighteenth century cared much for nature, unless it was enclosed and tamed in formal gardens. This is why passages like the following from Letter XXXVIII, Part One, made such an impact:

> [Here] I find the country more gay, the green more fresh and vivid, the air more pure, the sky more serene. The song of the birds seems to be more tender and voluptuous; the murmur of the brooks evokes a more amorous languor; from afar the blooming vine exudes the sweetest perfumes; a secret charm either embellishes or fascinates my senses. One would say that the earth adorns itself to make for your happy lover a nuptial bed worthy of the beauty he adores and of the passion which consumes him.

Rousseau made Europe suddenly aware that mountains and untamed woods were beautiful.

When Wordsworth went to France 30 years later, he was not only ecstatic about the French Revolution, which had got rid of the parasitic aristocracy, but about the possibility that this new vision of nature could transform human beings into something more noble and godlike. Society itself would change, and men would at last discover the secret of happiness as they learned to trust the highest that was in them: 'Bliss was it in that dawn to be alive/But to be young was very heaven.' The new spirit was soon christened romanticism, and in the hands of poets like Byron and Shelley, it taught Europe to see visions and dream dreams.

Then something strange happened. With the death of Shelley and Byron, all the optimism evaporated. Suddenly, the poets became convinced that it had all been an illusion, a beautiful dream, and they were now awake in a world of dreary ordinariness. Surely, to be a poet or an artist was tantamount to inviting an early death? For nothing in this boring practical world could bring the ecstasy of dreams. A pall of pessimism, like the smoke from an industrial city, descended over the nineteenth century.

This was my starting point in *The Outsider*, the epidemic of suicide and misfortune and madness that destroyed so many of the best minds of the age of romanticism. Yeats called the poets of the 1890s 'the tragic generation'.

In England, at least, the twentieth century brought a reaction against the sense of defeat as Shaw and Wells and Chesterton found again the vision of social change that had inspired Rousseau. But by the end of the First World War their optimism seemed naïve and outdated, and was replaced by the darker vision of Eliot, Joyce and Hemingway. As Edmund Wilson noted in *Axel's Castle*, the new generation had returned to the spirit of romantic pessimism. And as we look back on the 1920s and 1930s, we can see that literature has left the heights of the early nineteenth century, and gone into a long and slow descent towards the featureless plains.

The defeat of Hitler renewed Europe's political optimism. But when I went to London in 1951, there was still no sign of a new literary generation. It seemed that the optimism that had inspired Rousseau and his descendants, then reignited in Shaw and Wells, had burned itself out.

Now came the generation that is the subject of this book – Amis, Tynan, Osborne *et al* – and it seemed clear to me that they had simply failed to detect new pathways into the future. They had come to a halt in front of this great fallen tree of pessimism that blocked the road, and assumed, like Beckett's tramps, that there was 'Nothing to be done.'

The only one of my contemporaries with any claims to be a thinker was Iris Murdoch. But her case provides an interesting and instructive example of what had gone wrong with the postwar generation.

Iris declared herself an existentialist, and began her career with a small book on Sartre. He, of course, had proclaimed himself, like Camus, an atheist. So did Iris. 'There is no God in the traditional sense of that term,' she says in *The Sovereignty of Good* (1967). In *Under the Net*, she accepted this as her own foundation. Jake admits that we are in a meaningless world, and proclaims his admiration of Beckett's *Murphy,* where 'the sun shone on the nothing new.'

I have tried to show how hard she struggled to escape this cul-de-sac she had landed herself in. Jake concludes that the sight of a cat licking its kittens proves that the world is not entirely meaningless. In *The Sandcastle* the protagonist's daughter has second sight and can perform acts of magic, which seems to indicate something Sartre left out of account. In *The Bell,* the hero has no doubts about the validity of religious and mystical emotion, and the author seems to sympathise. The foundation of *A Severed Head* is a Blakeian sexual vision that is certainly a decisive extension of Sartrian existentialism, in which sex was always portrayed with a grimace of disgust. (Sartre admitted that he never much enjoyed it.)

But it is in her 1968 novel, *The Time of the Angels,* that her limitations suddenly become clear. The central character is the Rev Carel Fisher, who describes himself as 'a priest of no God', but who tries to escape his sense of meaninglessness by making determined efforts to be a sinner. He sleeps with the coloured maid Pattie and treats her as his slave. He seduces his brother's wife and drives him to suicide by getting her pregnant. Later he seduces the child she has borne – ostensibly his niece, although he knows she is his daughter. He even tries devil worship. Yet, like Stavrogin in Dostoevsky's *The Possessed,* none of his acts of immorality succeeds in making him feel a sense of sin. Even when, like Stavrogin, he commits suicide, the reader finds it impossible to take him seriously, or to suppose that his creator did, for Iris has just not succeeded in making either the clergyman or his problems real.

This failure, we feel, is part of her existentialist heritage from Sartre and Camus. They were convinced that the world is exactly what it appears to be, and there is no 'higher realm' of morality and meaning. Which is why the reader of *The Time of the Angels* declines to believe in her wicked clergyman and his attempts to be sinful, and the novel collapses like a badly baked cake.

We can see the problem. In swallowing postwar existentialism, Iris had accepted the non-existence of God. This is not in itself a radical step for a philosopher. But it also involved accepting the non-existence of *meaning* – that is to say, meaning as an objective datum, something that really exists 'out there', and is not merely a creation of the human mind. And as far as philosophy is concerned, that amounts to destroying your own foundations.

What are the foundations? They are implicit in a letter of August 1918 from Bertrand Russell to Constance Malleson:

'I must, I *must,* before I die, find *some* way to say the essential thing that is in me, that I have never said yet – a thing that is not love or hate or pity or scorn, but the very breath of life, fierce and coming from far away, bringing into human life the vastness and fearful passionless force of non-human things.'

This is the vision of philosophy, and it is based upon a sense of immense meaning, meaning stretching to infinity – a meaning that would exist even if there were no human beings there to see it. It is what saints mean when they speak of God.

This is also clearly what Proust is talking about when he describes the *moment bienheureux* that comes to Marcel as he tastes the cake dipped in tea:

'. . . at once the vicissitudes of life had become indifferent to me, its disasters innocuous, its brevity illusory – the new sensation having had on me the effect which love has of filling me with a precious essence, or rather, this essence was not in me, it *was* me. I had now ceased to feel mediocre, accidental, mortal . . .'

The taste has given him a sense of magnificent *objectivity*, of infinite meaning.

If the philosopher denies this vision of meaning, dismissing it as a human intellectual artefact, then he is condemning himself to entrapment in the triviality that constitute ordinary human life.

Even the arch-existentialist Heidegger recognises this when he speaks of the fundamental human problem as being 'forgetfulness of Being', a forgetfulness that is due to our involvement in triviality, which condemns us to mechanical awareness.

Sartre, too, admitted that he had never felt so free as when he was a member of the Resistance, and was likely to be arrested and shot at any moment. But he failed to ponder its implications and integrate them into his philosophy. And that, as we shall see, would have serious consequences for existentialism.

This explains why Iris, in spite of proclaiming herself an existentialist, failed to get to grips with its essence, and why the endless adulteries of her novels strike us as repetitive variations upon the same rather trivial theme. Although I was deeply saddened to hear that she was suffering from Alzheimer's in the mid 1990s, I felt that her valuable work had been over for decades.

Sartre himself was partly to blame. Although he was himself aware of this detrivialising effect of death – which he uses in the title story of *Le Mur* – he failed to recognise its centrality to philosophy.

This in turn may be blamed on his failure to understand the implications of the central concept of Husserl's phenomenology, 'intentionality'. By this Husserl meant the 'grasping activity' of consciousness. If you read a paragraph in a newspaper without intentionality, you fail to 'take it in', and have to read it again. The second time you read it, you take care to summon intentionality. Without intentionality, the world looks blank.

Now Sartre made this fundamental error at a bad time, the very start of his career, in a small work of 1937 called *The Transcendence of the Ego*. (This did not appear in English until 1957, four years after Iris's little book on Sartre and, since it appeared originally in *Recherches Philosophique*, was probably unknown to her.)

If consciousness is 'intentional' – that is, it could be compared to an arrow fired at a target – then it would seem clear that there must be an archer. This archer behind consciousness is what Kant and Husserl meant by 'the transcendental ego'. Sartre flatly denied that there is such a thing.

How could Sartre arrive at such a conclusion? Mainly because of the kind of person he was. Sartre had nothing of the introvert about him. Like Kingsley Amis, he hated being alone. He could happily write in a café full of people. He liked to be surrounded by what he called his 'family', a group of disciples and mistresses. From this we may deduce that, like Amis, he suffered from low self-esteem. He hated the very idea of what the philosopher Maine de Biran called 'inward sense' (*sense intime*). He even rejected the Freudian Unconscious.

Which explains why, although he accepts that consciousness is intentional, he does not agree there is a 'you' behind it. The 'you', Sartre says, is a notion that we arrive at by seeing ourselves in the mirror of other people's eyes. It is a construct.

Then what *does* lie behind intentionality? Nothing, says Sartre. If I wake up feeling dazed and bewildered, the world seems meaningless. Then 'intentionality' switches on, like the daylight coming through the curtains, and I remember where I am. Intentionality is like a light *without a source*. We resemble Peer Gynt's onion; peel away the outer layers and you find the centre is missing.

Such a concept sounds absurd to us, although David Hume said something of the sort. To the French it has been around ever since 1748, when La Mettrie wrote a book called *Man the Machine,* arguing that we can be explained entirely in mechanical terms. He was followed by a group known as the Ideologues, Etienne de Condillac, Destut de Tracey and Pierre Cabanis. Condillac argued that our so-called mental life is merely a matter of physical sensations, and Cabanis that the brain secretes thoughts as the liver secretes bile.

Amusingly enough, Rousseau deserves some share of the blame, for in his novel about education *Émile* (1762), which was as popular and influential as *La Nouvelle Héloïse*, he had embraced the ideas of the English philosopher John Locke who said that 'there is nothing in the mind that was not first in the senses', and that our minds start off as blank slates. This is obviously fairly close to saying that there is no 'real you'.

Now in the early nineteenth century, Maine de Biran, who was a follower of Cabanis, came to object to this notion. He pointed out that when I am making some kind of real effort (*effort voulu*), I have a clear feeling that it is I who am doing it, not a machine. I may feel mechanical when I'm doing something boring and automatic, because a robotic level of my mind takes over, but as soon as I exert my will, I become aware that I'm not a robot – that I possess an active power.

Sadly, this insight failed to make much impact on the mainstream of French philosophy, which continued in the mechanistic tradition. This explains how Sartre could assert something apparently so illogical as that that is no 'you' behind consciousness, not even an unconscious mind.

But if there is no 'archer', then what is it that gives us the impression that consciousness is 'directed'? Well, Sartre claims, there is the fact that something can 'arrest' your attention. That is to say, it *pulls* your interest towards it, as the moon pulls the tides.

This, of course, fails to meet Maine de Biran's objection that when I make an active effort of will, it feels quite different from doing something mechanically.

All of which explains why, in spite of insistence that we possess freedom, Sartre's existential psychology really denies it. It also explains why a novel like *The Time of the Angels*, which should have been a major analysis of the problem of good and evil, free will versus mechanicalness, is so oddly disappointing and unconvincing.

This is a pity, for no one else of Iris's generation was capable of raising in dramatic form the questions probed by Dostoevsky, and expressed by Kirilov in *The Possessed* – whether, if God does not exist, man is forced to accept that he must be God?

Once we can see how this question of the freedom of the will has been vitiated by post-romantic philosophy, with its inbuilt tendency to laziness and boredom, we can also see how it came about that existentialism found itself in a hole of its own digging, and how the philosophical developments since then have amounted to walking in circles round that hole.

First came Foucault, with his post-Marxian determinism (history divides neatly into cultural units called *epistemes*), Derrida's Deconstruction, with its anti-metaphysical bias and its insistence that we are tools in the hands of language, then Jean-François Lyotard's post-modernism, which amounts to an 'incredulity towards metanarratives' (i.e., towards a bird's eye view of truth that transcends mere 'language games'), which boils down to a foundationless relativism that leaves everyone feeling confused and depressed. This, it seems, is the philosophy of today's younger generation of novelists.

In view of this drift into post-modernism, we can begin to see the period of the Angry Young Men in a rather more sympathetic light. Osborne's work may be little more than a surrender to negative emotion, but at least he regrets that 'there are no good, brave causes left'. Tynan's central motivation may have been an obsession with celebrities, but at least he thought that Marxism might be the route to a more serious art. Braine may be naïve about the trappings of success, but at least he always preserved an appealing kind of innocence about them. Larkin's pessimism may be admission of defeat (and a way of guaranteeing it), but at least it produced some excellent poems. Trocchi may have destroyed himself in the hedonistic pursuit of sensation, but he was driven by a positive vision of the evolution of consciousness.

As for Amis, the only one about whom I find it difficult to find anything positive to say, the lesson of his career is that he allowed himself to be hypnotised by the cynicism of his intellectual mentor Larkin, and firmly stuck to this unfruitful position to the end . . .

What happened to the British novel in the post-modern period is competently chronicled in D J Taylor's *After the War, The Novel and English Society since 1945*. Chapter Eight, 'The Search for Value', begins with a quotation from Graham Greene complaining that since the death of Henry James, the religious sense has vanished from the English novel, and that character has been replaced in E M Forster and Virginia Woolf by 'cardboard symbols' in a world that is 'paper-thin'.

Taylor goes on: 'Character, according to Professor Joachim in Malcolm Bradbury's *Stepping Westward*, is an out-dated concept. By "character", of course, Joachim means people's sense of their inner selves.' He contrasts this with the Victorian age, and novels like *Vanity Fair* and *The Last Chronicle of Barset*, with their awareness of moral values. Compared to these, Jim Dixon and Charles Lumley 'are generally helpless in the face of events, victims of circumstance, people to whom things happen.'

Pamela Hansford Johnson is discussed as an 'old-fashioned novelist', whose *The Humbler Creation,* although aware of the forces of disintegration, nevertheless operates on the level of religion and morality. By contrast, Golding's characters live in a world of 'unappeasable dark forces', of 'civilised values put to the test and found wanting'. Greene and Waugh make an attempt to return to religious values, but their work is vitiated by a kind of Catholic snobbery, in which there is 'something rather *distingué* in the idea of being damned'.

Wain is considered as 'a more deserving candidate for the title of "English moralist"' than Amis, but found wanting, since his idea of decency seems to consist of making his provincial characters prefer the provinces to London, hardly an important moral decision.

The chapter concludes with a section on the work of Martin Amis, as an example of the problem 'of writing moral fiction in a moral vacuum'. 'Amis's chief characteristic is an intense and fascinated disgust, in which the exposure of his characters' appalling behaviour is invariably followed by retribution and, occasionally, outright obliteration', as when the inhabitants of a rectory in *Dead Babies* are destroyed by the man they assume to be the impresario of their decadence. But Taylor notes that 'disgust is not necessarily a moral statement', and goes on to remark that 'Amis's fiction is built on the assumption of impending social and ethical collapse'.

Taylor notes of Amis's novel *Success* that if it has a 'moral' 'it is that triumph debases you even more than failure'. '*London Fields* discloses a more subtle yet equally depressing purpose, much of it detectable in the gargantuan figure of Keith Talent, a sublime barbarian – criminal, womaniser, cheat . . .' And he concludes his analysis of Talent's destructive amoralism : 'If there is a consolation it lies in the fact that these are not real people – certainly not in the sense achieved by Pamela Hansford Johnson's characters. Amis's people cannot better themselves. They cannot even make choices. They can only be extinguished . . .'

Taylor concludes: 'The protagonists of the immediately postwar novel might have been distinguishable by their inability to live moral lives . . . Their late 1980s successors have even less ability to make moral choices, and consequently even less sense of possessing lives of their own. In any fictional battle involving moral relativism, unfortunately, the only victor is the author.'

It seems sad that, since Martin Amis is one of the most intelligent literary critics since V S Pritchett, his skilful novels should be devoted to conjuring up negative states of mind and some of the nastiest people in modern fiction. The satisfaction we are supposed to derive from them is the dubious one of seeing them getting their come-uppance. This, Taylor seems to feel, is typical of the post-modernist literary milieu.

By way of distancing ourselves from this Dantesque vision of the hopeless and the damned, let us, as an exercise in imagination, try to envisage what might have happened if Maine de Biran's protest about free will had been taken seriously by the French philosophical establishment, which was still, in the tradition of Condillac and Cabanis, materialist and determinist. Maine de Biran asserted that man's inner world, governed by intuition, is more important than the external world, to which most men feel enslaved. *It is because we do not recognise our freedom that we fail to use it.* The situation is rather like that of a bird that has forgotten that it can fly.

Even so, by the year 1900, intellectual prospects had brightened. Henri Bergson, born in 1859, was a direct philosophical descendant of Maine de Biran (via his teacher Ravaisson), born 1859, began as an atheist and positivist. But when he became a schoolmaster in the Auvergne, and began to take long walks, the peace of the countryside and the magnificent scenery, his atheism dissolved away, and he began to grasp an insight that would change philosophy.

It was this. As an instrument for grasping reality, the rational mind is a blundering incompetent. We know, for example, that mathematically speaking, a line consists of millions of points, yet when you draw it, you see it as continuous. It is the same with time. How long does twelve o'clock last? It doesn't, for you can imagine a millionth of a second to twelve, or a billionth. Yet as you watch the hand of a clock, twelve o'clock comes and goes. Reality is a *flow*. A positivist would say that the beauty of a sunset is a purely subjective feeling, whose reality is energy vibrating in space. He would also say that a symphony consists of sound waves in the air. These two examples make us aware *that when we try to grasp reality with the mind, we falsify it.* Even to try is like trying to pick up a peeled soft-boiled egg with fire-tongs. Our most valuable and important experiences cannot be grasped with thought, only with intuition.

Once we have grasped this we have released ourselves from the trap of positivism. And we can instantly see that Maine de Biran's recognition of free will fits comfortably into the new picture, whereas the materialist psychology of La Mettrie and Condillac, like a square peg in a round hole, is simply inadequate.

Now in 1927, the nineteen-year-old Sartre was an enthusiastic disciple of Bergson; when he first read him he felt that 'the truth had come down from the heavens'. And indeed, Bergson was an important influence on what came to be called existentialism. If all had gone well, existentialism might have become the flexible and fluid philosophy that the twentieth century most needed, and the collapse into post-modernist relativism might have been averted.

Unfortunately, Sartre failed to understand Husserl's intentionality, largely because of clashes within his own temperament, which is oddly pessimistic. He told Simone de Beauvoir: 'We are as free as you like, but helpless.' This is surely a self-contradictory absurdity, like telling someone who is bound hand and foot: 'You are free – get up and walk.'

Sartre's problem here is a misunderstanding about the nature of freedom. The philosopher Fichte remarked: 'To be free is nothing. To *become* free is heavenly.' If I say 'I am free' I usually mean something negative: 'I am not doing anything at the moment.' This is quite different from the shock of freedom experienced by a man who has been reprieved from a firing squad – or indeed, the sense of freedom we experienced when we set out on holiday. This is positive freedom, and the distinction is vital. Sartre's failure to bear the difference in mind means there is a fallacy at the very foundation of his philosophy.

Freedom in the positive sense is like an awakening, or like an engine roaring into life. It brings a surge of vitality.

Sartre's failure to grasp this can be attributed to the fact that he suffered many of the same weaknesses as so many of the writers in this volume – alcoholism, tobacco and drugs.

A list of his daily intake quoted by philosopher Michel Onfray includes two packs of strong cigarettes and numerous pipefuls of brown tobacco, more than a litre of alcohol – wine, beer, vodka, whisky, etc. – 200 milligrams of amphetamines; 15 grams of aspirin; several grams of barbiturates, without counting the coffees, teas and other fats of his daily dietary intake.

Sartre's lack of interest in hygiene is reminiscent of many nineteenth century artists and poets. 'In Germany, he had let filth and smell set in to the point that his biographer could speak of his "pestilential room" and weeks on end passed without washing', says Onfray. 'His nickname was "the man with the black gloves" because his lower arms were black with filth.'

Any psychiatrist would recognise that these signs indicate a depressive who finds consciousness too much of a burden to be borne without stimulants. All this explains why Sartre did not believe in free will.

By his early sixties he was suffering from high blood pressure and periodic strokes, which he ignored; until by the age of 71 he was dead.

Since Sartre made no attempt to understand the 'young Turks' who were treading on his heels – Barthes, Foucault, Derrida – he also made no attempt to oppose the return of the relativism they represented, and abnegated his responsibilities towards post-existentialism. As a result, a century and a half of interesting innovations since Maine de Biran were swept away in the flood of structuralism, deconstruction and post-modernism that followed each other as relentlessly as a landslide. This could have been avoided if Sartre had opened the pages of *Les Temps modernes* to discussion of these new ideas; but he was, as always, too preoccupied with his own notion of revolutionary politics, denouncing the *salauds* of the bourgeoisie, and declaring that true progress lay in the attempt of the coloured races to free themselves through violence.

Oddly enough, Beckett played a central role in the rise of the new philosophy. On 29 May 1966, *L'Express* came out with a headline: THE GREATEST REVOLUTION SINCE EXISTENTIALISM, above a huge picture of Michel Foucault. It was about a book called *Les Mots et les Choses* (translated into English as *The Order of Things*). This represented Foucault's attempt to dethrone Sartre, and it succeeded. It argues that man is in the grip of immense historical forces that he cannot escape, and which periodically replace one epoch (or *episteme*) with another. It sounds a little like Karl Marx, but Foucault also attacks Marx as being trapped in his epoch 'like a fish in water' – a sideswipe at Sartre's Marxism.

But it was *Waiting for Godot* that had first inspired Foucault with the conviction that Sartre's notion of 'commitment' could be ignored; *Godot* seemed to be saying that history is meaningless. By that time, linguistic discoveries of a long-dead Swiss professor named Ferdinand de Saussure had been disinterred from his notes, and suddenly everybody was talking excitedly about signifiers and signified, *langue* and *parole*. We must think of language (*langue*) as a living reality, pulsing with life like some gigantic mass of protoplasm, not as a dead structure preserved in libraries. Language is a living structure – which is why its study engendered a concept called structuralism.

Foucault would find Saussure as useful as Beckett in building a siege-engine to storm the ramparts of existentialism.

Another major influence was the anthropologist Claude Lévi-Strauss, because 'who says man says language, and who says language says society'. He attempted to use the methods of linguistics to study primitive societies – for example, kin structures and myth. In this sense, structures might be compared to what Freud meant by the unconscious mind – unseen forces below the surface. Structuralists were creating their own kind of psychoanalysis. The prey they hunted were not neuroses but 'codes'.

Now structuralism is closely related to Husserl's phenomenology, in that what we see is determined by what we 'intend'. Blake said: 'The fool sees not the same tree that the wise man sees.' Kant argued that the world we see is determined by underlying structures called 'categories'. But since Sartre denied the existence of a 'real me' he was in no position to engage in this new kind of philosophical analysis, and he simply condemned the structuralists for lacking a historical sense and failing to grasp the importance of revolution.

By far the most influential of the post-Sartrians was Jacques Derrida, a Husserlian who, like Sartre, disbelieved in the transcendental ego. And as an anti-metaphysical materialist, he also rejects wholesale anything that sounds like a platonic belief in a world of ideas and essences. His technique of 'deconstruction' is aimed at pricking such metaphysical concepts like so many balloons.

But he accepts Saussure's notion of language as a living, pulsating reality, to such an extent that he believes that it is the true moulder of consciousness. Which is why he asserted that we do not speak language; language speaks us.

We can see that the post-Sartrian landscape is even bleaker than the world of Sartre's atheistic existentialism. It is difficult to see how philosophy could extricate itself from such a totally negative position.

However, a glance back into the past provides a vital clue, by enabling us to see how this situation came about, and just where and when philosophy found itself on the downhill slope towards relativism.

To begin with, we note that the problem seems to originate in La Mettrie's argument that human beings are machines. But then, 60 years later, Maine de Biran showed this to be absurd when he pointed out that we can *feel* the difference between doing something mechanically and making an effort of will.

If free will exists, there must surely be an 'essential me' from whom it emanates? If so, then this should be the foundation stone of a new philosophical synthesis.

Its first step would be to dismiss any philosophical position that is based on the contrary assertion – and that would include Sartre, Foucault and Derrida, as well as La Mettrie and the Ideologues of the late eighteenth century. This leaves us with the phenomenology of Edmund Husserl, with its recognition of the transcendental ego, and the intuitionism of Bergson, with its recognition that the thinking mind is inadequate when it tries to grasp the nature of reality.

Bergson is particularly important, since he developed Maine de Biran's insight about free will. His *Time and Free Will* (1889) concludes with an assertion of the reality of freedom, while his *Introduction to Metaphysics* (1903) defines metaphysics as the science that uses intuition. *Creative Evolution* (1906) speaks of the essentially dynamic nature of the Self – what Buckminster Fuller seems to have meant when he said 'I seem to be a verb' – and introduces the concept of the *élan vital*, the force that lies behind the evolution of intelligence.

This notion has been attacked by biologists – like Julian Huxley, who claimed it explains nothing. But we can grasp its importance as soon as we reflect on the concept of futility in post-modernism, which Camus called 'the absurd' – that is to say, meaningless, boring repetition. This same meaninglessness Sartre calls 'nausea', and he even makes Mathieu, the hero of *The Age of Reason*, speak about his need for 'salvation'.

In a context of atheistic existentialism, that word can only mean the opposite of boredom and futility: the sense of purpose: what Shaw means when he talks about the human 'appetite for fruitful activity and a high quality of life'. It reminds us that man is the only animal whose craving for a sense of purpose is as basic as his need for food and drink.

Again, Jung, commenting on the number of his patients who suffered from a sense of suicidal meaninglessness, remarked that 'The soul has a religious function,' by which he meant that man seems to differ from animals in needing a sense of evolutionary purpose before he can feel fulfilled. And Julian Huxley once defined religion as 'the organ by which man grasps his destiny'.

William James makes the same point when he comments in 'The Energies of Men':

> In some persons this sense of being cut off from their rightful resources is extreme, and we then get the formidable neurasthenic

and psychasthenic conditions, with life grown into one tissue of impossibilities, that so many medical books describe.

Stating the thing broadly, the human individual thus lives usually far within his limits; he possesses powers of various sorts which he habitually fails to use. He energizes below his maximum, and he behaves below his optimum. In elementary faculty, in co-ordination, in power of inhibition and control, in every conceivable way, his life is contracted like the field of vision of an hysteric subject — but with less excuse, for the poor hysteric is diseased, while in the rest of us it is only an inveterate habit — the habit of inferiority to our full self — that is bad.

As to how we can learn to break this habit, Dr Johnson pointed us in the right direction when he commented: 'When a man knows he is to be hanged in a fortnight, it concentrates his mind wonderfully.' Any stimulus that concentrates the mind has the effect of making us aware of the reality of free will.

Which brings us back in a full circle to an observation made at the beginning of this book: that for Rousseau, the notion of sexual freedom precedes that of social freedom. When St Preux envisages possessing Julie, he glimpses the essence of freedom, the *moment bienheureux* that will make him 'cease to feel mediocre, accidental, mortal' and raise his life to a new level. This is why the theme of sexuality has run like a thread throughout this book, and why D H Lawrence and William Blake made unexpected guest appearances in the chapter on Iris Murdoch.

It is a pity that this primary insight of Rousseau's was so quickly diluted by his muddled, unrealistic philosophy of social freedom that was to inspire Karl Marx, as well as contemporaries like Sartre, Tynan, Debord and Trocchi, whose deficiencies I have tried to allow to speak for themselves.

It is appropriate to quote Dr Johnson in this context, for in 1759, two years before the publication of *La Nouvelle Héloïse*, Johnson had written a novel that is effectively a refutation of Rousseau's social doctrines. It was called *Rasselas, Prince of Abyssinia*, and the prince of its title lives in a 'Happy Valley' that sounds like Rousseau's idea of paradise. Its inhabitants have everything they need to be contented: a perfect climate, magnificent scenery, beautiful palaces, interesting entertainment, wise teachers. Yet the young prince admits to feeling oddly bored and frustrated, and comments: 'Man surely has some latent sense for which this place affords no grati-fication; or he has some desire, distinct from sense, which must be satisfied before he can be happy'. And he plots to escape to the outside world.

This 'latent sense' is what Jung means when he says 'the soul has a religious function' – the craving for purpose.

If there was a pill that could put us in touch with our 'rightful resources', and fill us with a sense of reality, the problem would vanish. But pills – or drugs – do not strengthen the will: they make us passive.

When we survey all the possible answers, we have to admit that those who have come closest to a solution have been certain saints and ascetics. Gurdjieff taught that 'normal' consciousness is a form of sleep, and his disciple Ouspensky, in *Tertium Organum*, wrote: '. . . in reality, all that proceeds around us we sense only very confusedly, just as a snail senses confusedly the sunlight, the darkness and the rain.'

For more than 50 years my own work has been concerned with this problem. From the beginning, I was aware that one effective method of 'breaking through' to reality is by deliberately inducing 'crisis', as Graham Greene did when, as a clinically depressed teenager, he played Russian roulette with a revolver that contained a single bullet. When the hammer clicked on an empty chamber, he experienced a revelation of sheer relief and delight, writing: 'It was as if a light had been turned on . . . and I felt that life contained an infinite number of possibilities.'

But ascetics are aware that there are less risky methods of achieving the same result. The Japanese master Ikkyu was asked by a workman to write something on his tablet. He wrote: 'Attention.' The workman looked disappointed. 'Can't you write something else?' So Ikkyu wrote: 'Attention, attention.' The workman asked: 'But what does attention mean?' Ikkyu replied: 'Attention means attention.'

When I came upon that comment, some 30 years ago, I tried putting it into practice in my afternoon walks over the cliff, paying attention to the scenery. Yet no matter how hard to tried, I did not seem to be able to maintain 'attention' for long; clearly I had not got the hang of what Ikkyu meant.

Then, in the New Year of 1979, I stumbled on the solution by accident. I had driven over to lecture at a farm in North Devon at a place called Sheepwash, and when we all woke up the next morning, the snow was two feet deep. We were all forced to stay another night. On the third day, with the help of shovels, we managed to clear a path along the mile-long farm track to the road. I was the first to leave, and I found myself driving along a narrow country road between snow-filled ditches that made it impossible to guess where the road ended and the ditch began. I knew that if I went into the ditch I might spend the night there. So I drove with intense, deep concentration for mile after mile.

When I finally arrived back at the main road, where the snow had been turned into slush by traffic, I was at last able to relax. And I realised that all this fierce 'attention' had raised my consciousness to a higher level. Everything I looked at seemed fascinating, even telegraph poles. This is clearly what Ikkyu meant: *concentrated* attention. It lasted all the way home.

Naturally, I assumed that what had enabled me to achieve this level of concentration was my sense of urgency. And later, on a trip to London, I achieved it again by concentrating hard. But again, I assumed that this was because I had plenty of time to devote to it.

Then, one day, I discovered this was untrue. It was simply a matter of practice, and could be done on a country walk, or on a drive to the supermarket. What happens is that concentration brings a glowing sense of energy, such as an athlete feels when pushing himself to effort, and the effort seems self-sustaining.

This is not, I must emphasise, some kind of mystical state; it is simply a sense of possessing large reserves of energy, which can be accessed by an effort of will.

Maine de Biran was right. When we make an effort, we can *feel* that free will is a reality. What Maine de Biran did not understand, probably because he was often in poor health, was that this sense of freedom can be increased with practice. But Bergson understood it. So did William James, in that extraordinary essay 'The Energies of Men', which is virtually an instruction manual for achieving higher levels of energy. What they understood is that the mind has gears, exactly like a car engine. I added to that my own discovery: that these gears can be made to work through the muscles of the face, particularly the lips. The face is the gearbox of the soul.

It is not my intention to assess the writers I have discussed according to this standard of awareness, except to say that I find it in the work of Doris Lessing, the early novels of Iris Murdoch, and in a certain fascination with the future in the plays of Arnold Wesker – even in his title *I'm Talking About Jerusalem*.

For indeed, Jerusalem – in Blake's sense – is precisely what we are talking about.

H G Wells – as noted earlier – summarised our present stage of evolution when he said: 'The bird is a creature of the air, the fish is a creature of the water, and man is a creature of the mind.' But in his *Experiment in Autobiography* (1935) he agreed that we are not yet creatures of the mind. Rather, we are like the earliest amphibians, who dragged themselves out of prehistoric seas because they wanted to become land animals. But having flippers instead of legs, they found this new element exhausting, and had to keep returning to the sea, even though they hated their dependence on it.

I have tried to show how, for more than two centuries, certain human beings have come to hate their dependence on the material world, and struggled to escape it. I called them Outsiders. This was the true meaning of the revolt called romanticism, which began so promisingly with Rousseau, then collapsed into tragedy and defeat. Yet looking back, we can see that what was really happening was that a new kind of creature was struggling to be born, trying to turn his fins into legs.

And the discovery that the mind has 'gears' constitutes the basis of the evolutionary leap, through which a new species of humans will emerge.

It seems that the Master Ikkyu knew the answer all the time.

Select Bibliography

Allsop, Kenneth. *The Angry Decade: A Survey of the Cultural Revolt of the 1950s*. Peter Owen, 1958.

Alvarez, Al. *Samuel Beckett*. Collins, 1970.

Amis, Kingsley. *What Became of Jane Austen, and Other Questions*. Harcourt Brace, 1970.

— *Memoirs*. Hutchinson, 1991.

— *The Letters of Kingsley Amis*. Ed. Zachary Leader, HarperCollins, 2001.

Amis, Martin. *Experience*. Jonathan Cape, 2000.

Bair, Deirdre. *Samuel Beckett: A Biography*. Harcourt Brace, 1978.

Booker, Christopher. *The Neophiliacs*. Collins, 1969.

Bradbury, Malcolm. *Possibilities: Essays on the State of the Novel*. Oxford, 1973.

Bradford, Richard. *Lucky Him*. Peter Owen, 2001.

Brophy, Brigid. *Don't Never Forget: Collected Views and Reviews*. New York, Holt, Rinehart & Winston, 1966.

Carpenter, Humphrey. *The Angry Young Men: A Literary Comedy of the 1950s*. Allen Lane, 2002.

Conradi, Peter J. *Iris Murdoch, A Life*. HarperCollins, 2001.

Dossor, Howard F. *Colin Wilson: the Man and his Mind*. Element Books, 1990.

Feldman, Gene and Gartenberg, Max (eds.). *Protest, the Beat Generation and the Angry Young Men*. New York, Senior Press, 1959.

Hanson, Gillian Mary. *Understanding Alan Sillitoe*. USA, University of South Carolina Press, 1999.

Heilpern, John. *John Osborne: A Patriot for Us*. Chatto & Windus, 2006.

Holroyd, Stuart. *Contraries: A Personal Progression*. Bodley Head, 1975.

Jacobs, Eric. *Kingsley Amis: a Biography*. Hodder & Stoughton, 1995.

Larkin, Philip. *Selected Letters*. Faber & Faber, 1993.

Lessing, Doris. *Walking in the Shade* (autobiography 1949–62). HarperCollins, 1997.

Lewis, Peter. *The Fifties*. Heinemann Ltd, 1978.

Logue, Christopher. *Prince Charming: A Memoir*. Faber & Faber, 1999.

Maschler, Tom (ed.). *Declaration*. MacGibbon & Kee, 1959.

— *Publisher*. Picador, 2005.

Morgan, Ted. *Literary Outlaw: The Life and Times of William Burroughs*.

New York, Henry Holt & Company, 1988.

Motion, Andrew. *Philip Larkin: A Writer's Life*. Faber & Faber, 1993.

Murray Scott, Andrew. *Alexander Trocchi: The Making of a Monster*. Polygon, 1991.

Osborne, John. *A Better Class of Person*. Faber & Faber, 1981.

— *Almost a Gentleman*. Faber & Faber, 1991.

Rickards, Jocelyn. *The Painted Banquet: My Life and Loves*. Weidenfeld & Nicolson, 1987.

Ritchie, Harry. *Success Stories: Literature and Media in England 1950–59*. Faber & Faber, 1988.

St Jorre, John de. *Venus Bound: the Erotic Voyage of the Olympia Press and its Writers*. New York, Random House, 1994.

Salwak, Dale. *John Braine and John Wain, a reference guide*. USA, G K Hall & Company, 1980.

— *John Wain*. USA, Twayne Publishers, 1981.

— *Interviews with Britain's Angry Young Men, John Braine, John Wain, Bill Hopkins, Colin Wilson, Kingsley Amis*. USA, Borgo Press, 1984.

— *Kingsley Amis: Modern Novelist*. Harvester Wheatsheaf, 1992.

Shellard, Dominic. *Kenneth Tynan: A Life*. USA, Yale University Press, 2003.

Taylor, D J. *After the War: the Novel and English Society since 1945*. Chatto & Windus, 1993.

Thwaite, Anthony (ed.). *Selected Letters of Philip Larkin 1940–85*. Faber & Faber, 1992.

Tynan, Elaine (Dundy). *Life Itself*. Virago Press, 2001.

Tynan, Kathleen. *The Life of Kenneth Tynan*. Weidenfeld & Nicolson, 1987.

— (ed.). *Letters of Kenneth Tynan*. Weidenfeld & Nicolson, 1994.

Tynan, Kenneth. *Curtains*. Longmans, 1961.

— *The Diaries of Kenneth Tynan*. Ed. John Lahr. Bloomsbury, 2001.

Wain, John. *Sprightly Running: Part of an Autobiography*. Macmillan, 1962.

Wardle, Irving. *The Theatre of George Devine*. Cape, 1978.

Wesker, Arnold. *As Much As I Dare: An Autobiography 1932–59*. Century, 1994.

Index